Trial and Error

Trial and Error

The Case of John Brownfield and Race Relations in Georgetown, South Carolina

Tom Rubillo

Charleston The History Press London

Published by The History Press
18 Percy Street
Charleston, SC 29403
866.223.5778
www.historypress.net

Cover Image: "Slab Town" section of Georgetown where John Brownfield, his wife Sibby and sister Anna lived, circa 1900. *Courtesy of the Georgetown County Library Morgan Collection*

First published 2005

Manufactured in the United Kingdom

ISBN 1.59629.035.8

Library of Congress Cataloging-in-Publication Data

Rubillo, Tom.
Trial and error : the case of John Brownfield and race relations in Georgetown, South Carolina / Tom Rubillo.
p. cm.
Includes bibliographical references and index.
ISBN 1-59629-035-8 (alk. paper)
1. Brownfield, John--Trials, litigation, etc. 2. Trials (Murder)--South Carolina--Georgetown. 3. Georgetown (S.C.)--Race relations--History--19th century. I. Title.
KF224.B764R83 2005
345.757'8902523--dc22
2005007096

CONTENTS

Prologue

FIVE RIVERS CONVERGE ON THE South Carolina coast to form Winyah Bay. At its headwaters is an oak-shaded colonial town. Many homes there date back to the early 1700s. That community, Georgetown, is the seat of government for the 864-square-mile county bearing the same name. Around fifty thousand people live in the county today. That is twice as many inhabitants as lived in the area in the eighteenth, nineteenth and early twentieth centuries.

One of the rivers flowing into Winyah Bay is named the Sampit. It is a relatively short and naturally deep waterway that drains the lowlands in the western half of the county. There is a pedestrian boardwalk along that river. Historic markers along this walkway offer the accepted version of local history. The walkway immediately behind the town's clock tower describes the years of antebellum as "a glamorous and genteel era of enormous wealth, aristocracy and plantations" and as the "most gracious and colorful chapter in Georgetown's history."

The description distorts reality. Throughout most of its recorded history, the economy of Georgetown County has been under the exclusive control of a small minority of white men. These few men amassed fortunes on the labors of a multitude of blacks, who endured lives of drudgery, poverty and mistreatment. Until 1865, as many as nine out of ten of Georgetown's residents did not have control over their fates or futures, or lives or labors. They were not entitled to accumulate wealth or own property. Instead, like farm animals, they were chattels driven by taskmasters. First they were forced to clear tens of thousands of acres of ancient cypress swamps. Next, they dug canals, built impoundments and created complex tidal-controlled irrigation systems. That work done-work comparable in enormity to construction of the great pyramids-they cultivated annual rice crops that produced fortunes for the "aristocracy" of slavemasters who reaped the profits of the cruel harvests of the Georgetown rice fields.

In July 2003, President George W. Bush visited Goree Island in Senegal at the westernmost tip of the continent of Africa. There, he stood in the "Door of No Return." Over the centuries, millions of people passed through that door in chains on their way to lives of misery. President Bush then gave a short speech. In it, he lamented that "for 250 years the captives endured an assault on their culture and their dignity."

"Small men took on the powers and airs of tyrants and masters. Years of unpunished brutality and bullying and rape produced a dullness and hardness of conscience," Bush continued. "Christian men and women became blind to the clearest commands of their faith and added hypocrisy to injustice. A republic founded on equality for all became a prison for millions."

When this speech was reported on July 9, 2003 in the *New York Times*, the quotation (with its source identified) was clipped from the newspaper and securely taped onto the historic marker on the Sampit River. The next morning, it was gone. It was taped onto the marker again. It was removed again, and so on for about a month. The views of the president of the United States about the "most glamorous era" in local history were not welcome in Georgetown.

With the end of slavery in 1865, Georgetown's economy began to disintegrate. "Without slave labor to cultivate the rice crop, most of the plantations were doomed," the historic marker on the Sampit grudgingly admits. In this one sentence, a fundamental historical truth is revealed: the accomplishments of the county's "most glamorous era" were the product of the knowledge, skills and abilities of black labor, not that of the "small men [who] took on the powers and airs of tyrants and masters."

When, in 1865, Georgetown's slaves were finally emancipated, they outnumbered their former captors by a ratio of around to nine to one. Their superior numbers notwithstanding, the newly released slaves were not free. Only their physical shackles had been removed. They had nowhere to go. They had few material resources. Denied an education and possessing little, if any, capital, the newly emancipated slaves remained under the economic control of their former taskmasters. Fearful of change, local whites were relentless in their efforts to keep former servants in a subservient role. That struggle to maintain white supremacy continued for decades. In some ways, it continues to this day.

This book explores important events in the history of race relations in Georgetown. That history reveals an alchemy that turned the Golden Rule into lead. Greed and cruelty were smelted in a caldron of oppression. The pungent scent of the victims' resentment filled the air. Once that happened, the alchemists began to worry that the product of their own creation was explosive-that what they had done to others might be done to them in return. All this fear and resentment fostered a mutual mistrust that has proven persistent.

This legacy of suspicion is not unique to this community. It is the product of a time-tested, volatile combination of ingredients that has been mixed together around the world throughout human history. In some places, tribal differences have been used to rationalize cruelty to others. In other places, religious differences were considered justification. In still other places, ethnocentricity has been stirred with violence. Human beings can be very creative when it comes to developing reasons to look down their noses and hurt their neighbors. In Georgetown, simple greed rationalized and fed the initial notions of racial superiority. Those actions have left behind a bitter toxic waste.

The following pages tell how this volatile process destroyed the lives of two men, one black and one white. It is a true story, one of many of its kind. It is told by quoting original sources and participants as much as possible. Readers may find some of the language used in those times offensive. These words are used here so the attitudes of those who lived through these events will resonate as their stories are retold. In this way, perhaps their legacy, and the influence of that legacy on today's society, can be understood a little better.

Chapter I

"Small men took on the powers and airs of tyrants and masters."

President George W. Bush,
Goree Island, Senegal, July 8, 2003

Throughout most of its history, Georgetown was almost totally isolated from the outside world. It is surrounded by rivers, swamps, marshes and dense forests. A large bay is found at its heart. This brackish estuary was pristine until the latter part of the twentieth century. At that point, the appearance of heavy industries along the bay's tributaries caused abrupt and dramatic changes in its natural environment. These changes occurred in just one human lifetime, leaving the area and its once abundant wildlife threatened by thoughtlessly discarded hazardous and toxic waste.

Archeological evidence reveals that the shores of Georgetown's waterways have been inhabited by humans for thousands of years. Ancient pottery shards, circular mounds of oyster and clam shells and centuries-old campsites can be unearthed on nearly every bluff overlooking flowing water. Local lore has it that Pedro de Quexos, under the command of Vasquez de Ayllon, sailed up Winyah Bay in 1521, seized 140 Indians and sold them as slaves in the West Indies. The story goes on to say that in 1526, de Ayllon established a sizeable settlement, but it was overrun after the Spanish stole corn from the aboriginals.[1] No physical evidence supports this adventurous version of local lore.

The first relics of European colonization of the area date to the middle 1600s when English settlers staked their claim to the land by slaughtering, enslaving and spreading disease among the indigenous population. Ultimately, natives who were not sold, dead or dying were ethnically cleansed along a trail of tears headed west. By whichever genocidal cause, the social order that had existed in the area for more than ten thousand years—the Seewee, Santee, Sampa, Weenee, Pee Dee and Waccamaw tribes—was gone in little more than 150 years after Europeans first appeared in Georgetown County.

Amid this process of conquest and colonization, the city of Georgetown came into being. Established on 274 acres of high ground at the head of Winyah Bay, the city was laid out by the son of a Baptist preacher who did not own the land.[2] In what may have been one of America's first land swindles, he executed a deed to the town to three men: George Pawley, William Swinton and Daniel LaRoche. They, in turn, sold individual lots to unsuspecting buyers, all to the consternation of the land's rightful owner, John Cleland. In 1737, Cleland arrived from England to claim his property. He ran into a problem. Swinton was a descendant of the Royal House of Stuart. Cleland was not. Swinton's connections apparently were helpful. The matter was resolved when those who had purchased individual lots paid a small fee to Cleland.[3] Swinton and his partners, meanwhile, paid nothing and retained their profits. So did the preacher's son. Cleland then expanded the town by several blocks.

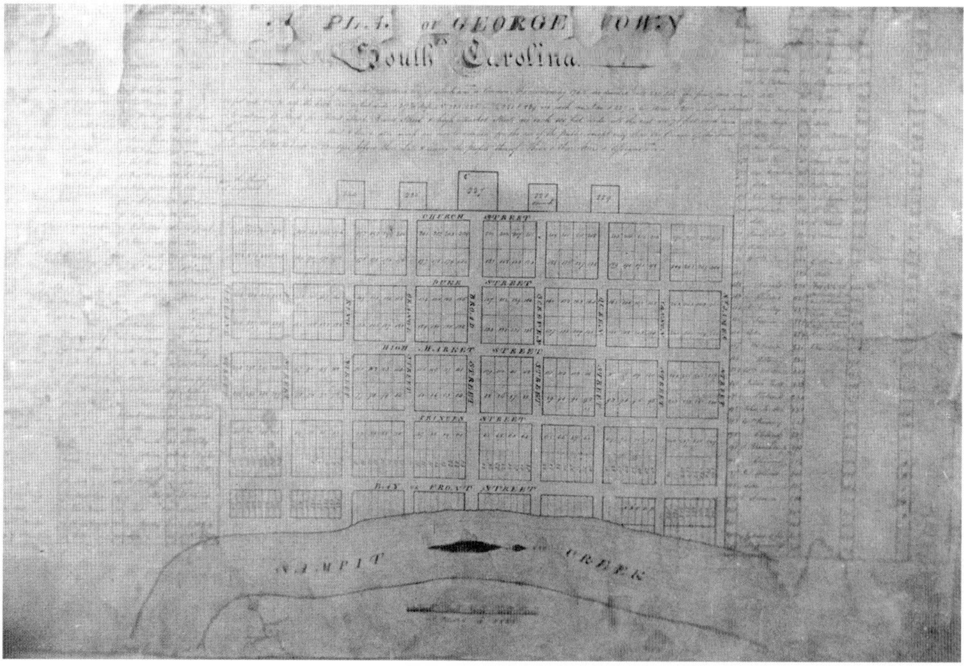

Plat, city of Georgetown, circa 1884. *Courtesy of the Georgetown County Library Morgan Collection.*

In the early 1700s, Georgetown—along with Charleston as well as Philadelphia, Pennsylvania—was an official "port of entry" for immigrants, indentured servants and, until their importation was banned, slaves. Indigo, rice and naval stores were loaded on outbound ships. Cotton, turpentine and lumber were added to the list of exports, and a plantation economy developed. That economy thrived for more than 150 years, ended only by the unsuccessful separatist movement of the slave-holding states and the resulting end of slavery in North America.

Without slave labor, white planters were not able to maintain their crops, their plantations or their way of life. Efforts to keep blacks working the rice paddies were not particularly profitable. Then, during the latter part of the nineteenth century, a series of devastating hurricanes struck the area. Rice fields were inundated with saltwater driven by storm surges, and salt contaminated the soil. The complex of canals, irrigation ditches, dikes and other earthworks of the rice fields were destroyed. Rice crops failed. The economy that fed both blacks and whites fell on very hard times.

Because the plantations were dying, the local economy had to go through a dramatic transition if the community were to survive. Fortunately, change came. It began in the late 1880s and continued through the first decade of the twentieth century. The transition was dominated by the efforts of one man, William D. Morgan. Morgan served as the chief executive of the City of Georgetown from 1891 to 1905. Numerous improvements in the public infrastructure, port facilities and transportation arteries occurred during his tenure. These improvements, along with the area's abundant pine forests, attracted a major industry that saved the area's economy from collapse. At the turn of the twentieth century, Georgetown became home to one of the world's largest lumber mills.

Atlantic Coast Lumber Company served as the bedrock of the local economy until the Great Depression. When the company closed, the local economy nearly collapsed again, only to be rescued by another saving industry when a paper mill was built on the outskirts of the city. To this day, the paper mill's pungent aroma "smells like bread and butter" to local residents. In the 1970s, the paper mill was joined by a steel mill, which was sited in the center of town. A finely grained, rust-colored dust has since rained on the town whenever the mill has been in operation. The smallest granules of this dust are classified as a toxic waste by the federal Environmental Protection Agency. That waste is supposed to be bagged, hauled off and disposed of only in approved landfills. That has not always been the case. For a number of years, local government officials looked the other way while the company dumped waste in an unlined county landfill on the outskirts of town, poisoning the wells of adjacent homes in the process. The site is now what is called a "brownfield" in federal law—it is a location in need of reclamation before it can be used for human habitation.[4] As interim measures, the dump site was quietly capped with asphalt and the drinking wells closed.[5] A few years later, water was piped to neighboring homes from the municipal waterworks without cost to the homeowners, but also without explanation.[6] Since those actions were taken, the steel mill filed for bankruptcy protection, was permitted to abandon its toxic waste and stopped paying the water bills.[7]

Georgetown County owns the landfill. Because of the bankruptcy of the steel mill, the county is now straddled with responsibility for cleanup of this brownfield.[8] Unable to afford that very expensive task, the county is using the relatively modest fund set aside for cleanup by the steel mill to monitor the situation. In the interim, it constructed tennis courts and baseball fields on adjacent property-without posting notice of the nearby toxins.

In the early 1980s, an oil refinery with a production of thirty thousand barrels per day sought permission to locate its operations on the shores of the Sampit River just outside of town. Daily, it planned to spill at least thirty pounds of oil and grease into the river and six tons of pollutants into the air.[9] Brigadier General Forrest T. Gay III of the U.S. Army Corps of Engineers' South Atlantic Division barred the refinery from its systematic pollution. He recognized that the estuary was a "truly unique environment"[10] that was in need of, and deserved, protection.

Ironically, at the same time as the Army Corps was carefully studying the fragile environment of the bay, the local paper company decided to reconfigure its plant.[11] It was manufacturing brown paper and boxes. The mill had become outdated and insufficiently profitable. After the paper company spread alarming rumors that it might close the Georgetown mill, gaining apparent advantage during union negotiations,[12] the company announced it planned to reconfigure the plant to make bleached white paper. That process involves, in part, using chlorine (now in the form of chlorine dioxide). Because of the scare about the mill closing, no one asked about the chemical process involved in bleaching paper.

The combination of chlorine and heat produces dioxins, primary ingredients of Agent Orange, the defoliant sprayed on the jungles of Southeast Asia by the U.S. military in the 1960s and 1970s. Dioxins are deadly compounds. They cause cancers, deformities and miscarriages when ingested in parts per quadrillion.[13] Dioxins are not water soluble or otherwise biodegradable. Instead, like DDT, they

Rural road, Georgetown County, circa 1900. *Courtesy of the Georgetown County Library Morgan Collection.*

persist in the environment. Over the years that followed, the mill was repeatedly listed as one of the biggest producers of dioxin pollution in the nation.[14]

In addition to dioxin, one tributary of the bay—the Sampit River—is contaminated with lead, cadmium, chrome and other heavy metals from the steel mill that sits in the center of town. Because of the presence of mercury in the estuary, warnings about eating fish from local waters are issued periodically but go largely unheeded. "Sometimes you think about it," said one fisherman, a cigarette dangling from his lips, as he baited a hook for his son. "But I've been eating the fish for years and I've got no problems," he told the reporter and photographer who prepared the story about the health hazard.[15]

Until the early twentieth century, sailing ships were the principal means by which people entered or left the county. The extreme density of the underbrush in its semitropical forests and the generally swampy nature of much of its abundant lowlands have made it almost impossible to enter or leave Georgetown County without traveling by water at some point. Even the few narrow dirt roads that led out of the county were interrupted by rivers that had to be crossed by ferry. The only other way out was by booking passage on a ship sailing to sea. These physical features made a land escape from Georgetown almost impossible, both for slaves and, after abolition, anyone seeking to leave on foot, by horse or, later, by horseless carriage without being seen and easily tracked. This physical isolation also limited the flow of information from the outside world to that which the editor of the local newspaper decided to publish and that which filtered in through the mail.

The first land connection with the outside word was made in 1924 when a bridge was constructed over the Black River about ten miles to the west of town. The bridge replaced ferry service there. The next connecting bridge was about twenty-five miles to the north of town. It was built over the Pee Dee River delta at the county line at a place called Yauhannah. The next bridges opened in 1928 spanning the North Santee and South Santee Rivers about a dozen miles south of town and connecting Georgetown to Charleston County.

These structures completely changed Georgetown, transforming it from a remote backwater of South Carolina to a place that is open to the outside world and its influences. During the past several decades, many retirees have moved to the area from colder climes. Largely because of the kind of suspicions that accompany xenophobia, the customs, mores, habits and interrelationships of a large majority of Georgetown's population, both black and white, have remained fairly static nonetheless. The way of life was forged over four centuries, so many in the population resist change. But they are changing, albeit slowly.

Chapter II

"Oppression makes a wise man mad."

Ecclesiastes, 7:7

The first commercial crop harvested in Georgetown was indigo, a plant used in the cotton mills of England to dye cloth. Then, spurred by the importation of a targeted population of slaves from West Africa's grain coast[1] where rice had been grown for thousands of years, plantation owners soon found rice was much more profitable. By 1850, the "rice culture" was firmly established with 87 major plantation owners profiting from the toils of 12,199 slaves. By 1860, the number of slaves in Georgetown County had increased to 18,109.

South Carolina's rice crop was cultivated in what originally was a vast swamp infested with snakes, alligators, horseflies and mosquitoes. Once cleared of ancient cypress trees and impounded with massive earthworks, cultivation began. Planting took place during moderate spring weather. Attending and harvesting of rice occurred during the deadliest months of the year. That time—the months of August through November—was known as the "sickly season." Those months were when yellow fever, smallpox, malaria and other diseases were rampant in the Carolina Lowcountry. Slaves did not have special immunity to these afflictions. They worked the rice fields anyway, while their owners summered in Newport, Rhode Island, or in the cooling breezes of South Carolina's nearby barrier islands. Tropical diseases were so rampant, in fact, that nearly one-third of newly arrived slaves died within three years of arrival.[2] By 1860, in Georgetown County, less than 8 percent of the slave population survived beyond age fifty.[3]

The hard work on rice plantations was performed on a "task" basis. Each slave was given a specific amount of work to perform each day. The work had to be completed, no matter how long it took. If it was not done, the slave was punished. According to Plowden C.J. Weston, the owner of Hagley Plantation on the Waccamaw River, a task was "as much work as the meanest hand can do in nine hours, working industriously"[4] -in nine hours, that is, in the opinion of someone who did not perform the work. Another planter, James Sparkman, boasted that his slaves could "easily" complete their tasks "during the winter months in eight to nine hours and in summer my people seldom exceed 10 hours of labor per day." Slave accounts, on the other hand, reported being in the fields from sunrise to sunset and, at harvest time, working eighteen hours a day.[5]

Thanks to the efforts of a Federal Writers Project of the 1930s, the recollections of a few survivors of slavery were preserved. These include narratives of those who toiled in the South Carolina Lowcounty, including Georgetown County.

Ben Horry was born into slavery on December 13, 1852. He was a teenager when emancipated and lived more than 104 years. At age 104, he was interviewed by Genevieve Chandler at his cabin on King's Road in Murrells Inlet, Georgetown County. "I the oldest liver left on Waccamaw Neck that belong to Brook Green, Prospect, Longwood, Adderly Plantations. I been here! I seen things! I tell you. Thousands of them things happen but I try to forget 'em."

According to Mr. Horry, a full task spanned a half acre of land each day if the work involved "mashing raw ground" with a hoe, making it ready for planting. "Cutting rice [grueling work requiring] half acre a day."

Former slave Ben Horry at age 104. *Courtesy of the National Archives.*

Sam Polite was ninety-three years old when interviewed by Chlotilde R. Martin in Beaufort County. He was born on Fripp Plantation on St. Helena Island. According to Mr. Polite, "Every slave have task to do, sometime one task, sometime two task, sometime three. You have for work till task through."

Prince Smith was one hundred years old when interviewed. He described three ways of assigning a day's work. A person in his prime was given a whole task or even two tasks. Each task involved the cultivation of between twenty-four and twenty-five rectangles, each of which was thirty feet by twenty-five feet. Young children between ages five and twelve were given three-quarters of a task. Old slaves were assigned a half task.

Work was supervised by an overseer. It was his job to punish those who did not complete their assigned tasks. Prince Smith told of people being nailed into a sweat box that was placed in the sun during hot weather or in the dampest available spot when the weather turned cold. He recalled the use of a stock, where the victim was placed on his back, his hands and feet tied, with a heavy weight placed on his chest. An even worse punishment involved putting a person in shackles and making the victim stand on a high, narrow scaffold for hours. Those who could not remain still and keep their balance would fall and be killed or seriously injured.[6]

"If slave don't do task, they get licking with lash on naked back," Sam Polite said. "Driver nigger give licking, but Master most always been there....Can't be no trouble between white folks and nigger in slavery time, for they do as they choose with you."

In his 1863 book *50 Years of Slavery*, Francis Frederic wrote:

> *Many masters possessing large plantations, and some hundreds of slaves being desirous to divest themselves as much as possible of the cares of managing the estate, hire white men, at a salary of from 1,200 to 1,400 dollars per annum, to look after the whole property. These are the best and most humane overseers. But other slave proprietors, in order to save the cost of an overseer, but chiefly to extract as much work as possible out of the niggers, make a nigger an overseer, who if he does not cruelly work the slaves is threatened with a flogging, which the master cannot give to a white man. In order to save his own back the slave overseer very often behaves in the most brutal manner to the niggers under him.*
>
> *My grandmother's master was one of the hard kind. He had made her son an overseer. Consequently, my grandmother having committed the crime of attending a prayer-meeting, was ordered to be flogged by her own son. This was done by tying her hands before her with a rope, and then fastening the rope to a peach*

> *tree, and laying bare the back. Her own son was then made to give her 40 lashes with a thong of a raw cow's-hide, her master standing over her the whole time blaspheming and threatening what he would do if her son did not lay it on.*[7]

Mom Hagar Brown did not know how old she was when she was interviewed. "I too glad my chillun ain't been here Rebs time. Give you task, you rather drown than not done that task. Ma say Auntie poor weak [creature], couldn't strain. Ma had to strain to fetch sister up with her task. Dere in rice field.... Don't done you task, diver wave that whip, put you over the barrel, beat you so blood run down."

(Singing)
Stay in the field
stay in the field
stay in the field til
the war been end

Moses Grandy wrote an autobiography, *Life of a Slave*, in 1843. In it, he reported that "MacPherson [the overseer] gave the same task to each slave; of course the weak ones often failed to do it. I have often seen him tie up persons and flog them in the morning, only because they were unable to get the previous day's task done: after they were flogged, pork or beef brine was put on their bleeding backs, to increase the pain; he sitting by resting himself, and seeing it done. After being thus flogged and pickled, the sufferers often remained tied up all day, the feet just touching the ground, the legs tied, and pieces of wood put between the legs. All the motion allowed was a slight turn of the neck. Thus exposed and helpless, the yellow flies and mosquitoes in great numbers would settle on the bleeding and smarting back, and put the sufferer to extreme torture. This continued all day, for they were not taken down till night."

Margaret Bryant did not know her age when interviewed at her home in Georgetown County. "When freedom come, I been here. Not big 'nuff for work for the Reb, but I been here Reb time." The punishment she recalled most vividly was being put in a "bull pen." "Hab 'em a place can't see you hand before you. Can't turn around good in there. Left you in there till morning. Give you sixty lash and send you to work. You ain't done that task, man and woman lick!

"Couldn't manage my ma. Oberseeher want to lick ma, Mary One say, 'going drown meself.' I done my work! Fore I take a lick, rather drown meself.

Woman pounding rice on plantation. *Courtesy of the Georgetown County Library Morgan Collection.*

Oberseeher gone tell the doctor. Tie her long rope. Right to Sandy Island. Man hold the rope. Gone on. Jump in river."

This lack of respect did not end with the life of the slave. "When nigger dead, you can't knock off work for bury 'um. You have to wait till nighttime to put 'um in the grave. You bury 'um by the light of torch," Sam Polite recalled.

The extreme cruelty of the slave drivers and physical hardships suffered by slaves quickly bred fear. That, in turn, resulted in a seething resentment and sullen defiance.

A society's fears often can be found in its most repressive laws. Today, so-called "Patriot" laws seek to limit individual rights in exchange for security.[8] In colonial South Carolina, frightened by the hatred that their brutality had created, white planters turned to the law for help. The South Carolina legislature was more than willing to provide it.

One of the first laws addressing resistance by slaves was adopted in 1715. Its preamble explains its purpose. It says, "the detestable crime of poisoning hath of late been frequently committed by many slaves in this Province and notwithstanding the execution of several criminals for that offense, yet it has not been sufficient to deter others from being guilty of same." Accordingly, to deter the slaves from poisoning their owners, it became unlawful to employ any person of color in an apothecary and a capital offense for anyone of color to procure, furnish or convey poison.[9]

Next, in 1722, the South Carolina legislature adopted "An Act for the Better Ordering and Governing Negroes and Other Slaves." The law began by acknowledging the total dependence of whites on blacks. Its preamble admits "the plantations and estates of this Province cannot be well and sufficiently managed and brought into use, without the labor and service of negroes and other slaves." It then condoned white brutality by alleging that those "brought unto the people of this Province for that purpose are of barbarous, wild and savage natures, and such as render them wholly unqualified to be governed by the laws, customs and practices of England." Based on that notion, the legislature concluded that it was "absolutely necessary that such laws and orders should be made and enacted, for the good regulating and ordering of them, as may restrain the disorders, rapines and inhumanities to which *they* are naturally prone." (Emphasis added.)

To control the enslaved and preserve the prosperity of the small white minority, the law provided, among other things, that "all negroes, mulattoes, mestizoes or Indians, which at any time hereafter shall have been sold, and now are held and taken to be, or hereafter shall be bought and sold for slave, are hereby declared slaves; and they, *and their children*, are hereby made and declared slaves, to all intents and purposes."[10] (Emphasis added.) The law made no distinction between children born of fathers who were slaves and children sired by white masters or others who were otherwise legally free to "take pleasure" from slave women. Unlike today, a father's citizenship status did not attach to his child under these latter circumstances. Indeed, even if most white men wanted all their children to be free, the law could not have made that possible without an acknowledgment of paternity by the father.

The updated law also prohibited any slave from travel outside of his or her owner's property "without a ticket or leave in writing from his master or mistress, or some other person by his or her appointment, or some white person in the company of such slave to give account of his business." A slave caught in violation of this restriction was subject to a whipping "not exceeding twenty lashes."

"In 'Reb Time' you know, when they sell you bout-massa sell you all about. Broke through them briar and branch and thing to go to church. Them patrol get you," said Mom Hagar Brown when telling of her days in bondage to a biographer from the Federal Writer's Project.[11]

Corporal punishment was not the only instrument of control. As has been the case in places like Ethiopia, Somalia, North Korea and various other iron-fisted dictatorships, food stocks were used on the plantations as a show of power. Whites held all the supplies. Subsistence rations were distributed each week on Saturday afternoon. They had to last all week. John D. Magill of Georgetown County, for example, handed out a peck of sweet potatoes and a dozen salted fish *per family*, adding a peck of grits and a piece of fat back to families with a baby, and a peck of meal and a quart of syrup for each family in the "sickly season" of summer. Others allocated varying quantities of the same sorts of bland and monotonous, minimal provisions.[12] If those ran out and sufficient vegetables were not grown behind the slave's cabin during the very few off hours, there were three choices: beg the master for more (which he was free to give or withhold according to his whim), steal food or go hungry.

Stealing food was risky business, hungry family or not. By law, any "negro or other slave" believed to have stolen a pig, cow or sheep could be branded with an "R" on the right cheek "with a red hot iron" for the first offense. The accused could be branded on the left cheek and given up to forty lashes for the second offense. Death was the permitted punishment for the third offense. Stealing corn or rice could also result in branding but was punishable by only thirty-nine lashes, rather than forty. Again, death was an acceptable punishment for the third offense.

Running away was not a good option either. Water, swamps and dense forests surrounded the plantations. "Beat companies" made up of five-man patrols rode the few narrow dirt roads between the plantations looking for trouble. By 1819, the law required that all white males older than age eighteen participate in the patrols. Those who did not own slaves became exempt after age forty-five. While the main aim of these patrols was to capture and punish runaways, they served a secondary role of keeping "vagabond whites" from slave women, preserving them for masters and overseers.[13]

Surviving slave Hagar Brown talked about one escape attempt. "May say some dem plan to run way. Say, 'Less run! Less run!' Master ketch dem and fetch dem in. Lay 'em cross barrel-hogsket barrel-Christ! They ramp wash in blood!"

Albert Caroline told of when he left his plantation without a pass. "Patrols come riding down th' road. Sour plait whip. Two big dog. White pat-roller. Ketch without pass, they whip me. Crawling. But I walk then and walk ever since. Bo-cart. Dat's what they call it-Bo-cart [a homemade baby walker that he had to use to walk after being permanently crippled by this beating]. 'Bout seventy-seven years since I start."

Mariah Heywood was born in 1855 and was "Alston labor" in Georgetown County. "I hear 'bout them slave try to run way. Aunt Tella Kinloch eye sho out. Baby cry. Mother say take her apron and stuff the child mouth. Blockade [runaway slave patrol] wuz hiding. Shot in range of that sound. Pow. Pow. Pow. Put everything in jail. All in jail. Mr. McCuskey tell us. He wuz one of the men help lynch...Nemo Ralston....They running away from Oregon Plantation—Dr. McGill place. Say they put four horse on him—one to each limb. Stretch 'em. And cut horses and each horse carry a piece. Mr. McCuskey was one help lynch Nemo."

Ben Horry said: "Got to have paper. Dem patroller put you cross a log. Beat you to death. I see them beat Ben Sharp. Beat 'em till Ben kin hardly git across fence. Jump over fence give 'em last chop! Patrol jess like road men [KKK] now. If I much of age reckon they have to kill me."

In 1735, a twenty-shilling bounty, payable by the slave's owner, was placed on the head of any runaway slave.[14] Making it easier to collect that bounty, the statute made it "lawful for any white person to beat, maim, or assault any slave who endeavors to avoid such white person by running away; and if any such slave shall resist with a stick or other instrument or weapon, that then it shall and may be lawful to kill any slave or slaves so resisting"[15] and still collect the reward. The law did not require proof of resistance by the slave as a prerequisite to killing him. The bounty was still due and payable.

Food, flogging and lynching were not the only acts of terror used against slaves. The possibility of rape was ever present. As Ben Horry reported: "The worst thing I members was colored oberseeher. He was the one straight from Africa. He the boss over all the mens and womens....My mother won't do all he say. When he say, 'you go to barn and stay till I come, she ain't do 'em. So he have it in for my mother and lay task on 'em she ain't able for do. Then for punishment my mother is take to the barn and strapped down on thing called the pony. Hands spread like this and strapped to the floor and...both she feet been like this. And she been give...sixty lashes till the blood flow And my father and me stand right there and look and ain't able to lift a hand. Blood on floor in that rice barn when [it was burned] down [by the property owner during the 1930s]. I see gash so long in my mama—my own mama. I shame for Miss Jinny! If one them driver want you [pointing to a black woman named Lillie sitting nearby] they give you task you can't do. You getting this beating not for you task—for you flesh."

Miss Lillie replied, "That why nation get mix up so" with mulattoes.

Ben Horry continued: "Susan wuz a house woman....To my knowing she had three white chillun. Not want 'em. Hab 'em. Boy near bout clean as them boy of missus....Woman over-power."[16]

The law did not forbid the rape of slave women, only white women. Slave women who attempted to fight off a white attacker fared even worse. By law, if a slave raised a hand against a white, she would "be severely whipped, and have his or her right ear cut off" for the first offense and could be killed for the second.

Committed
To the Gaol of Georgetown a Negro Woman named VIOLET, who says she belongs to Mr. White Scott of Williamsburgh District. She is about 5 feet 2 to 3 inches high and stoutly made. The owner is requested to pay charges and take her away.
Robert Huggins
Georgetown District Gaoler

Advertisement in Georgetown newspaper, August 12, 1826.

If a white person was bruised, wounded, maimed or disabled, the punishment was death.[17] Because of continuing resistance, this law was made even harsher in 1740. After that date, any slave who struck or assaulted a white could be "lawfully killed" on the spot without regard to whether the white was injured.[18]

At the same time, any white person who killed a slave for no reason simply had to pay the victim's owner "the full value of such negro so killed"[19] for the owner's financial loss, but was not otherwise punished for the murder.[20] If the killing occurred while a white was inflicting punishment authorized by the slave's owner, the statute said that "no person whatsoever shall be liable to any penalty."[21]

In order to deter other forms of resistance, the amended law added the burning of stocks of rice, tar kilns, barrels of tar, pitch or turpentine by slaves to the list of capital offenses.[22]

As the years passed, the law was further amended to ban meetings behind closed doors by slaves, free blacks or other people of color "for the purpose of mental instruction." A black student could receive up to twenty lashes for trying to learn to read, write or count.[23] The law was also amended to prohibit blacks who had been freed and left the state from ever returning.[24] It banned any free persons of color from entering the state.[25] It prohibited anyone from teaching a slave to read or write.[26] It barred anyone from employing a person of color in a store or shop.[27]

"Steal off slavery time in they own house and have class meeting. Driver come find 'em, whip 'em," former slave Albert Caroline told his biographer.

Such were the customs, mores, manners and laws of the "gracious" and "genteel" society created by Georgetown's "aristocracy."

CHAPTER III

"THEIR SPIRIT DID NOT BREAK."

President George W. Bush,
Goree Island, Senegal, July 8, 2003

BY 1820, THERE WERE 17,603 PEOPLE LIVING in Georgetown County. Of those, 1,830 were white. Another 227 were free persons of color. The remainder, 15,456, were slaves.[1] "For the slaves who produced the crop, rice planting meant grueling labor in steaming heat amid swarming horseflies and mosquitoes in one of the deadliest, most disease-ridden places on earth this side of the Black Hole of Calcutta," Richard N. Côté wrote in his 2001 book *Mary's World*.[2]

With a tiny minority reaping all the benefit from the toils of this harsh bondage, fear and resentment sometimes boiled over. South Carolina's leading historian Walter Edgar described the cycle of events this way: "white fears grew more pronounced about what the black majority might do; therefore, to prevent the unthinkable, the white minority resorted to intimidation to keep blacks in line." This did not help. "As control over the slave population increased, so did tensions. When blacks reacted in an 'insolent or mischievous' manner, whites clamped down even more. This, in turn, led to further black resistance."[3] Thus Georgetown, along with the rest of South Carolina, became engulfed in the cycle of violence—oppression, retaliation, reaction, retaliation, reaction, retaliation and so forth—that, to this day, continues to spiral out of control in other places around the world.

In Georgetown County, white fear led to the creation of a special posse. Emboldened by superior weapons, arrogance and silver badges, the posse rode the roads in search of unescorted blacks who did not have a pass. These patrols did not stop efforts to escape. Newspapers regularly contained notices of runaways.

Five Dollars Reward
Runaway from the subscriber on the 1st inst.,
his fellow MORRIS, an African. He is about 5 feet 4 or 5 inches high, well known about this place. Morris is supposed to be lurking somewhere about the free negro settlement on the Hill, as he has been seen there.
JAMES CORSON

Advertisement from Georgetown newspaper, August 12, 1826.

Not all resistance was individual. During the summer of 1829, Captain William Vaught of the Lower All Saints' Beat Company "accidentally discovered" information about an uprising that was being planned. His informant reportedly was a slave woman. Why she told him of the plot is not known.

Believing there was "barely enough time to obviate the terrible consequences of [the] contemplated insurrection,"[4] Vaught dispatched Sergeant Joseph Peake to raise a company. Peake took Vaught's horse and rode his steed "extremely hard, so much so that to my knowledge she [the horse] has not been able to do one day's work since."[5] The Committee on Claims of the South Carolina legislature later recommended that Vaught be paid $100 for the loss of his horse.[6] The money was given to the sheriff to be turned over to Vaught.

Being so heavily outnumbered by their slaves, the prospect of an uprising was frightening to the white planters. Eight years earlier, a group of slaves had killed George Ford, owner of a plantation on the Black River. It reportedly cost $500 to pay a militia for the two weeks it took to catch the runaway rebels who had killed Ford before fleeing into the swamps.[7]

As a result of the 1829 plot, fifteen slaves were arrested, including Quacooo and Mood. They were 2 of the 338 slaves of Francis Kinloch, then the owner of Kensington, WeeHaw and Rice Hope Plantations. Also arrested was Charles Prioleau, a slave of John Coachman. Quacooo, Mood and Charles were charged with "aiding in raising an insurrection." Another slave (whose identity is unknown) was charged with assaulting the woman who had disclosed the plot. The penalty upon conviction for either charge was death. The law required that the defendants be ready to go on trial for their lives within six days of their arrest.

The rights not to be tortured but, rather, to be free from self-incrimination, to confront accusers and to be tried by an impartial jury were each guaranteed to the people of America by both the United States Constitution and the constitution of the State of South Carolina at the time of these arrests. There was, however, a small "technicality." It had to do with definitions. To be protected by the law, defendants had to be "people."[8] This distinction made all the difference in the world.

In the cases of Quacooo, Mood, Charles and the others, they were chattel, not "people." Meaning they had fewer rights than horses, cattle, sheep and goats. As just one example, rape of an animal was classified as a common law "crime against nature," so farm animals were protected. Rape of a slave was not a crime at all.

In an era where physical brutality against slaves was routine, a slave's confession or the testimony of any other slave "attended with circumstances of truth and credit" was "deemed good and convincing evidence" at any capital or criminal trial against a black (although not against a white person).[9] The law did not limit the methods that could be used to extract confessions or the statements of witnesses. A decision as to whether the bounds of propriety had been crossed was left to the discretion of the court.[10]

The plan for the Georgetown insurrection was uncovered July 23, 1829. Mood was tried and convicted on July 26, 1829. He was not tried by impartial judges and jurors. The same planters who would have been targets of the proposed insurrection filled those roles. Plantation owners William S. Harvey and John R. Easterling served as justices, and slaveholders Eleazer Waterman, Thomas Goddard, W.W. Trapier, Joseph W. Allston and Davison McDowell were the jurors. They sentenced Mood to be hung. He was executed on the same day as convicted. He had no right to appeal.[11] His owner, Francis Kinloch, filed a petition with the South Carolina legislature and was paid the maximum amount allowed by law in compensation for the loss of his property—$122.45.[12]

In the case of Charles Prioleau, the same justices presided along with two of the same jurors. Edward T. Heriot, R.W. Allston and Stephen Ford (whose kin had been killed by slaves eight years earlier) were replacement jurors in the Prioleau case. The outcome was the same as the trial of Mood. Charles Prioleau was condemned to be hanged. The sentence was carried out September 18, 1829. In between the time of sentencing and the hanging, an appraiser placed a value on him of $122.45.[13] After the execution, the South Carolina Senate paid John Coachman for his lost property.

One other slave—the one whose name does not appear in the available historical record—was similarly tried and executed, but not because of participation in the plot. He was convicted of assaulting the initial informant.

Additionally, other alleged conspirators were named Nat and Robert. They were sentenced to be transported out of the United States.

The trial of Quacooo was delayed because "so many were concerned in the plot or conspiracy, that it appeared evident that the public safety required this delay, in order to find out the ramifications of the extended conspiracy, and to get the whole of the plot discovered."[14] Also, it was the "sickly season," a fact that contributed to the trial being delayed about a week.

Francis Kinloch did not like being deprived of his property without being paid. In an effort to collect, he hired an attorney and sent his counsel to speak with Quacooo at the jail. The presiding magistrate would not allow the lawyer to see Quacooo or anyone else. The trial proceeded. The evidence included unsworn testimony of several codefendants. There was no cross-examination. The record does not say what prompted the cooperation of the codefendants. They were, however, acquitted.

These unchallenged witnesses said that they had attended one meeting in June or July, allegedly speaking out against the rebellion. They claimed "all upon the log"—meaning Quacooo, Charles and Mood—had answered, "[W]e can soon collect Negroes enough to commence it, as there are ten blacks to one white." These same witnesses also said the "mode of attack, who would be killed first, next, etc." and "how to follow up the work of death and plunder so none would be spared" were also discussed, the latter subject at the second meeting. The court's record does not reveal how these witnesses, who claim to have attended only one meeting, knew about what was discussed at the second. Today, second-hand information is usually objectionable as hearsay.

Quacooo was convicted and sentenced to be transported—he was banished and lived out whatever life he had remaining by performing hard labor in the tropics.

Kinloch sought further review of the decision in Quacooo's case. He could not bring a direct appeal. That was not allowed. Instead, Kinloch sought a writ of prohibition—an order that would stop local officials from carrying out the "transportation" of his property. He raised three arguments: First, he said the trial was unfair because the regular rules of evidence had not been followed. Second, he said the law did not allow for "transportation" of a slave convicted of plotting an insurrection; death was the only penalty permitted by law. And third, if Quacooo were hanged, Kinloch could petition the president and members of the senate for payment of the fair market value of his property, as he had done in the case of Mood and as John Coachman had done in compensation for Charles.[15] But if Quacooo were sent away, Kinloch would not be reimbursed.

The state appellate court dismissed Kinloch's petition. As to the claim about the rules of evidence, the court said the complaint

> *seems to imply that the persons brought forward for trial for these offenses were entitled to the rights of citizens, secured by the magna charta or the common law of the land, whereas they have no rights, other than those which their masters or owners may give them. They are the property of their masters or owners, and are considered in this State, in law, as goods and chattels, and not as persons entitled to the benefits of freemen. Hence it arises that they are not entitled to the privileges of the common law, further than the rights of humanity, and the principles of benevolence and natural justice require be exercised toward them. In fact, in all countries where slavery is permitted, or established by law, the leading principle by which they are governed, is a sense of coercive necessity; which, leaving no choice of action, supersedes all questions of absolute right. Every endeavor, therefore, to extend positive rights to this class of people, is an attempt to reconcile inherent contradictions.*
>
> *The great security and happiness of the slave is the humanity and kindness of his master and [the] interest he has in the preservation of his health and bodily labor; which, in return, requires of his master's protection, kindness, and every necessary support for his sustenance and comfort.*[16]

As to the procedural issues Kinloch raised, the court said the local tribunal had "the power…to dispense with the common law rules of evidence entirely, by admitting of testimony, without oath, of Indians and slaves;[17] and instead of making up their sentences and judgments according to the rules of law and evidence, their consciences are made the rule of action, from whose sentence or conviction the [law] allows no appeal. Their judgments are final."

Permitted punishments included death by "consigning him to the gibbet" to be hung, but also could include "within the benefit of clergy" more "usual and common" ones like "whipping, branding, cropping or other infamous punishments." Portending the reasoning of the post-September 11, 2001 U.S. Justice Department, the South Carolina Supreme Court in 1829 wrote "when the dreadful nature and consequences of the insurrection…are taken into consideration…the judges of the Superior Courts ought to be extremely cautious in interfering…in the exercise of these summary jurisdictions; and they ought not be too eagle-eyed in viewing their proceedings, and in finding out and supporting every formal error or neglect, where the real merits have been duly and fairly attended to, and determined according to justice."[18]

This same kind of callous disregard for basic human rights was demonstrated again by the U.S. Supreme Court two decades later. In 1858, that court issued its infamous Dred Scott decision. Dred Scott had been born into slavery in the South. He then was moved with his owner to a free state where he enjoyed a taste of freedom. When his owner decided to return to a slave-holding state some years later, Scott refused to go, claiming that since he was in a free state, he was free.

The court ruled to the contrary. In his majority opinion, Chief Justice Taney reasoned that the only people protected by the federal Constitution were white males descended from the original colonists. Women, the descendants of post-colonial immigrants, Indians, blacks and even mulattoes were second-class citizens or, worse, the property of one of those old colonial families. They were not, Taney said, intended by the founding fathers to enjoy federal constitutional rights.

Taney was a strict constructionist. He believed that the Constitution could only be properly interpreted by unwavering devotion to exactly what was in the minds of the document's colonial drafters at the time they wrote it. This approach chisels the law in stone and does not allow it to change with changing times. Following that manner of thought, Taney reasoned that neither Dred Scott nor any other slave could obtain federally protected civil rights by moving to a so-called "free" state or territory. Once a slave, always a slave.

So it was with Quacooo, Mood, Charles and their co-conspirators. They had no legal rights. As to them, the South Carolina Supreme Court reasoned that "[t]he great security and happiness of the slave, is the humanity and kindness of his master."

As 104-year-old Ben Horry recalled, "Bury live? I did hear some talk o' that. I didn't know whether they bury 'em to scay (scare) 'em or what. I did hear tell bout it....Some these white people that day something. They either manage you or kill you."[19]

This brutality had its desired effect. "All evidence points to the fact that by the 1840's the slaves were submissive and content [sic]. The system, which had been worked out by the laws of the 1820's, was beginning to bring results in the sense that the slave population was passive and quiet," George C. Rogers wrote in his book *The History of Georgetown County*. "The institution was more firmly fixed, perhaps eradicable only by war."[20]

George Mason, a slaveholder from Virginia and delegate to the federal Constitutional Convention, foresaw the result of this disregard for basic human rights. He predicted "by an inevitable chain of causes and effects, providence [will] punish national sins by national calamities."[21] Time proved him to be right.

CHAPTER IV

RED BLOOD, NOT BLUE

"POLITICIANS START WARS; SOLDIERS FIGHT AND DIE IN THEM."

Colin Powell, My American Journey

THE DRED SCOTT DECISION FANNED the flames of the heated national debate over slavery. In the North, a seemingly limitless flow of immigrants from Ireland provided a cheap, readily dispensable source of labor for industrialists. Hoveled in cold, crowded, filthy tenements and paid starvation wages for long hours, those who worked twelve or more hours a day, seven days a week in the North were little better off than their economic counterparts in the South. Northern workers were, of course, free from beatings and less susceptible to forcible rape. They were also free to toil, freeze and starve wherever they could find a job. If they complained or organized, they were fired and blacklisted. "If you don't come in on Sunday, don't come in on Monday" was the mantra of the sweatshop.

Unconcerned with the well-being of their own workers, wealthy Northerners nonetheless found time to look down their noses on the exploitation of slaves by wealthy Southerners. The summer luncheons of the wealthy at Newport, Rhode Island, turned unpleasant.

"By the 1830s Newport's 'Southern colony' had become fully-organized," Côté writes in *Mary's World.* "Most South Carolina planters stayed in the large hotels or as house guests or tenants in private homes. In the mid-nineteenth century, the city was an international watering hole where the rich—like the Pringles, Middletons and Alstons—could watch the super-rich hold court and practice conspicuous consumption. There, South Carolinians spent their money 'lavishly, even wastefully.'"[1]

Courtesy of the Georgetown County Library Morgan Collection.

Harriet Beecher Stowe had published her antislavery novel *Uncle Tom's Cabin* in the early 1850s. Its publication fueled the heated national argument over slavery. One response came from a Harvard student from South Carolina, Edward Pringle. He circulated a pamphlet titled *Slavery in the Southern States*. He anchored his thesis in the concept of noblesse oblige, then recited the classical antebellum litany of Southern arguments in defense of slavery:

1. *It was God's will, sanctioned by the Bible.*
2. *Negro brains weighed less than white brains.*
3. *Negroes were intellectually inferior to whites.*
4. *Blacks themselves sold fellow blacks into slavery.*
5. *Chattel slavery in the South was no worse than wage slavery in the factories of the north.*
6. *Slaves on the Southern plantations were more likely to be kept together as families than were white Northern factory workers.*
7. *Men who purchased slaves incurred a heavy obligation of social welfare and Christian duty.*
8. *Real abuses of slaves were rare.*
9. *Blacks were better suited to manual labor in hot climates than whites.*
10. *Southern agriculture would be paralyzed by emancipation of slaves.*[2]

Another response to abolitionist sentiment was penned by South Carolinian William S. Pettigrew. He wrote, "The institution of slavery is unquestionably justified by Scripture, both by precect [sic] & example. The sin does not consist in holding that description of property, but the guilt lies in trespassing on it."[3]

William J. Grayson wrote a poem *The Hireling and Slave.*[4]

If bound to the daily labour while he lives,
His is the daily bread that labour gives;
Guarded from want, from beggary secure,
He never feels what Hireling crowds endure,
Nor knows, like them, in hopeless want to crave,
For wife and child, the comforts of the slave,
Or the sad thought that, when about to die,
He leaves them to the world's cold charity,
And sees them forced to seek the poor-house door
The last, sad, hated refuge of the poor.

This genteel recitation of pieties reached its crescendo with the election of Abraham Lincoln as president of the United States. Lincoln's campaign had been silent on the issue of the rights of workers in the North. He had, however, spoken about slavery. His in-laws owned slaves, giving him a family connection to the practice. While opposing slavery, he campaigned on a practical platform advocating a gradual end to the institution, the harshness of the lives of hundreds of thousands of slaves in the meantime notwithstanding. But even this moderate solution was too radical for plantation owners.

In his comprehensive work, *South Carolina, A History,* Walter Edgar explained events this way:

> *South Carolinians left the Union in order to preserve, protect, and defend themselves, their families, their homes, and the good order and harmony of their community from the horrors they feared a Republican administration would bring: race war, economic disaster, political subjugation, and social equality. With freedom, the state's black majority would turn on its former masters and butcher them, as had occurred in Haiti. Not only would South Carolinians' capital investments in slaves be lost, but without slavery blacks would not be an effective labor force; therefore, the value of the agricultural land, buildings, and machinery would decline. Working-class whites and yeoman farmers would have to compete with free blacks in the labor market. If black Carolinians were given the right to vote, their*

> *numbers would overwhelm the white majority in two-thirds of the state's thirty districts. Any statewide elections would be controlled by the black majority. Social equality would bring with it the possibility of racial amalgamation.*

Displeased with the outcome of the election, on December 20, 1860, the South Carolina General Assembly met and voted to secede from the Union. Its resolution asserted that with Lincoln's inauguration: "The guarantees of the Constitution will then no longer exist; the equal rights of the states will be lost. The slaveholding states will no longer have the power of self-government and the federal government will have become their enemy."

Framed in this way, the issue of secession has since been rationalized by some as involving "states rights" rather than slavery. That is a half truth. The "state's right" at issue was the right of whites to own and keep slaves and continue to profit from the labors of those held in bondage.[5]

In an effort to get Southerners who did not own slaves to join the movement for secession, Edisto Island planter John Townsend made a blatant appeal to racism. "In no country in the world does the poor white man, whether slaveholder or non-slaveholder, occupy so enviable a position as in the slaveholding States of the South. His color admits him to social and civil privileges which the white man enjoys nowhere else....[T]he status and color of the black race become the badge of inferiority, and the poorest non-slaveholder may rejoice with the richest of his brethren of the white race, in the distinction of his color."[6]

Three Georgetown planters signed South Carolina's Ordinance of Secession: Samuel Taylor Atkinson (1822-1880) of Prince George Parish, Francis Simons Parker (1814-1865) of Prince George Parish and John Izard Middleton (1800-1877) of All Saints Parish.

War broke out. "Politicians start wars; soldiers fight and die in them," Secretary of State (and former Army General and Chairman of the Joint Chiefs of Staff) Colin L. Powell said in his 1995 autobiography.[7]

The South never had a chance, regional chauvinism and bravado notwithstanding. Like Japan when it brought the United States into World War II by bombarding Pearl Harbor some eighty years later, the South was vastly outnumbered, under financed, poorly armed and lacked the economic might to wage an extended war against the dominant industrial power it chose as an enemy when it bombarded Fort Sumter. In fact, the South was so short of manpower that, early in the war (September 1862), the 2nd Confederate Conscription increased the age to which men would be eligible for the draft to forty-five.[8] Meanwhile, by pressing into service its poor residents as well

Dead soldiers on the battlefield. *Courtesy of the National Achieves.*

as those in the steady flow of newly arriving immigrants, the North could maintain the stream of fresh, relatively young replacements to the front lines. Its incentive for doing so: Northern industrialists, bankers, mine owners, arms makers, shipbuilders and merchants stood to reap huge profits by financing and supplying a protracted war of attrition, with the financial and industrial base of the North growing stronger with each passing year. The South, meanwhile, had to obtain a significant part of its military supplies by running blockades and debated whether to draft slaves for combat in exchange for their freedom. Fear of how armed blacks would aim their weapons prevented that. Fear of black dissent found expression in Georgetown in the fall of 1862 when three escaped slaves returned for their wives and were caught. They were promptly executed. "Blacks were encouraged to attend the execution" so "the effect [of the hangings would] not be forgotten," William Kaufman Scarborough wrote in his book *Masters in the Big House.*[9]

In the war, the Northern economic interests prevailed. While Southern troops-the vast majority of whom never owned a slave or even cared about the issue[10]-won many battles, they were ill-equipped and undermanned, and, not surprisingly, lost the war. In the process, a half-million brave young men suffered, bled and died, each believing God was on and at his side.

CHAPTER V

"MASSA BEEN HIDE. BEEN IN SWAMP."

Former slave Ellen Godfrey,
at age ninety-eight

AS IN ALL WARS, THE blood was red. Blue blood almost never stains battlefields. While they may urge armed conflict and their profits are frequently enhanced by it, the well-connected and the well-heeled do not dirty their hands with war, at least not in a way in which they are likely to get hurt. During the War Between the States, Northern sons of the wealthy avoided the draft by purchasing a replacement. This use of money to stay safe had its more modern counterpart during the Vietnam War when draft deferments to attend college and influence peddling to get into the National Guard were the techniques used by the well-to-do to keep their sons out of harm's way. On that subject, Secretary of State Colin Powell has written:

> *I particularly condemn the way our political leaders supplied the manpower for that war [in Vietnam]. The policies—determining who would be drafted and who would be deferred, who would serve and who would escape, who would die and who would live—were an anti-democratic disgrace. I can never forgive a leadership that said, in effect: These young men—poor, less educated, less privileged—are expendable (someone described them as "economic cannon fodder"), but the rest are too good to risk. I am angry that so many of the sons of the powerful and well placed and so many professional athletes (who were probably healthier than any of us) managed to wangle slots in Reserve and National Guard units. Of the many tragedies of Vietnam, this raw class discrimination strikes me as the most damaging to the ideal that all Americans are created equal and owe equal allegiance to their country.*[1]

Georgetown Confederate War Monument, circa 1900. *Courtesy of the Georgetown County Library Morgan Collection.*

During the conflict of the 1860s, those wealthy Southern planters who did serve used their wealth to raise troops and were appointed as commanding officers where the risk was lower. While not disclosing how many were older than age forty-five and, therefore, ineligible for the draft (and/or otherwise unable to volunteer), one historian reports that of the 339 Southern slaveholders who owned more than 250 slaves at the outbreak of hostilities, only 4 were killed in action during the war. Only twenty of them lost sons.[2]

According to the Confederate War Memorial at Church and Screven Streets in Georgetown, of the twenty-five officers and noncommissioned officers of Company A, Georgetown Rifle Guards under the command of Captain (and later Governor) Plowden C.J. Weston, one was killed.

Of the 113 privates in the company, 41 were killed, wounded or captured, for a total casualty rate of 36 percent. Those who died included A.P. Skipper who was killed at Chickamauga, Georgia, and T.J. Harris, W.J. Clarkson and James Mulken, all of whom died at Murfreesboro, Tennessee. J.B. Thomas was captured at

Gilbert Johnson, seated at center front row, circa 1900. *Courtesy of the Georgetown County Library Morgan Collection.*

Missionary Ridge, Georgia. I.M. Cook was captured at Murfreesboro and never returned. The bugler boy, C. Tabler, was reported as missing and never found.

Meanwhile, Captain Joshua Ward of the Waccamaw Light Artillery missed so much time that, in October 1863, several men in his company filed charges against him. Although his commanding general ordered an investigation, Ward was not removed or demoted, instead in April 1864, he took an indefinite leave of absence, never to return to his company. He resigned his commission and asked for a passport so he could leave the country. "I have had repeated attacks of chills and fever," Ward wrote as his reason for resigning his commission, "which has completely undermined my constitution, and as I am desirous of going over to Europe for a change, hope that my resignation will be accepted."[3]

One Georgetown boy who actually fought was Gilbert Johnson. He served in Company B of the Brooks Rifle Guards.

After being involved in a number of smaller skirmishes, Gilbert Johnson arrived at Murfreesboro. His chronicler explained what happened this way:

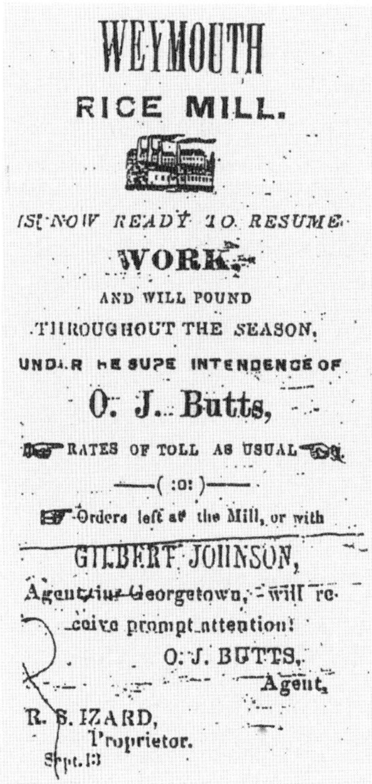

Advertisement appearing in Georgetown newspaper, December 1876.

> *At Murfreesboro there was a terrible battle....For two-and-a half miles there were dead bodies and pools of blood. In that country there were beautiful large hogs and they feasted on the dead, which was an awful sight to see.*
>
> *At Missionary Ridge, Mr. Johnson was wounded in the left shoulder and taken to Marietta Hospital in Georgia....Gangrene set in...and the doctors said his shoulder would have to be amputated and got all the instruments ready for the operation. Mr. Johnson looked in a corner of the room and saw many arms, fingers, and legs that had been cut off by the doctors, and he protested against his shoulder being cut. The doctors insisted. He pulled out an old Colt pistol from under his pillow and said he would kill any man who attempted it. The doctor turned on his heel and said, "Die then."*[4]

Johnson survived the war, returning home to operate a rice mill on Weymouth Plantation on the Pee Dee River.

While Gilbert Johnson and other sons of Georgetown were fighting, suffering and, in many instances, dying, Georgetown County itself remained relatively peaceful. Most of the military activity in the county involved garrison duty and occasional pursuits of blockade-runners around Murrells Inlet at the northern border. What happened there revealed a fundamental truth about war. While weapons, warriors and causes change, war doesn't. It breeds senseless brutality. A fairly typical example of this was recounted by a former slave being interviewed as part of the Federal Writers Project during the Great Depression. She told of Yankee soldiers walking on the beach. When they came over a sand dune, a Confederate battery at Laurel Hill Plantation opened fire, denying the Yankees an avenue of retreat. The rebels captured two prisoners. "Hang one colored man and one white man to Oaks seashore. White man...sergeant or big cap'n," the woman recalled.

What that incident actually involved was part of a naval encounter between the federal gunboat *Perry* and a blockade-runner named the *Cecilia*. The *Cecilia* was out of Nassau in the Bahamas. When the shooting ended, the captain of the *Perry* dispatched twenty-two seamen to set fire to the *Cecilia*. The ensign in charge of the party sent some of his men to the *Cecilia* and took the remaining twelve down the beach to look around. He and his party were captured. During that confrontation, Seaman John Pickham was injured. He could not get up when ordered, so a Confederate captain summarily shot and killed Pickham. Today, that would be a war crime. The other seamen, save one, were taken prisoner and later sent to Georgia's Andersonville prison, a place notorious for, among other things, its "deadline" that resulted in death if crossed. One black sailor named George Brimsmaid was separated from the rest of the prisoners by two Confederate soldiers and a civilian. This trio pushed took Brimsmaid into the woods and lynched him.[5]

In response to the execution of prisoners of war, on December 14, 1864, "a big streak come over" as the Yankee gunships fired an artillery barrage in retaliation. This act of retribution did no harm to the Confederates. Instead, it resulted in what is commonly called "collateral damage." Innocent noncombatants became victims. Some in the slave quarters were killed, including a woman named Judy and the brother-in-law of the former slave, Miss Georgie, who lived to tell the tale.[6]

In late February 1865, Georgetown fell under Union control. An expedition composed of the USS *Pawnee*, the USS *Nipsic*, the USS *Mingoe*, the USS *Catalpa* and the USS *Harvest Moon* led by Admiral John A. Dahlgren steamed to Winyah Bay.[7] Ensign Allen K. Noyes took a party of ten sailors into Georgetown and demanded its surrender. "Town officials turned over their authority to Noyes with no arguments and gave him the keys to town hall. Noyes sent three seamen inside the building to raise the American flag on the bell tower. When the flag unfurled, the seamen gave three cheers and fired a volley from their muskets." Although a small band of Confederate horsemen raced down the street and opened fire on the sailors, the raiding party quickly retreated when shots were fired in return. According to a March 8, 1865 report in the *Charleston Courier,* the rebels "hastily evacuated the town." The admiral sent his gunboat up the rivers to try to cut off the Confederate horsemen, but they had already fled into the swamps, taking Seaman Morris Sullivan with them as a hostage.[8]

The murder of two prisoners of war, one senseless act of destruction of a rice mill,[9] some small skirmishes and a postwar incident involving the sinking of the *Harvest Moon* constituted the entirety of local resistance. Instead of fighting, wealthy slaveholders—who had urged going to war but stayed at home during the fighting—fled at the first sign of danger. Ninety-nine-year-old Ellen Godfrey said when the Yankees finally came, "Massa been hide. Been in swamp."

Ben Horry recounted the time: "Two Yankee gun boats come up Waccamaw River. Come by us plantation. One stop to Sandy Island, Mont Arena landing. One gone Watsaw [Wachesaw landing]. Old Marsh Josh and all the White buckra gone to Marlboro County to hide in a boat by name *Pilot Boy*. Take Colonel Ward and all the cap'n to hide from gun boat till peace declare."[10]

In her reminiscence of war years for the Daughters of the Confederacy, Margaret Blanch Rouquie, told of the "Yankee Gunboats" that steamed up the Black River "burning and plundering as 'the spirit moved them' to punish 'the damned Rebels.' They stopped at Rural Hall. My granduncle, accompanied by 'old Daddy Abram,' the foreman of the slaves, went down to the landing to meet them. The Union officers were received with the courtesy and tact so characteristic of this 'old Southern gentleman.' They were invited up to the house and entertained, sampling with great relish my uncle's excellent wine. The slaves were then summoned and questioned about their treatment."

Whether out of intimidation or affection, they "declared that they had 'no fault to find with Massa.' He was 'good' to them, and they 'loved him.' After taking all they wanted, the 'Gunboat' passed on to the next plantation, leaving it in ashes."[11]

With only isolated resistance, and a great deal of expectation by slaves and foreboding by whites, Georgetown quickly came under Federal control.

Mariah Heywood recalled the day as a bright and a sunny Sunday. "Big guns shooting! House jar...water shake out the glass. Miss Susan take her spyglass and stand behind one of them big posses [posts] and spy them big boats shooting! And boss say don't get in front of them posses—they might shoot you....

"That day, all the right hand servant always take they massa title." The old people declared, "Thank God!" Others cried out: "Massa, He Coming (meaning freedom)!! He Coming!!" The children said: "What coming? What coming? What coming, grandma?" She assured them: "You all will know. You all will know!"

Chapter VI

Potter's Raid

Not everyone shared the joy of Union occupation. In April 1865, about two miles south of the city of Georgetown, Ben Smith left his plantation to go to Six-Mile Creek north of the city to "see about some cows." His sister Donie, his wife Sallie and his baby son John remained behind. Sallie Smith's brother, John Bourne, had not yet returned from the war, but had sent home a gold watch and a good suit of clothes for safekeeping. A short while later, as the women were attending to household chores, Donie Smith heard "a confused noise of geese and chickens squawking, turkeys yelping, the din of many voices and the tramping of hundreds of feet. Running to the window and looking out, she saw a sight which struck terror to her heart."

"'Sallie, Sallie,' she called, 'Come and see. The negro raiders are coming on us. What shall we do?'"[1]

"Potter's Raid" was an offshoot of Sherman's march through South Carolina. Beginning on April 5, 1865, Union General Edward E. Potter led fifteen thousand troops, including colored troops and freed slaves, on a raid that began in Georgetown and ended in North Carolina, supplying themselves at the expense of the population living along the way. Its beginning was described this way in Nannie Beaty's *Recollections and Reminiscences*:

> *Coming down the road was a motley array of negroes of all sizes and ages. About five hundred ignorant negroes inflamed with idea of their power, feeling that they could rob, pillage and burn with no fear of punishment now that the Northern army was victorious.*

> *This was known as Potter's Raid. They had visited other plantations and taken whatever they wanted. The chickens, turkeys and geese had been taken on their progress through the county and carried along in wagons, also taken from their former masters.*
>
> *They came up to a plantation where there were only defenseless women and children, as at Ben Smith's, took everything in the house or on the place that they wanted, went in the stables, got the horses or mules, hitched them to wagons or carts and, loading in all they had gathered, drove on with it to the next plantation, where they could commit any dreadful crime or burn the house and go unmolested.*

During the pillaging of her home, Miss Smith managed to save John Bourne's gold pocket watch by slipping it "in the bosom of her dress. It was done so quickly that it was not noticed by Richard Grant [one of the leaders of the raiding party] and his companion [a tall, slim black man named Sancho]."[2]

The raiders finally left, warning that the men of the household "had better come back here and take the oath, or before God, we are coming back and kill every one of them. You tell 'em so." The oath was the pledge of allegiance to the United States.

"When Ben Smith returned home that evening to find his house stripped and desolate and his wife and sister terrified, his astonishment and anger knew no bounds," Beaty continued. "He was full of regret that he had not stayed at home that day. How often we would act differently if we could look into the future and see what was in store for us and our dear ones; and yet if he had been at home, he would have tried to defend his home and dear ones and would almost certainly have been killed."

Potter's army marched through to North Carolina and returned to Georgetown sixteen days later. The only local resistance was encountered April 16, 1865 at Potatoe[3] Bed Ferry. Three of Potter's men—Private J.C. Johnson, Private Jeff White and a lieutenant named Rogers—were wounded.[4] No local militia was injured.

Potter returned to Georgetown on April 21, 1865. By the time he had returned, Potter had been joined by six thousand former slaves.[5] On his return, Potter traveled to Charleston, turning over command of his troops to Colonel P.P. Brown. Thereafter, Georgetown was occupied by white brigades from New York and Massachusetts Volunteers—the 157th and 54th, respectively—and thirteen companies of U.S. Colored Troops.[6] Those troops seized the cannons in the massive earthworks at Battery White, a few miles south of the city of Georgetown along the shore of Winyah Bay. Because this artillery was too heavy to move, the soldiers pushed the cannons off their parapets into the marsh. They were left there to rust, untouched for more than sixty years before retrieved and remounted.[7]

As the city was being turned over to the Army by the Navy, Admiral Dahlgren lost his flagship. The USS *Harvest Moon*, under the command of Captain John K. Crosby, was struck by a Confederate torpedo and sank. One version of local history has it that this was an act of resistance carried out by a small band of rebels who in "the chilly predawn darkness" floated a torpedo into the ship's path. "It struck her amidships and she went down in."[8] Another version holds that the sinking was an accident.[9] Either way, the torpedo "blew a hole through the starboard quarter, tearing away the main deck over it." This caused the ship "to sink in five minutes in two and a half fathoms of water."[10] One sailor, a steward named John Hazzard, lost his life. He may have been the last sailor of the U.S. Navy to die because wealthy plantation owners, including those in Georgetown, did not want to free their slaves. The smokestack of the USS *Harvest Moon* is still visible at low tide from Battery White. Whether accidental or as a last act of defiance, the sinking did not stop the inevitable course of events.[11]

When Federal troops took control of the city of Georgetown, they confiscated several buildings. Two stand directly across the street from one another at the corner of Cannon and Prince Streets in the heart of the old part of town. One is the Winyah Indigo Society building, a meeting place for local genteel society. The organization predates the Revolutionary War. Its building was constructed in 1857 and used by Union troops as a headquarters. The other was "the old Rouquie house" that had been owned by a Confederate soldier, Stephen William Rouquie. It was used as a hospital, and one upstairs room in the house served as an operating room. The blood of Union soldiers reportedly still stains its floors. The homes are also said to be haunted by Union soldiers, just like the entire region is still haunted by the War Between the States.

(Singing):
Freedom forever!
freedom ever more!
Want to see the devil run
Let the Yankee fling a ball
The Domocrack will take to the swamp![12]

Chapter VII

"Providence punishes national sins by national calamities."

Virginia slaveholder George Mason, 1787[1]

IN 1565, THE FINAL WESTWARD DRIVE of Islam was halted when Christianity's Knights of Saint John of Jerusalem defeated Sultan Suleyman the Magnificent at the island of Malta in the Mediterranean Sea. A month into the siege, the sultan's men overran the 129 knights who were holding Fort Saint Elmo on one side of the harbor. The Muslims decapitated their prisoners and set their bodies adrift on crosses toward Fort Saint Angelo where the remaining Christian defenders were holding out. In retaliation, the Knights of Saint John cut off the heads of their Muslim prisoners, stuffed the heads into cannons and fired them back across the waterway. The military jihad continued for another two months until Christian reinforcements arrived from Sicily, ousting the Muslim invaders.[2]

This gruesome event is just one of the hundreds of thousands of examples in human history demonstrating how readily one act of brutality breeds another. Modern examples abound around the world. Recognizing the danger, in his second inaugural address, President Lincoln urged everyone to forgive one another for the horrors and suffering of the previous four years: "With malice toward none, with charity for all, with firmness in the right as God gives us to see the right, let us strive on to finish the work we are in to bind up the nation's wounds, to care for him who has borne the battle and for his widow and his orphans—to do all which may achieve and cherish a just and lasting peace among ourselves and with all nations."

A lesser soul disagreed. Rather than look Lincoln in the eye and say so, a self-possessed actor crept up from behind Lincoln in a dark theater, quietly raised a pistol and shot him in the back of the head. The assassin then leaped to the stage of the Ford's Theater in Washington, D.C., and fled into the dark, taking the nation's opportunity to heal with him.

The period that followed was as turbulent as any postwar era in a country ravaged first by oppression and then war. Military battles ended. Hatred did not. The federal Constitution was amended in an effort to provide the same legal protections to everyone. These were very positive changes, albeit much too late for Quacooo, Mood, Charles, Dred Scott and the millions of others who had suffered and died while bullied by the whims of "small men who had taken on the powers and airs of tyrants and masters."[3]

At the end of the War Between the States, the U.S. Congress was dominated by the Republican Party. It, in turn, was in the hands of "radicals." Unlike President Lincoln, these ideological purists sought retribution rather than reconciliation. Initially, the property of white Southerners was seized and they were disenfranchised. Postwar social and economic chaos drove the weak Southern economy to its knees. Those who managed to hold onto their land had no work force. Newly freed slaves had no land and no work. As newly emancipated T. Thomas Fortune wrote in his book *Black and White: Land, Labor, and Politics in the South* in 1884, "To tell him he was a freeman and at the same time shut him off from free access to the soil upon which he had been reared, without a penny in his pocket and with an army of children at his coattail—some of his reputed wife's children being the illegitimate offspring of a former inhuman master—was to add insult to injury, to mix syrup and hyssop, to aggravate into curses the pretended conference of blessings."

Two and a half centuries of imprisonment, brutality and humiliation of blacks left all Southern whites fearful of the sullen, resentful and suspicious black majority that fewer than 9 percent of their fellow whites had imported and enslaved. Each side eyed the other suspiciously. In the standoff that resulted, crops failed and people went hungry.

"When the freedom [came] I was twenty-three-over the twenty-five," according to the *Recollection of Ellen Godfrey, Age 99*." Great God, have-a-mercy! McGill people have to steal for something to eat."[4]

Faced with a growing humanitarian crisis, the local white press offered a solution. The June 17, 1869 edition of the *Georgetown Times* urged white planters who found themselves in trouble because they had exploited one race of people to exploit another in its place. Complaining that "free negro labor" was "unreliable" and "the North [had] monopolized the influx of Irish and Germans" to work in its factories and fields, the *Times* advocated the importation of cheap Chinese labor:

> *[While] John Chinaman...will steal; so will the negro. He will lie; so will the negro. But work, indefatigable, persistent labor, seems to be an inherent characteristic of the Chinaman. With the negro, it is, for the most part, compulsory.*
>
> *The labor is the cheapest in the world. They are capable of adapting themselves to any pursuit, being among the most ingenious people on the globe. They will ditch, dig, plough and attend to all the requirements of agriculture while they are useful in the factories. For rice culture, they would far excel Cuffee and Sambo, both in thrift and powers of endurance.*
>
> *We are certainly in need of such laborers, particularly so for our rice fields; and the time is not far distant when the Celestials will find their way to the cotton and rice fields of the South....*
>
> *As regards the political bearings of the subject, this is a problem for politicians to work out and we will soon see how the 15th amendment [voting rights for former slaves] will apply, but the present indications are that Asia will soon pour upon and over us, countless thousands of her superfluous, cheap-living, slow-changing, un assimilating, but very useful laborers.*

In Washington, D.C., the Thirteenth Amendment to the U.S. Constitution abolishing slavery throughout the Union was adopted and promptly ratified by the states. Slaves held by Lincoln's in-laws in the border state of Kentucky were freed for the first time. The Fourteenth Amendment—extending all existing legal privileges, immunities and protections to everyone—passed and was ratified, as was the Fifteenth Amendment, extending the right to vote to males without regard to prior condition of servitude.

These changes dealt with the legal relationships between people. They acknowledged that blacks were people, at least in the eyes of the law. However, the end of warfare and the changes in the law did nothing to provide meaningful employment, educational or social opportunities to anyone who had not enjoyed them before. The changes did nothing to improve the day-to-day existence of working people, be they black, white, yellow or red. The War Between the States had not been a revolution. All the other distinctions based on race, class and gender remained intact. Women, immigrants and blacks remained subservient to white males. For those lacking land or money—regardless of age, gender or color—the only equal right they shared was the right to work long hours for starvation wages in dangerous conditions, and that's assuming they could find work. Even for those with a job, employment seldom provided meaningful opportunity for personal advancement. At the same time, federal

Georgetown workers circa 1900. *Courtesy of the Georgetown County Library Morgan Collection.*

and state legislators lined their pockets with dollars from powerful business interests, protecting the profits of corporate barons and their investors in exchange for campaign contributions or simply bribes. Business was largely unregulated. Insider trading, profit skimming, shady accounting practices and phony investment schemes flourished, and large fortunes were amassed.

Compounding the problems of these times, child labor was permitted, there weren't any provisions to care for injured workers and violence was a common response by employers to any efforts at concerted action by workers. To keep workers in check, legislatures declared labor unions to be criminal conspiracies, unlawful restraints on trade and/or an illegal interference with the right of "freedom of contract."

While the methods used may have differed, the result was the same in the North and the South. When emancipated by Northern soldiers, Mariah Heywood, and other "Alston laborers" were encouraged by their liberators to "[s]ign a contract for you boss you would work the same and get pay the end of the year-and [their former masters would] tend you when you sick all the same."[5]

Under slavery, blacks had been fed, housed and clothed until death, albeit minimally and cruelly. This disappeared with emancipation. The newly freed slaves found themselves in the same position as other impoverished people in America. If they stayed on the land, they became sharecroppers. If they moved north, they were "free" to work long hours, at low wages, in dangerous working conditions, living in employer-furnished housing and obtaining extensions of credit at employer-owned stores. If they complained, they would be fired and their names circulated on black lists.

As one Welsh immigrant miner wrote in December 1874:

> *We in this country had to bend to the ground under the burdens placed on us by the avaricious, tyrannical masters. We were forced throughout the years to work for low wages which were hardly enough to keep body and soul together; to accept those wages in script which was worthless outside the local trading circle of the company; and to buy all ours good from their store and pay 25 percent more than we could get in other places; together with robbing us of half of our coal, taxed for what we knew not, without any receipt.*
>
> *Also to show us their power, they forced us to sign the contract...that if any misunderstanding occurred between master and workman, the latter had to leave his house with ten-days notice according to the contract law, whereas the state government [otherwise] allowed three months.*
>
> *But although we suffered the above without grumbling throughout the years, it was not enough to satisfy the greed of the masters, for early this winter they rushed on us with fierceness of a lion on its prey, lowering us to 20 percent and also threatening us with 10 percent and forcing us to bind ourselves not to accept money for our labor until May 20, 1874....*
>
> *When they understood that one and all refused the above terms, they put the screw to work, that is, warning us to leave our houses within ten days; and when the time came and we had not left our houses, summoned us before the judge to demand why we refused to obey the warning. The cruel judge would not listen to us as he had been bought body and soul by the company, and gave judgment against us, together with having to pay all costs. So hundred and hundreds of families were forced to leave their homes to look for fresh houses amid the snow and ice. What a terrible sight it was to see hundreds of innocent men, women and their children having to break up their comfortable homes without knowing where to go....*
>
> *P.S. In the circumstances, I thought it better to send my family back to Wales. I heard that the ship had left, but nothing more, and if anyone reads these lines, news of them would be welcome, whether they are dead or alive.*[6]

Georgetown workers, circa 1900. *Courtesy of the Georgetown County Library Morgan Collection.*

As newly freed slave T. Thomas Fortune, observed,

> *[The industrial working conditions are] a slavery more excruciating in its exactions, more irresponsible in its machinations than that other slavery which I once endured. The chattel slaveholder must, to preserve the value of his property, feed, clothe, and house his property, and give it proper medical attention when disease or accident threatened its life. But industrial slavery requires no such care. The new slaveholder is only solicitous of obtaining the maximum of labor for the minimum of cost. He does not regard the man as of any consequence when he can no longer produce. Having worked him to death, or ruined his constitution and robbed him of his labor, he turns him out upon the world to live upon the charity of mankind or to die of inattention and starvation. He knows that it profits him nothing to waste time and money upon a disabled industrial slave. The multitude of laborers from which he can recruit his necessary laboring force is so enormous that solicitude on his part for one that falls by the wayside would be a gratuitous expenditure of humanity and charity which the world is too intensely selfish and materialistic to expect of him.*
>
> *Here he forges wealth and death at one and the same time.*[7]

Laborers in both the North and the South were tied to their employers by employer-dictated terms. Those who did not like those terms were "free" to exercise their "right of contract," quit, get blackballed and starve. Those with children could watch their little ones starve, too. It took an actual civil war—the very violent labor movement—a stock market crash and a severe economic depression to begin to empower workers. Today, corporate greed again threatens American workers, this time appearing in the form of "outsourcing" of work to places lacking age, safety, minimum wage or environmental regulations.

Because of the labor-intensive nature of rice cultivation, at the end of the war, blacks outnumbered whites in Georgetown County by eight or nine to one. Counterbalancing the perceived raw physical threat were money and land, which remained in the control of whites, the actions of the Freedman's Bureau notwithstanding. Occupying Federal troops, meanwhile, filled the thankless task of peacekeepers while the process of nation rebuilding was being sabotaged by bribery, corruption, power grabbing and political infighting. What followed was the period of "good stealing" called "Reconstruction" when predators of all types and stripes, including an awful lot of whites, descended upon the carcass of the South.

CHAPTER VIII

A FEW GOOD MEN

THE OLD ORDER OF THINGS had been overturned. The Fifteenth Amendment to the U.S. Constitution guaranteed black males the right to vote. In Georgetown, simple arithmetic added up to dramatic change. By 1867, there were 457 whites registered to vote in Georgetown County. At the same time, 2,922 blacks appeared on local voter registration rolls. Now a political majority, blacks took public office.

Into this abrupt upheaval stepped Joseph Hayne Rainey. Rainey was born June 21, 1832 in Georgetown to Edward and Teresa Rainey. His father was a barber who purchased freedom for his entire family. A free man, in 1859, Rainey traveled to Philadelphia, Pennsylvania, to marry. He then returned to South Carolina, even though doing so was in violation of an 1823 law forbidding free persons of color who left South Carolina from returning. Influential friends reportedly kept him from being prosecuted.[1]

When the War Between the States broke out, Rainey was drafted by the Confederacy to work on earthworks fortifying Charleston.[2] Within a short time, he was reassigned as a steward on a Confederate blockade-runner.[3] Unhappy with conscription, he jumped ship in Bermuda. He remained there until the end of the war, working at the Hamilton Hotel as a barber and bartender.[4]

Rainey was described by a contemporary as "a light mulatto with regular features; bright genial eyes; pleasant expression; broad, clear brow; and a profusion of silky hair. He was of medium height, with a graceful and easy

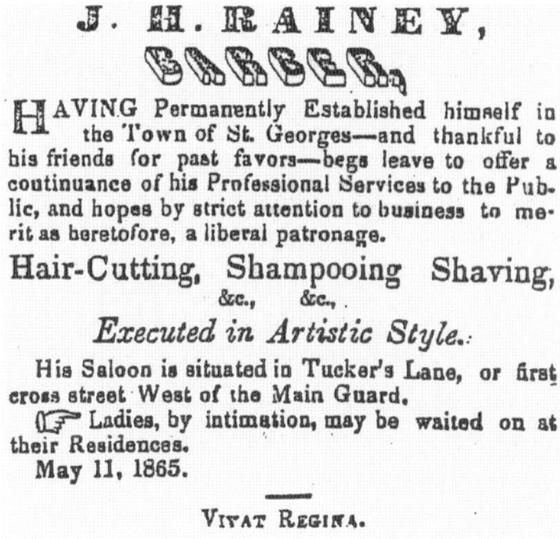

J. H. RAINEY,

BARBER,

HAVING Permanently Established himself in the Town of St. Georges—and thankful to his friends for past favors—begs leave to offer a continuance of his Professional Services to the Public, and hopes by strict attention to business to merit as heretofore, a liberal patronage.

Hair-Cutting, Shampooing Shaving, &c., &c.,

Executed in Artistic Style.

His Saloon is situated in Tucker's Lane, or first cross street West of the Main Guard.

☞ Ladies, by intimation, may be waited on at their Residences.

May 11, 1865.

VIVAT REGINA.

Advertisement in Bermuda *Royal Gazette,* July 11, 1865.

carriage and with very small hands which he used effectively in gesturing. He was courteous and suave rather than aggressive, but could defend himself well if necessary. As a speaker he was fluent and even eloquent on occasion, moderate but earnest, and held his own with opponents even in impromptu debate."[5] Another described him as "below the medium size, of a dark olive complexion, straight, black hair, finely chiseled features, modest in manners, and dignified in his deportment."[6]

In 1866, Rainey returned to South Carolina, first to Charleston and then to Georgetown where he became involved in politics. He was selected by the local Republican Party as a delegate to the South Carolina constitutional convention and subsequently elected to the state senate. Then, in July 1870, he was nominated by the Republicans to fill a vacancy in the U.S. House of Representatives. He received nearly nine thousand of the seventeen thousand votes cast in the election that fall. He was reelected and served four and one-half terms from 1870 to 1879 representing the First Congressional District, then composed of Georgetown, Horry, Marion, Williamsburg, Darlington, Chesterfield, Marlboro, Sumter, Clarendon, Kershaw and Lancaster Counties-geographically the northeastern third of the state. His record in Congress is impressive, even noble.

One of the items that came before the 42nd Congress early in 1871 was the Ku Klux Klan Act. It was an effort to stem the rising tide of white violence against blacks throughout the South. Men who hid their faces behind white sheets struck fear into the hearts of many Southerners. Blacks feared being the Klan's next victim. Whites were afraid to speak out against the brutality, fearing they would be shunned or worse. Rainey, on the other hand, faced the threat boldly, addressing the U.S. House of Representatives, saying:

> *The enormity of the crimes constantly perpetrated [by the KKK in the South] finds no parallel in the history of this Republic in her very darkest days...I need not, Mr. Speaker, recite here the murderous deeds committed both in North and South Carolina. I could touch the feelings of this House by the story of widows and orphans now wandering amid the ravines of the rural counties of my native State seeking protection and maintenance from others who are yet unable, on account of their own poverty, to grant them aid. I could dwell upon the sorrows of poor women, with their helpless infants, cast upon the world, homeless and destitute, deprived of their natural protectors by the red hand of the midnight assassin. I could appeal to you, members of this floor, as husbands and fathers, to picture to yourselves the desolation of your own happy firesides should you be suddenly snatched away from your loved ones. Think of gray haired men, whose fourscore years are almost numbered, the venerated heads of peaceful households, without warning murdered for political opinion's sake.*
>
> *When myself and colleagues shall leave these Halls and turn our footsteps toward our southern homes, we know not but that the assassin may await our coming, as marked for his vengeance. Should this befall, we would bid Congress and our country to remember that t'was-"Bloody treason flourished over us."*[7]

As a result of the efforts of Rainey and others, the KKK Act—America's first antiterrorist legislation—was signed into law by President U.S. Grant on April 20, 1871. It gave the president the power to declare martial law anywhere the Ku Klux Klan was deemed to be in rebellion against the United States. The act also made it a crime for two or more persons to conspire—by threats, intimidation or force—against anyone running for or holding public office, participating in political campaigns or voting.

The KKK Act proved to be of little help. Rather than abating, the violence increased. Rainey addressed Congress again about the problem. "Because we have thus acted, and have dared as men, on the establishment of our manhood; to declare our sentiments to the country and cast our ballots as we think best, we have been persecuted, maltreated, murdered, and in every way abused, not only men, but helpless women and children, be it said to the shame of these white citizens of South Carolina who perpetrated these atrocities."[8]

Upon returning home to campaign for reelection in 1874, Rainey traveled by horseback on the road from Cheraw to a stop in Bennettsville. He was met along the way by about sixty blacks who warned him area whites had been bragging for days that they were going to break up the Republican rally. When Rainey and his men arrived in Bennettsville, they were met by a very large crowd of white men on horseback. The whites were armed and menacing. Only the appearance of a company of U.S. Army soldiers stopped blood from flowing. "The presence of the troops was most providential. I am confident that members of both parties who are alive at this time, if it had been otherwise, would have been numbered among the dead," Rainey reported.[9]

Racial violence was not the only problem Rainey courageously confronted. Other forms of racial discrimination were rampant too. Speaking of how he was treated in the nation's capital, Rainey complained: "Why is it that colored members of Congress cannot enjoy the same immunities that are accorded to white members? Why cannot we stop at hotels here without meeting objection? Why cannot we go into restaurants without being insulted? We are here enacting laws for the country and casting votes upon important questions: we have been sent here by the suffrages of the people, and why cannot we enjoy the same benefits that are accorded to our white colleagues on this floor?...Why this discrimination against us when we enter public conveyances or places of public amusement? Why is a discrimination made against us in the churches; and why in the cemeteries when we go to pay that last debt of nature that brings us all upon a level?"[10]

On one occasion, Rainey was charged fifty cents for a five-cent beer at Ralf's, a popular Congressional drinking spot opposite the U.S. Post Office. He asked the waiter if he was being overcharged because he was "a colored man" and was insultingly told "yes." On other occasions, he was barred from riding street cars in Richmond, Virginia. He was denied the first-class train passage. On a boat from Washington to Norfolk, Virginia, he was told he had to wait for the second seating rather than eat with first-class passengers. He refused, saying he would rather starve. And in what may have been America's first sit-in demonstration, he had to be forcibly ejected from a hotel dining room in Norfolk that had refused to serve him.[11]

One of the proposals fueling the flames of racism was the postwar drive by Northern Republicans to strip Southern whites of their lands and the right to vote. Rainey was against this effort. Rather than trying to take away the legal rights of his white neighbors, Rainey supported granting them amnesty for their rebelliousness, allowing them to keep their land and restoring their right to vote. As one of his first acts in the U.S. Congress, when an amnesty bill came to the floor of the House of Representatives in 1872, Rainey spoke in favor of its passage. In doing so, he expressed the same sentiments that would earn Nelson Mandela and the Reverend Dr. Martin Luther King separate Nobel Peace Prizes during the next century. "It is not the disposition of my constituents that these disabilities should longer be retained. We are desirous of being magnanimous; it may be that we are so to a fault. Nevertheless we have open and frank hearts toward those who were our former oppressors and taskmasters. We foster no enmity now, and we desire to foster none, for their acts in the past to us or to the Government we love so well."

But Rainey asked for similar consideration.

> *While we are willing to accord them their enfranchisement and here today give our votes that they may be amnestied, while we declare our hearts open and free from any vindictive feelings toward them, we would say to those gentlemen on the other side that there is another class of citizens in the country, who have certain rights and immunities which they would like you, sirs, to remember and respect.*
>
> *The Republican members of this House will give their votes for the passage of the amnesty bill. The majority of them are also in favor of civil rights, which my people, the colored people, are desirous of having. We are in earnest about this matter. We are earnest in our support of the Government. We were earnest in the hour of the nation's perils and dangers; and now, in our country's comparative peace and tranquility, we are in earnest for our rights. We now invoke you, gentlemen, to show the same magnanimity and kindly feeling toward us—a race long oppressed; and in demonstration of this humane and just feeling, I implore you, give support to the civil rights bill, which we have been asking at your hands, lo! these many days.*[12]

When all the votes were counted, Southern whites had their land and their right to vote restored to them. The civil rights bill did not pass for several more years, only to be stricken as unconstitutional by the courts.[13] Nearly a century elapsed before the kind of civil rights act envisioned by Rainey was adopted. That 1964 law has reshaped society, even though its letter and spirit are still resisted at barber shops, beauty parlors, by funeral directors and in all but national cemeteries. In Georgetown, like elsewhere around America, those remain strictly segregated by race to this day; as do many churches.

Joseph Hayne Rainey. *Courtesy of the Library of Congress.*

In nineteenth century Georgetown, Major Charles Alston, late of the Confederate forces, was the last planter to accept the offer of amnesty. Former slave Aunt Mariah Heywood described what happened:

> *Major Charles say he'd die in Sunnyside yard fore he'd go there [to Georgetown] and take off his hat and 'swear against my swear.' He'd die in Sunnyside yard. My Massa, Major Charles Alston, was the last one to gone Georgetown and gone under that flag. He was Charles Jr., but after Confederate war he was Major Charles. Major Charles the last man of Waccamaw gone under the flag! At Georgetown. Went down in row-boat. My father gone and tell old man Tom Nesbitt to have his boat and four of his best mens. Got to go off a piece. Pa gone. Have boat ready. Ma got up. Cook a traveling lunch for 'em. Fore day. Blue uniform. Yellow streak down side—just like this streak in my dress. Yellow bar. Most of 'em had to rob dead Yankees or go naked. Last gentleman gone under the flag.*[14]

Regardless of if he understood or appreciated the fact, Charles Alston was able to rejoin the American economic mainstream because his neighbor, Rainey, lived by the Golden Rule. Regrettably, Rainey's fundamental decency remains largely unheralded in American history.[15] There is one exception to this undeserved historical anomaly. In his political autobiography, then Speaker of the House James G. Blaine wrote: "The colored representatives, who had been slaves, were willing to release their task masters from every form of disability, but the immediate friends of the masters were unwilling to extend the civil rights of colored man. So far as chivalry, magnanimity, charity, Christian kindness, were involved, the colored men appeared at an advantage. Perhaps it is not surprising that lingering prejudice and the sudden change of situation should have restrained Southern white men from granting these privileges, but it must always be mentioned to the credit of the colored man that he gave his vote for amnesty to his former master when his demand for delay would have obstructed the passage of the measure."[16]

Chapter IX

A Few Bad Men

While Joseph Hayne Rainey was working for everyone's benefit in Washington, others at home in Georgetown were creating trouble.

William H. Jones was elected to the South Carolina Senate to fill the vacancy created when Rainey went off to the U.S. Congress. James A. Bowley had moved to Georgetown from Maryland after the war and had been elected to the South Carolina House of Representatives in 1872. Each had his own constituency. Initially, the three men—Rainey, Jones and Bowley—got along and worked cooperatively. But once elected, Bowley acquired a reputation for accepting bribes, and neither did Jones enjoy a sterling reputation. Both lived in large and lavish homes, well beyond the means of even the most industrious black entrepreneur, all while other newly freed Georgetonians continued to live in severe poverty.

In August 1874, Bowley called a meeting one Wednesday evening at the Georgetown County Court House as part of his reelection effort. Jones sent some of his followers to the meeting armed with Winchester rifles and Colt revolvers to break up the gathering. A fight broke out; many were injured.

When news of what happened spread, Jones's supporters armed themselves and went looking for Bowley. According to news accounts: "Exasperated females brandished their clubs and sliced the unoffending air in a manner imitative of what they wished to do with the corpus of Bowley. So many threats were made that the property owners—both white and colored—were apprehensive that incendiaries would be at work during the night. The closing shades of night, however, summoning this noisy multitude to their homes, the excitement subsided and comparative quiet reigned throughout the town. Thursday, the excitement, to a great extent, was renewed, caused principally by fresh arrivals of blacks armed with miscellaneous weapons. In the afternoon some of those engaged in the Court House row were indicted and brought before Trial Justice Gipson. The Court House was crowded, and the number of clubs displayed on the occasion indicated the intention of those who held them, in case another row occurred. The counsel for the defendants, seeing how matters stood, very wisely asked a postponement of the case, which was granted. The case was adjourned till 10 A.M. Monday. "[1]

That evening, Bowley's supporters gathered, and a little after midnight. "[T]he quiet slumbers of our citizens were disturbed by the shooting of muskets and pistols in the northern part of town. The shooting was continued from about half past twelve until nearly daylight. Few, at the time, thought that midnight assassins were at their horrible work. But such was the case."[2]

Streetlights surrounding the home of Senator Jones were shot out by the marauders, "in order more effectively to conceal themselves and the deformity of their evil deeds." A man named Harrison was severely wounded in the head. The senator's house was struck by more than two hundred bullets. "Inside, books, beds and sofas were perforated with the balls, and picture frames, windows, glasses, etc. were smashed to pieces. The balls even splintered the gilded pinions of Jones' wooden eagle, which has clawed the floor of his upper piazza for, lo! these many weeks past,"[3] the Charleston newspaper reported.

Sheriff S.R. Carr, Georgetown Intendant George R. Congdon and Congressman Rainey wrote the governor about this "dastardly assault."[4] The black militia was called out and, by nine o'clock in the morning, its members, along with the sheriff, were making arrests, Bowley included.

"A fearful riot prevailed"[5] and the scene around the jail was one of great excitement. Jones was a colonel in the state militia, and many of his supporters were members of the militia, too. They assembled at the jail and tried to take it over, while their friends stood cursing, swearing, calling for vengeance and occasionally emphasizing the point by throwing a brick at the jail. "Laborers, forgetting their work, thronged the streets. Women, prompted by the feeling of the moment, left their children to take care of themselves, rushed out to add to the crowd, and gave vent to the hate and malice raging in their breasts. The dusky Amazons from the country, armed with their favorite weapon, the rice hook, followed in the wake of the militia."

In the news reporter's opinion, "more awful curses and foul language cannot be found recorded in the journals of hell." When the exasperated crowd finally realized that Bowley could not be seized and lynched, it reassembled around his house and began to tear it down. "This fine residence has for a long time been the object of envy," the news reported.[6]

Georgetown was "in a state of revolt, civil officers having no control whatsoever; the jail...in the hands of the militia, and the Sheriff very much demoralized, declaring he had no power to do anything in the premises," the state adjutant and inspector general (himself black) reported to the governor. Sheriff Carr became "so panic-stricken as to have so far lost all manhood and courage" and fled town.[7]

To restore order, the governor dispatched the U.S. Revenue Cutter *Moccasin* from Charleston to Georgetown. When it arrived, it fired a signal (or warning) shot. This had "the very salutary effect on the crowd of rioters, stopping many who were on the outskirts of town and about to enter; and causing those already assembled to retire," the press reported.[8]

Because "the lives of Bowley and his friends were not safe in the jail, guarded, as they were, by an infuriated and hostile militia, who had threatened their lives," a major general named Swails had Bowley and his men transported on the *Moccasin* to Charleston.[9]

As the prisoners passed on their way to the cutter, Jones's supporters filled the streets, "evidently in a state of suppressed excitement, but they made no unlawful demonstration."[10]

After the ship sailed, everyone gathered at the county courthouse. Once there, General Swails told the crowd that he "deplored the disgrace which had been brought upon the colored people by the lawless and outrageous conduct" of the various rioters. He assured everyone that he would exercise his authority to the utmost to maintain order. He also rebuked Jones and his militiamen for acting unlawfully and promised they would be punished. Swails promised "such other steps...as might be necessary to vindicate the majesty of the law and preserve the peace of the country."[11]

General H.W. Purvis spoke next. He, too, criticized militia members, characterizing what happened as "the riotous proceedings of an irresponsible mob with arms in their hands, who had assumed the authority of converting the jail of the county into a military garrison." Purvis promised, "As officers of the militia, their straps and epaulets will be taken from their shoulders; as to the privates, their arms will be taken from them and their company disbanded."

Congressman Rainey spoke last. He said Georgetown's blacks had been made free by the accidents of history, and that "while no combination of circumstances could ever place them again into slavery, that many of the privileges of freedom might be taken away if the people of the whole country found that they abused the rights conferred upon them." He went on to say that people of color were "on trial before the world, and it depended upon the manner of their conduct whether some of the rights they now enjoyed would not be curtailed." He then spoke a fundamental truth, advising all those present that if they "expected to hold on to the rights and privileges which the law had conferred" upon them, they "must obey the law."[12] Today, prisons overflow with those who fail to recognize this social axiom.

Peace was restored in Georgetown but not without a price. The riots and lawlessness brought about by political rivalries among blacks terrorized whites, whose fears of helplessness galvanized them into action. They had, according to the Charleston newspaper, become "pretty apprehensive of incendiarism and other crimes" and were "glad that the cutter had arrived." It was, some whites said, "the first time since the war that they felt that they had a government to protect them."[13]

Within weeks, the first meeting of an all-white militia was convened at the courthouse. It adopted the name of the military company Plowden C.J. Weston had organized during the Civil War—the Georgetown Rifle Guards. Its aims were discussed in a news article commemorating its first anniversary. "In cases of emergency, the Georgetown Rifle Guards would be a dangerous and formidable foe to contend with. The powerful and unerring Remington and the rapid and deadly Winchester are a host in themselves while those long glittering bayonets do not look as though they would improve on close acquaintance."[14]

W.D. Morgan, who was later to become Georgetown's mayor, was appointed as the first warden of the Rifle Guards and given the rank of sergeant. To enhance its military aura, the guard decked itself out in single-breasted, gray frock coats trimmed with green cord, a single row of brass palmetto buttons down the front and smaller buttons on the sleeves. This array was topped off with a gray felt hat, looped on the side with cross guns, with a green feather in the left side of the hat flowing over the top in the front and bottomed off with black pants. Officer uniforms were the same except they were trimmed with gold cord and contained an insignia of rank.[15]

From the next eight years, the Rifle Guards functioned as a quasi-military, semisocial club.[16] Its members would have regular drills, meetings, encampments and parades in furtherance of their primary mission of assuaging the fears of whites. When those military practices were concluded, receptions, dances and other activities typically followed. One newspaper account of the August 1875 meeting said, "When feed cakes, lemonade, etc.

Georgetown Rifle Guards, circa 1900. *Courtesy of the Georgetown County Library Morgan Collection.*

had regaled the party the fragrant weed was called into requisition, and speeches etc. were in order."[17] This activity would have been very much in line with one organizational purpose, as stated in the guard's constitution, of "the promotion of social intercourse."[18]

At the same time as they were organizing and arming, white residents sought to reach a peaceful accommodation with their black neighbors. They did this because they were hopelessly outnumbered and it would take a day or two to get the sort of military aid necessary to stop any outbreak of racial violence. In the meantime, the strife would exact a heavy toll on both sides, no matter what the outcome. A special meeting of the town council was convened at the county courthouse. There, a Committee of Safety was created. The founding resolution of the organization read:

> *Whereas, certain reports and rumors of an incendiary nature have been circulating through the town and country to such an extent that they are tending to engender feelings of distrust and alarm among the people;*
>
> *And whereas, we the citizens of the Town of Georgetown, disregarding questions of color or politics, believing the welfare of the races to be identical, and that they are bound together by common destiny, and that what destroys the prosperity of one injures the other;*
>
> *And whereas, the town council has deemed it expedient, through their proper officer, the intendant, to call a mass meeting of citizens of the town, irrespective of*

> *color or politics, to advise together for their mutual protection, and the enforcement of good order in the town; therefore, be it*
>
> *Resolved 1st, that we, the citizens of the Town of Georgetown, in mass meeting assembled, laying aside all political or race questions, and desiring to live in harmony and peace with all, do hereby pledge ourselves to each other to use every means at our command to prevent any open or general violation of the laws of the land, regarding any such attempt as an infringement of the rights and immunities which the constitution and laws guarantee to every citizen, without distinction of race, color or previous condition.*
>
> *2d, That we desire to harmonize (not to antagonize) the races with each other, and that in that direction all our energies will be bent; and although we deprecate violence of any kind, will be prepared to protect ourselves (should occasion require it) and will defend our persons and property from unprovoked insult and injury, exercising those powers which the laws give.*[19]

Ten whites—including the white Sheriff Carr, J.W. Tarbox, J.B. Steele, R.E. Frazer, Benjamin Hazard and J.L. Ward—and ten blacks—including Alonzo Johnson and James Brownfield, a man in his late thirties with a wife and three children[20]—were appointed to the resulting Committee of Safety.[21] They were all appointed because they were respected and respectable people. Rainey returned to Washington and continued to press the cause of civil rights for all. Meanwhile, in Georgetown, an informal "fusion," or power sharing agreement, began to take shape in which only whites ran for some offices and only blacks ran for others.

By 1880, the fusion had its desired effect and some modicum of social security was felt by all. After March 1880, the Georgetown Rifle Guards did not meet for the next nine years.[22]

Chapter X
One Last Try

As racial peace returned to Georgetown, white resistance to blacks joining the social mainstream increased throughout the rest of South Carolina and across America.[1] Intimidation was not limited to violence or threats of it. Wherever possible, whites resisted the efforts of their black neighbors to assert themselves at the polls. James G. Blaine explained the problem to Congress by saying: "[I]n South Carolina there seems to have been no election at all in any proper sense of the term. There was a series of skirmishes over the State, in which the polling places were regarded as forts to be captured by one party and held against the other, and where this could not be done with convenience, frauds in the count, and tissue-ballot devices were resorted to in order effectively to destroy the voice of the majority."[2]

Speaking on the same subject, Rainey said: "There is a constant effort to subjugate as much as possible the laboring classes, in order that they might keep alive in the breast the idea of the inferiority of the negro and his incapacity for any position apart from being a hewer of wood and a drawer of water. He is all desirable if he votes the democratic ticket, works the fields, and does the bidding of his former master. But as soon as he attempts to assert his manhood by advocating the claims of a republican for office, be his candidate ever so pure in character or even 'to the manor born,' from that day onward he is marked victim for the shotgun policy or the penitentiary."[3]

Reiterating his plea that Congress pass a comprehensive civil rights act, Rainey observed: "There are some things that are far more precious in the eye of the American citizen at least than all the wealth of the Indies, and those are human liberty and human rights. These are fundamental and much prized by my race; yes sir, superior to all pecuniary consideration, as the soul is to the body. For their possession and their complete exercise men and nations laid down their lives in all ages."[4]

Rainey's efforts at reconciliation went largely unheeded. The rhetoric against blacks escalated, along with the violence. In an editorial against passage of the civil rights act that Rainey was advocating, the September 10, 1874 *Atlanta News* said:

> *Radicalism has declared a war of extermination against the whites of the South. It proposes to punish rebels and make "treason odious" by the most vindictive measures its malignity can conceive. Our fate is to be less merciful than that of the Trojans, less sublime than that of the Carthaginians. We are not to perish by the sword as these people perished; we are to live, and live in degradation. Our helots and serfs of yesterday are to rule us politically and to sit beside us on terms of equality socially. All pride of race is to be crushed within us. We are to be the slave; the Negro is to be the master.*
>
> *History gives no precedent for this monstrous program.... [It] will not end in this civil rights bill. The next thing on the program will be to enact a compulsory education law, and compel us to send our children to public schools, there to herd with Negroes....*
>
> *Our only hope is in a stern resolute resistance—a resistance to the death, if necessary, with arms in our hands.*
>
> *Let there be White Leagues formed in every town, village, and hamlet of the South and let us organize for the great struggle which seems to be inevitable. If the October elections which are to be held at the North are favorable to the Radicals, the time will have arrived for us to prepare for the very worst. The radicalism of the Republican Party must be met by the radicalism of white men. We have no war to make against the United States government, but against the Republican Party our hate must be unquenchable, our war interminable and merciless. Fast fleeting away is the day for wordy protests and idle appeals to the magnanimity of the Republican Party. By brute force they are endeavoring to force us into acquiescence to their hideous program.*
>
> *We have submitted long enough to indignities, and it is time to meet brute force with brute force. Every Southern state should swarm with White Leagues, and we should stand ready to act the moment Grant signs the civil rights bill.... The signing of the bill will be a declaration of war against the Southern whites.*[5]

Rainey's response was already on record. "I say to you, gentlemen, that you are making a mistake. Public opinion is aroused on this question. I tell you that the Negro will never rest until he gets his rights. We ask them because we know it is proper, not because we want to deprive any other class of the rights and immunities they enjoy, but because they are granted to us by the law of the land."[6]

The civil rights bill extending legal rights to blacks did not pass until 1875—three years after amnesty was granted to Southern whites. Even then, it only passed after provisions calling for desegregation of public education and equality in jury service were taken out of the bill. It was ruled unconstitutional by the U.S. Supreme Court in 1883. T. Thomas Fortune, a former slave, described the result in his 1884 book titled *Black and White: Land, Labor and Politics in the South*. "While the white men of the South, the capitalists, the land sharks, the poor white trash, and the nondescript, with a thousand years of Christian civilization and culture behind them, with 'the boast of chivalry, the pomp of power,' these white scamps who have imposed upon the world the idea that they were paragons of virtue and the heaven-sent vice-regents of civil power, organized themselves into a band of outlaws whose concatenative chain of auxiliaries ran though the entire South, and deliberately proceeded to murder innocent men and women for political reasons and to systematically rob them of their honest labor because they were too accursedly lazy to labor themselves."

In response to the wounding and killing of blacks attempting to parade down Main Street in Hamburg on July 4, 1876, Rainey, addressed his fellow congressmen:

> *Why sir, Just think of it! What would be thought if here in Washington City, when a military company was parading on the Fourth of July, two men should come by in a buggy and demand of the officers that the company should get out of the way, and if they did not, should at once set to work and murder the men of that military company? I ask you, citizens of the United States, would you stand it? I ask you, brave men who fought for your country's liberties long before you took part in the war of the rebellion, would you stand it? I ask you, proud Southern men who boast of your gallantry and your intelligence and your superiority to my race, would you stand it? I ask you, men of the North who sacrificed your blood and treasure, who sacrificed the lives of your sons and your relatives, would you stand it? Do you, then, expect Negroes to stand all this? Do you expect my race to submit meekly to continual persecution and massacre by these people of the South?*

Are you not going to allow us any right of self-defense? In the name of my race and my people, in the name of humanity, in the name of God, I ask you whether we are to be American citizens with all the rights and immunities of citizens or whether we are to be vassals and slaves again? I ask you to tell us whether these things are to go on, so that we may understand now and henceforth what we are to expect.[7]

Chapter XI

Southern Strategy

From time to time, a presidential candidate who does not receive the most votes in the popular election becomes the president of the United States. That is possible because the president of the United States is selected by the Electoral College, not by citizens directly. While the citizens of each state vote for their candidate, what they are actually deciding are the political proclivities of members of the Electoral College from their state. Once the popular vote is counted, each state chooses delegates, equal in number to its total senators and representatives, who will then vote in the "real" presidential election.[1] The delegates typically vote in a manner that reflects the winner of the majority of popular votes in that state. This "winner-take-all" approach is followed in each state, except Maine and Nebraska, which apportion electors between the presidential candidates in a manner equal to the popular vote. If no one gets a majority of votes in the Electoral College, the election is to be decided by the House of Representatives.[2] The constitutional process is intended to prevent states with smaller populations from being ignored or marginalized in selecting the president.

Republican Rutherford B. Hayes did not receive a majority of the popular votes, had not carried the South and did not have sufficient votes in the 1876 Electoral College to become president. Nonetheless, in exchange for a promise to Southern white Democrats that he would withdraw Federal troops from the South, Hayes received the electoral support he needed to be declared to be the nation's chief executive. His ascension to office marked the end of Reconstruction in the South.

President Rutherford B. Hayes. *Courtesy of The Library of Congress.*

With occupying troops gone, the old political establishment was able to regain control of state and local government throughout the South. This was an important step to securing what wealth the states had retained.[3] In South Carolina, this chore fell to Confederate General Wade Hampton and his associates. However, with nearly one hundred thousand blacks registered to vote across the state, the task was not easy, particularly in the coastal counties where people of color held an overwhelming majority. In Georgetown County, whites made up less than 15 percent of all registered voters.

Hampton moved methodically. Initially, he courted black support by promising to protect everyone's right to vote and participate in government. He campaigned across South Carolina, including in Georgetown County. A Tilden and Hampton Reform Club was organized locally by, among others, W.D. Morgan (who later would become mayor) and three blacks: Alonzo Johnson and James Brownfield (both of whom had served on the biracial Committee on Safety organized in the aftermath of the Jones/Bowley riots) as well as Stephney Johnson, a store clerk in his thirties with a wife named Peggy.[4] Accepting office in the club, Johnson explained to the editor of the *Georgetown Times* that he "was not ashamed of his action in joining the club; he felt convinced in his mind that he was on the right side, and would work for its success. The white man gave him employment and paid him for his labor and by that means he was able to provide honestly for his family; he wished that his race would consider calmly their own condition, for he was satisfied if they would that a large number of them would join with the honest people to have better government."[5]

"The meeting was attended by a large number of colored citizens, and, during the proceedings, the utmost good feeling prevailed," the *Georgetown Times* told its readers.[6]

In October 1876, "Hampton Day" was celebrated in Georgetown. Wade Hampton came to Georgetown and made a speech. A parade was organized, and Johnson was one of the marshals.[7] Around the same time, Stephen B. Gipson of Georgetown reportedly advised the "radicals" in Georgetown that they should shoot whites.[8]

At the same time as they were luring Johnson, Brownfield and others into their fold, Hampton and his white supporters were working quietly to disenfranchise blacks. Hampton's "Conservative" (Democratic) and predominantly white political organization entered into fusion agreements with the black-dominated Republican Party across South Carolina. Under the fusion agreement in Georgetown County, whites controlled the sheriff's office, the clerk of court, two county commissioners and one member of the state House of Representatives. Blacks chose the local senator, one member of the House, the probate judge, the school commissioner and one county commissioner. This left whites with control over the office that investigated crimes, the county jail, all property records and the process for picking each jury venire—the large group from which the trial jury was to be selected. With a majority of county commissioners, whites also controlled the process of imposing local taxes. Black males sent their two most prominent politicians to the state capital and supervised the public schools otherwise funded by the county commissioners. The children of prominent whites attended private school at places like the Winyah Indigo Society.

Espousing inclusiveness, Hampton's forces set about diluting black influence at the polls by, among other things, adopting a system of multiple ballot boxes. This "eight-box election law" created abundant opportunities for fraud. It required voters to drop individual ballots in boxes designated from each office.[9] Poll managers could instruct (or misdirect) voters in any matter the managers chose, channeling only ballots believed to be favorable into the proper boxes. The practical effect of this law was to allow poll managers to vote over and over again for the candidate of the managers' choice and sway election results.

During the elections of 1883 and 1884, there was widespread fraud by white officials. State courts failed to prosecute those who participated. This emboldened those officials, and voting fraud flourished. Also in 1883, the U.S. Supreme Court declared the Civil Rights Act of 1875—the one Joseph Rainey had so eloquently supported—to be unconstitutional, further fueling the tempers of those in the white supremacy movement.

The effort to dilute black voting strength had strong editorial support across South Carolina. Just a few days before the general election in 1890, the *Georgetown Times,* on November 1, 1890, reprinted an article from the *Greenville News* on its front page. It appeared under the headline of "Negro Rule." It recalled the history of the period from 1868 to 1876—the time when Rainey campaigned in Congress for amnesty for whites and equality for blacks—as one

> *ruled by colored voters and politicians of the Radical party—carpet baggers and adventurers who came like birds of prey gathering upon a carcass, infamous scallywags who cut loose from all the ties of decency, who ignored all the demands of nature and humanity and helped in the plunder and degradation of their own State, their own race and their own people.*
>
> *The condition of affairs began bad and continually became worse....Public money was stolen recklessly and openly. Bribery of the Legislature became a habit. Every thief and pimp and lackey in the State of high or low degree, received a liberal share of the taxpayers' money on demand. The treasury was looted and emptied every year and the State's credit was strained to the breaking point to fatten and clothe and bedeck and enrich big and little robbers, native corn field hands and imported confidence men, and the gamblers and harlots who were their associates and pets. No country in any time of the world's history was ever cursed by more flagrant or nastier or more horrible debauchery and villainy than marked the period of negro rule in South Carolina.*
>
> *Nor was this the worst....The courts of the State were rotten from lowest to highest. There was no justice except where the longest purse or the strongest political pull was on the side of justice....The white man's home and family, his wife and children, were all at the mercy of the black man and his masters and backers who controlled and used every agent of the law and all its machinery.*
>
> *The situation did not improve. It grew worse every year.*

> *The experience of the past is a trustworthy guide for the future. Its teachings cannot be disputed when they are confirmed by the facts of the present....*
>
> *That experience is that there is no spirit of compromise in the negro and the facts of the present tell us that there is no hope that such a spirit will be developed in him....Here in South Carolina we offered the negro more than was offered anywhere and he rejected every offer. After we became tired of begging our rights and fought for them and took them and held them as we should have done at the beginning we tried the power of conciliation.*

The fact that the overwhelming majority of blacks had remained dirt poor while South Carolina's wealth remained in white hands was lost on the author of "Negro Rule." So was the fact that voting fraud was the primary method used by whites to regain public office—offices which they had theretofore controlled by manipulation and bribery of incumbents.

The Georgetown Rifle Guards called their first meeting in nearly nine years on January 23, 1889.[10] Because of relative peace and racial harmony for more than a decade, the guards had been relatively inactive. But in an atmosphere of growing racial hostility among whites statewide, some Georgetown whites let their animus get in the way of the lessons of local history. As a result, a whole new set of officers took command of a reactivated local militia.

Around this same time, manipulations of ballot counts by whites around the state and locally worked their intended wonders. In the 1890 election, for example, while there were 32,893 blacks and 7,695 whites in the Seventh Congressional District, "certified election returns" indicated that the white Democrat had defeated the black Republican candidate by some 1,305 votes.

Describing the outcome of the election, the *Georgetown Times* boldly stated: "The election law of South Carolina requires that a voter shall deposit his ballot in the right box, which is labeled for identification, or it shall be rejected. This educational qualification has proved annoying to ignorant voters and the men who have relied upon them for their support."[11]

By 1895, fusion agreements in most communities had served their purpose and were abandoned by whites. They had gradually regained control of all public offices without arousing disorder. The number of blacks registered to vote in South Carolina dropped sharply. For example, while comprising 80 percent of the population of Georgetown, by this time only slightly more than half the registered voters of the county were black. The eight-box election law and the fraud it perpetuated had prevented many ballots from being counted and discouraged many voters. Those not effectively disenfranchised in this way were shut out in others.

In 1895, the white-dominated South Carolina legislature wrote and approved a new state constitution. It was put into effect without being ratified by the general electorate. It contained an "understanding clause" as a prerequisite to voting. That clause required anyone who did not own more than $300 worth of land to be able to read, understand and explain any provision of the U.S. Constitution put before them. The aspiring voter also had to be able to write the same constitutional provision. This became known as the "literacy test." It was used to keep blacks and uncooperative poor whites from registering to vote in the South for the next seven decades. It proved particularly effective in Georgetown where, in 1900 for example, the budget for the education of white students was six times that for black students.[12]

In 1896, the U.S. Supreme Court decided the case *Plessy v. Ferguson*.[13] It was a death knell for equality and marked the beginning of the era of strict segregation by use of so-called "Jim Crow" laws. Louisiana had adopted a number of "separate but equal" public accommodation laws. One of those required the segregation of railroad cars for blacks and whites. If only one passenger car was available, it had to have separate black and white sections. The law further provided that "[n]o person or persons shall be admitted to occupy seats in coaches, other than the ones assigned to them on account of the race they belong to." Those violating the law could be fined $25 or, if they did not have money for the fine, imprisoned for up to twenty days. Train conductors were given the power of arrest.[14] The law was strictly enforced.

Homer Plessy had one black great-grandparent; the rest of his immediate predecessors were white. Nonetheless, he was classified as an octoroon and, therefore, black. One day while riding a train, Plessy sat in the all-white section. When he refused to move from his seat, he was arrested by the conductor. He was then tried and convicted of violating the new "separate but equal" law. He appealed his case all the way to the U.S. Supreme Court. Writing for the court's majority, Justice Henry Brown applied a lawyer's logic to justify segregation.

> *A statute which implies merely legal distinction between the whites and colored races—a distinction which is founded in the color of the two races, and which must always exist so long as white men are distinguished from the other race by color—has no tendency to destroy the legal equality of the two races or reestablish a state of involuntary servitude [banned by the Thirteenth Amendment]....*
>
> *The object of the [Fourteenth] Amendment was undoubtedly to enforce the absolute equality of the two races before the law, but in the nature of things it could not have been intended to abolish distinctions based upon color, or to enforce*

> *social as distinguished from political equality, or a commingling of the two races upon terms unsatisfactory to either. Laws permitting, and even requiring, their separation in places where they are liable to be brought into contact do not necessarily imply the inferiority of either race to the other....If this be so, it is not by reason of anything found in the act, but solely because the colored race chooses to put that construction upon it.*

While saying no indicia of inferiority was intended by the law, Justice Brown did nonetheless note what happens if someone is forced by the conductor to sit in the "wrong" place. "If he be a white man and assigned to a colored coach, he may have his action for damages against the company for being deprived of his so-called property [his reputation as a white man]. Upon the other hand, if he be a colored man and be so assigned, he has been deprived of no property [his reputation has not been harmed] since he is not lawfully entitled to the reputation of being a white man."[15]

In a strong, historic, prophetic dissent, Justice John M. Harlan said:

> *There is no caste here. Our Constitution is color-blind and neither knows nor tolerates classes among citizens.*
>
> *In respect to civil rights, all citizens are equal before the law. The humblest is peer of the most powerful. The law regards man as man and takes no account of his surroundings or of his color when his civil rights as guaranteed by the supreme law of the land are involved....*
>
> *In my opinion, the judgment this day rendered will, in time, prove to be quite as pernicious as the decision made by this tribunal in the Dred Scott Case....*
>
> *Sixty million whites are in no danger from the presence here of eight million blacks. The destinies of the two races in this country are indissolubly linked together, and the interests of both require that the common government of all shall not permit the seeds of race hate to be planted under the sanction of law. What can more certainly arouse race hate, what more certainly create and perpetuate a feeling of distrust between these races than state enactments which, in fact, proceed on the ground that colored citizens are so inferior and degraded that they cannot be allowed to sit in public coaches occupied by white citizens? That, as all will admit, is the real meaning of such legislation as was enacted in Louisiana....*
>
> *State enactments regulating the enjoyment upon the basis of race, and cunningly devised to defeat legitimate results of the war under the pretense of recognizing equality of rights [commonly called "Jim Crow" laws] can have no other result*

> *than to render permanent peace impossible and to keep alive a conflict of races, the continuance of which must do harm to all concerned.*

Justice Harlan's prediction came true. During the next sixty years, white supremacists spread their message of hate throughout America. Jim Crow laws segregating the races were passed throughout the South, border states and elsewhere. To discourage love, state constitutions were amended to forbid blacks from marrying whites.[16] Fueled by hatred, whites lynched 155 blacks in South Carolina, 84 in North Carolina, 83 in Virginia, 483 in Georgia, 299 in Alabama, 532 in Mississippi, 141 in Louisiana, 236 in Arkansas and 346 in Texas during the years that followed.[17] The notion of the inferiority of blacks became so insidious that, in 1906, the Soddy Baptist Church in Chattanooga, Tennessee, took up the question of whether "black people do have souls and can go to heaven." By a narrow three-vote margin, seventy-four to seventy-one, congregants conceded that blacks did and could. "Thank God for the Soddy Baptist Church," a prominent black lawyer responded, "I just hope they notified God about their decision."[18]

By 1890, the economy of Georgetown was forced to undergo a radical reconstruction or the town would wither and die. With the old forced-labor system gone and the rice fields being repeatedly battered by huge storms, the agricultural economy was nearing collapse. Recognizing that fact, the community entrusted the effort to bring Georgetown into the next century to William Doyle Morgan.

The son of Irish immigrants John and Mary Morgan, William was born February 5, 1853 in New York City.[19] His family moved to Georgetown when he was two months old. His father died in 1866, leaving a widow and four small children, of which William was the eldest.

He had been educated during the war years in a private school in Georgetown. His father, a well-educated man himself, added to Morgan's store of knowledge and molded Morgan's character. At age 15, Morgan went to work as a store clerk. His next job was in a local drugstore. Next, he took a job as a bookkeeper in a mercantile house, steadily working his way up the local economic ladder.

Morgan was active in politics from a young age. In 1874, he helped organize the Georgetown Rifle Guards and served as its first warden. In 1876, he was part of the Tilden and Hampton Reform Club ostensibly created to create "harmony and good feelings among whites and blacks." Morgan drafted the club's founding resolution.

W. D. Morgan (second from the right) and other officers of the Bank of Georgetown. *Courtesy of the Georgetown County Library Morgan Collection.*

In 1878, Morgan lost his left hand in an accident while hunting ducks on Thanksgiving Day. His use of an artificial hand, covered with a black leather glove, did not cripple him. To the contrary, his tenacity earned him even greater respect in the community.

In 1891, Morgan resigned his bookkeeping job to become president of the Bank of Georgetown. During this same decade, he served as a fire chief, was on the Commission of Pilotage and Port Warden, and was appointed as fire commissioner, organizing volunteer efforts.

Also in 1891, Morgan was elected to serve as intendant of the town. Writing to H.V. and H.W. Poor (co-founders of what is now Standard and Poors) at their Wall Street offices in New York on March 12, 1892 about Georgetown's financial condition, Morgan described the situation in Georgetown as follows: "Our town—which is an old one—has practically been at a standstill for the last 90 years, but a change is taking place—new people are coming in—new enterprises are being started—real estate is steadily enhancing in value and

The Port of Georgetown, circa 1900. *Courtesy of the Georgetown County Library Morgan Collection.*

stores & dwelling houses are being built in all directions. Our people are law abiding and pay their taxes promptly & cheerfully. The policy of our town government is to carry on improvements—which will help the town—rather than reduce debt."[20]

In 1892, the South Carolina legislature changed Georgetown's charter from that of a town to that of a city. Morgan served as mayor from January 1893 to January 1906. He was opposed only once, in an election to be discussed later.

During Morgan's term in office, electric lights, waterworks and a sewer system were installed throughout the city. New streets were added, and the existing ones improved. The police and fire departments were modernized. About two thousand shade trees were planted along the city's streets. Georgetown doubled in size.

Morgan's work on infrastructure improvement was not limited to streets and utilities. He was also largely responsible for securing appropriations from Congress to improve the shipping channel into Winyah Bay. This was accomplished by the construction of stone jetties. He also secured federal appropriations to increase the depth of the entrance to the bay from ten feet to twenty-one feet. Those tasks done, he was instrumental in chartering a railroad—the Georgetown and Lanes Railroad—connecting Georgetown to the outside world by rail for the first time.[21]

As a direct result of Morgan's work, a vibrant Port of Georgetown—long a dream of local merchants and businessmen—became a reality. Agricultural, lumber and other forest products began to stream out of Georgetown. Trade goods for trans-shipment throughout the South came in. All of this economic activity brought money and opportunity. A new economy centered on the port emerged.

For the first time, Georgetown began to develop a solid middle class, wedged between the haves and the have nots. That emerging middle class included the Fraser brothers, Robert and Samuel; J.B. Steele; and assorted members of the Kaminski family, Prussian Jews who had immigrated to Georgetown after the war. Working cooperatively, these men shaped and ensured Georgetown's economic future for the next half century.

While Morgan, Steele, the Fraser brothers and the Kaminskis worked with their neighbors in progressive and productive ways, they were, nonetheless, men of their times. They had not created the fears of whites, the resentments of blacks or the mutual mistrust that surrounded both. But they, like Rainey before them, had to cope with existing racial tensions if social peace were to be maintained.

Whether out of a sense of duty or, more likely, enlightened self-interest, the emerging middle class in Georgetown sought, and obtained, substantial political power. To do that, members of the middle class had to ride existing political tides. As the times (and *Times*) would have it, those tides were gradually washing blacks out of the voting booth and out of public office.

Chapter XII
Storm Clouds

The highest elevation in Georgetown County is around twenty-five feet above mean sea level. That physical fact leaves the area vulnerable to destruction by any hurricane that makes landfall. Such was the case August 27, 1893; October 13, 1893; September 26, 1894; and again September 28, 1898. During these storms, the levees impounding many rice fields were breached, allowing saltwater to contaminate the paddies. In the storm of October 1893, the Flagg family and their servants drowned when the house they were in washed out to sea, candles still burning in the windows.

At age 104, Ben Horry said:

> *Storm? Ain't I tell you I been here? Yes, sir. More than one storm I live through. Been through the Flagg storm....*
>
> *When the Flagg storm been, 1893, I was working for Ravanel and Holmes. I was taken up in that storm in a steamer boat. Leave Charleston generally about five in morning. That trip never reach Georgetown till nine that night. Meet a man on that trip got he wife hug to mast in a little kind [of] life boat. He had two chillun rope wrap 'em to mast. Save man and wife and chillun and gone back to save he trunk. After that they quit call me Ben; they call me Rooster.*
>
> *After Flagg storm, Colonel Ward take me and Peter Carr, us two and a horse, take the shore to Little River. Search for all them what been drowned. Find a trunk to Myrtle Beach. Have all kind [of] things n 'em; comb for you hair, thing you put on your wrist. Find dead horse, cow, ox, turkey, fowl—everything. Gracious God!*

> *Don't want to see no more thing like that....Find old Doctor [Flagg] body by he vest stick out of the mud; fetch doctor body to shore and he watch still ticking.*

As reported in the *Georgetown Times* of October 13, 1893:

> *The news from Magnolia Beach struck terror into every heart. Then it was asserted that the whole of Dr. Flagg's folks were washed away and drowned; that John Dozier's family were also lost, as well as others; that nothing had been heard of Robert J. Donaldson and family on Goat Island; that Wm. White and Josh Ward had been drowned while attempting to rescue people at Magnolia Beach and numerous other rumors of a more or less distressing character.*
>
> *Capt. S.M. Ward, who is more or less intimately connected with all these people, immediately got up steam on his boat and went off to the beach to render what aid could be given and left us all to wonder and talk over the rumors in the meantime. And little groups of men could be seen and observed all about, discussing every phase of the recent storm, and comparing notes. There was nothing else to do, everyone being desirous of catching the first news and eagerly asking for information.*
>
> *It is the general opinion that no rice will now be saved. The storm has probably ruined what was still left in the fields.*

These tragic events left everyone in Georgetown in the same boat. The destructive effect of the storms on the fields eroded the agricultural base of the economy. This left both blacks and whites to worry about the only meaningful economic color: green. The outlet for their mutual anxiety, unfortunately, continued to be one another.

It was the "sickly season" in Georgetown once again. On September 17, 1900, Dr. D.S. Black wrote to Mayor Morgan to report that he had treated three cases of hemorrhagic fever, Dr. T.P. Bailey had treated one and Dr. C. William Bailey had treated two more.[1] These were not the only problems confronting the community.

The dusty files of the Georgetown County clerk of court's office contain many old and crumbling documents. One is titled "Testimony of John L. Carter in the case against William Sumpter, Marsh Sumpter and George Carr." It reads as follows:

> *I had a warrant to arrest Ben Marsh. When I went to the house where he was, his mother told me he was in there. But I could not get him. I found William*

> *Sumpter, Marsh Sumpter and George Carr sitting on the piazza. William Sumpter seemed to be head of them and he told me he was a man and I could not get Ben that night. I had Mr. J.C. Scurry, Cap Snowden and Harry Holliday with me. I decided I would reinforce and made the second effort which had [drawn] quite a crowd....I found the same men there. The house was closed up and then [the] same men William Sumpter, Marsh Sumpter and George Carr were sitting on the piazza with their guns in their hands. We arrested them and after some little trouble we got their guns from them and then I arrested Ben Carr without any further trouble.*
>
> *s/ J.L. Carter*[2]

The record at the clerk's office does not reveal why Carter, Scurry and their companions sought to arrest Ben Carr. It does not explain the apparent belligerence of the Sumpter brothers and George Carr. All it reflects is that there was sufficient tension to result in an armed standoff between four white officers and three black men who were protecting a fourth.

Within a few weeks of this incident, white constable J.C. Scurry got involved in another confrontation with a black man, John Brownfield.

The Brownfield family first appears in the records of Georgetown when James Brownfield was appointed to serve on the Committee on Safety in the aftermath of the Bowley/Jones riot in 1874. James Brownfield next appears as an organizing member of the Hampton-Tilden Reform Club in 1876. The entire family tree is listed in the 1880 U.S. Census. Abram and Easter Brownfield were the family patriarch and matriarch. Abram was sixty years old at the time. Easter was fifty-five. They lived at home with their seventeen-year-old daughter May. They also had three sons, James, Philander and William. Census data identifies various members of the family as "negro" and others as "mulatto."

James was thirty-eight in 1880. He was married to a woman named Grace. They had three children: James Jr., age twelve; Timothy, age three; and Elizabeth, age two. Philander was a carpenter. His wife was named Sepia. They had five children, including a son John, age three. William was a twenty-six year old shoemaker. He and his wife Minerva had two sons, William Jr., age four, and Joseph, age two.

On the morning of September 29, 1900, barber John Brownfield, age twenty-two, kissed his young wife Sibby goodbye and went to work at Washington's barber shop. The shop was located on in the northernmost side of the 700 block of Front Street in Georgetown. A two-story wooden hotel was located right next door.[3]

Hotel in 700 block of Front Street, circa 1900. The unidentified black man standing in the gate to the left is dressed in the sort of attire that a barber would wear. *Courtesy of the Georgetown County Library Morgan Collection.*

There was a sign painted on the side wall of the third floor of a brick commercial building almost directly across the street from where the barber shop once stood. Painted around 1900, the sign is faded today. It reads: "Coca-Cola. Relieves fatigue." At the time, Coke pepped its consumers up thanks to the cocaine in its formula.

At the turn of the twentieth century, almost all black men in Georgetown engaged in dangerous, sweaty outdoor occupations that involved getting their clothes, hands and nails dirty, and resulted in thick calluses forming on their palms. The overwhelming majority of them were farmers, whose fortunes depended upon their crops (or their share of crops); worked for modest wages in the timber or forest industry as laborers; or were employed as longshoremen or in some other kind of heavy manual labor.

Brownfield was an exception to this rule. As a barber, he worked indoors keeping his clothes, hands and fingernails clean. His cash income depended on the number and loyalty of his customers. Because of this, it was in his interest to be courteous and gregarious. From the following events, it appears he was well liked, at least in the black community. Because he was a volunteer fireman, whites would have had a reason to look upon him with at least a small amount of favor.

Saturdays were usually busy days for barbers. Men who worked in the forests, in fields or on construction projects usually did not enjoy the freedom to take time off during working hours and get a haircut. They waited until Saturday to take care of other personal business. A century ago, many a working man had to go to work on Saturday morning. Similarly, farmers had morning chores to do every day. This caused a backup in haircuts, with many done on Saturday afternoons.

At four o'clock in the afternoon on Saturday, September 29, 1900, Stephney Johnson was sitting in Washington's barber shop. Johnson was a store clerk who had served with Brownfield's uncle as an officer in the Hampton-Tilden Reform Club. Also present were a man named Dick Chapman and a few others.

By late September, the weather begins to moderate in the South Carolina Lowcountry. Thanks to Mayor Morgan, Georgetown had been "electrified" by this time, and with the sun still high overhead, the ceiling fan in the barbershop helped keep things cool. Brownfield was shaving a customer with a straight razor.

Brownfield could read and write, and was a registered voter. To become one in 1900, he had to either own more than $300 worth of land or be able to pass a literacy test.[4] Sibby was about two years her husband's senior. She was a housewife who could also read and write. They didn't have any children. The 1900 census indicates that Brownfield and his wife rented a house at 231 Prince Street. According to the records of the register of deeds of Georgetown County, Brownfield did not own $300 worth of real estate in Georgetown County. To qualify as a voter, therefore, he had passed the "literacy test" when he turned twenty-one. That meant that he could recite, write and explain whatever provision of the U.S. Constitution that had been put to him at the voting registration office.

In addition, the law required Brownfield to pay an annual poll tax. If he did not do so, he would be barred from voting in the upcoming general election. Poll taxes were not imposed anywhere in America until after Reconstruction. In 1882, South Carolina passed its first poll tax of $1 per year for every man between the ages of twenty-one and fifty.[5] The tax was not intended to be a source of income. Rather, it was one of the tools used to get around the Fifteenth Amendment's guarantee of the right to vote without regard to color. The tax relied on the basic needs of poor people, black and white. In a household with little money, using $1 to buy food was a lot more important than using it to pay for the right to vote.

Over the years, poll taxes, multiple ballot-box laws and literacy tests had the desired effect. Along with poor whites, the number of blacks registered to vote across South Carolina dropped dramatically. Among blacks, registration fell from a high of nearly one hundred thousand to less than fourteen thousand by the turn of the twentieth century.

Because of its overwhelming black majority, Georgetown bucked the trend of black disempowerment longer than other places. Political fusion remained alive locally until 1901. The events described below caused its rapid demise.

J.C. Scurry was a thirty-seven-year-old man who resided as a boarder in a house owned by Robert and Rosa Rouse on Cleland Street near Church in Georgetown. The Georgetown Public Library is located near the site today. Prior to 1900, Scurry worked at Jackson's Stables, which traded in horses, mules and ponies. The stable was located about a block from Washington's barber shop. Given Georgetown's semitropical, humid climate (and all the manure), the work environment at the stables would not have been pleasant. Around age thirty-five, Scurry left that job to become a constable for a local magistrate.

There is no surviving record of whether Scurry was a registered voter. Property records show he did not own $300 of realty. To vote, therefore, he would have to pass a literacy test and pay the poll tax, just like Brownfield.

Scurry was a member of the Georgetown Rifle Guards. Nothing in the historic record leads to the conclusion that Scurry's racial attitudes were any different from those of other young white men of his time. He, like his contemporaries, had been exposed to the ever-growing call for white supremacy in South Carolina.

From these brief occupational and civic histories, the reader is left to construct the attitudes and social status of the protagonists of the story that follows. Given the proximity of their places of employment in such a small town, each reader can speculate whether the two men knew one another beforehand.

Whether he stopped for a Coca-Cola before entering Washington's barber shop is unknown. But it is certain that late on Saturday afternoon, September 29, 1900, J.C. Scurry entered Washington's barber shop and attempted to arrest John Brownfield for not paying the dollar poll tax.

If arrested on a Saturday afternoon, Brownfield would have had to sit in jail until a judge was available to review the legality of the matter and set bond. Brownfield protested. Johnson, Chapman and the others in the store later said Scurry was very belligerent, pulled out his service pistol, put it to Brownfield's head and said something like, "I'll show you whether I can arrest you or not." A scuffle broke out and Scurry was shot. Brownfield ran out of the back door of the barber shop. Scurry started to give chase but collapsed outside.

Advertisement from Georgetown newspaper placed for Jackson's Stables by J.C. Scurry circa 1895.

A fading turn-of-the-century Coca-Cola sign as it appears today. *Photograph courtesy of Jeannette Ard.*

Brownfield fled across the barbershop yard and scampered over a high wooden fence. He was stopped by a black police officer whose curiosity was aroused by the sight of a neatly dressed, mulatto-looking man (who the officer knew to be Brownfield) climbing over a fence. When asked what he was doing, a shaken Brownfield told the officer what had just happened. The officer took Brownfield to the chief of police. Brownfield was placed under arrest and walked one-and-a-half blocks to the three-story brick building that served as the county jail.

In the meantime, someone summoned the doctor. Upon his arrival, Scurry was taken to his brother's house located diagonally across the street from what was then the county jail.[6] Doctors treated him there for several hours, but Scurry died of his wounds later that evening.

The *Charleston News and Courier* reported that Scurry had a warrant for Brownfield's arrest. He did not. Sections 347 through 361 of the Civil Statute Laws of South Carolina provided the method for collecting unpaid poll taxes. That law provided that whenever taxes went unpaid, the county treasurer could issue a "warrant or execution" for their collection. The terms "warrant" and "execution" were used interchangeably in the law to describe the procedure for collecting debts or taxes owed to a governmental body.

The process is entirely a civil matter, not a criminal one. Section 347 of the law directed that once the county treasurer issued the warrant or execution, the sheriff or his deputy was required "to levy the same by distress and sale of so much of the defaulting taxpayer's estate, real or personal, or other, as may be sufficient to satisfy the taxes." The defaulting taxpayer had to pay an extra dollar as a penalty or administrative cost. In addition, he had to pay the sheriff another dollar for serving the legal paper, plus mileage "at the rate of five cents for each mile actually traveled in executing the warrant." Another $3 had to be paid for the preparation of any required deeds or documents of title. An additional 5 percent was tacked onto the bill to cover the cost of collection.

This mechanism for mandating payment was not the only method of enforcement. If a person failed to pay the poll tax, he was barred from voting until those taxes, plus penalties, were paid in full. Therefore, Brownfield had nothing to gain by not paying. At the same time, if Scurry did not like the idea of blacks voting, he had nothing to lose if Brownfield did not pay. Therefore, Scurry's attempt to arrest Brownfield for not paying a poll tax made little sense.

The Charleston newspaper did not reveal its sources for its article about events in Georgetown. But it stated that Scurry had been looking for Brownfield to collect the overdue poll tax for some time. That, too, did not make much sense since Brownfield worked at a fixed location during fixed hours. He was easy to find. If Scurry had been to Washington's barber shop previously, there is no record of it. In any event, Scurry chose the end of a busy day to come and collect the $3.10 it would have taken to satisfy Brownfield's poll tax debt. A simple request for payment should have been sufficient.

At this point, two distinct stories about what happened began to emerge, one black and the other white.

The black version was that Scurry was a belligerent aggressor who grabbed Brownfield as the latter was shaving a customer, pulled a gun, put it to Brownfield's head and demanded payment. A startled and frightened Brownfield defended himself, and Scurry was shot in the ensuing scuffle.

The white version held that the constable came into the shop and requested payment. Brownfield accidentally dropped the razor he was using. When a courteous Scurry bent over to pick it up, his pistol fell out of its holster. At that point, an irrational Brownfield seized the weapon and shot the peaceful, tax-collecting constable without warning. This version was repeated in the October 2, 1900 edition of the Charleston paper. According to the *News and Courier*: "Brownfield was shaving a Negro. Scurry, in picking up Brownfield's razor let his pistol fall. Brownfield picked up the pistol and in the twinkle of an eye has fired five times at Scurry."

No one wants to live in fear. To the contrary, every man, woman and child wants to feel safe and secure at home and while going about the business of daily life. Recognizing that there are dangerous people in the world, each community hires armed officers whose job is "to serve and to protect." The job is underpaid, misunderstood, dangerous and thankless. One of its few rewards is a high level of respect extended by polite society to law enforcement officers.

Because most people find it unsettling to think that armed law-enforcement officers are anything other than honest defenders of the public good, the benefit of doubt is extended to officers in questionable situations and they enjoy a "qualified immunity" from suit or prosecution.[7] This does not mean, however, that officers can act as they choose. Because the days of the Wild West are over, the law does not turn a blind eye to irrational, violent acts committed by law enforcement officers. So when, from time to time, these officers do something wrong, they are supposed to be punished. So too are those who lie to cover up the incident for the wrongdoer. The same is true for TV personalities, investment bankers, corporate officers, doctors, lawyers, members of the clergy, newspaper editors, bankers, car dealers and all other professions or occupations. The law is supposed to be evenhanded. It has to be because some people are simply bad apples who will abuse whatever trust is reposed in them. Just by way of example, in recent years in South Carolina, one Family Court judge was sanctioned for extorting women who were seeking custody of their children to go to bed with him.[8] A sheriff from an adjoining county and his chief deputy were sentenced to federal prison for dealing in narcotics. There was a notorious brothel in Georgetown County named Sunset Lodge. Its operations went unhampered for many years. During those years, the local "high sheriff" took control of the political and legal apparatus of the county, while white judges, prosecutors, lawyers and politicians were being entertained at the Sunset.[9]

In the case of the encounter between Scurry and Brownfield, there are several things about the white version that do not flow logically into one another.

First, there was no reason for Scurry to arrest Brownfield. The document Scurry is said to have possessed could not have been an arrest warrant. It was a civil process for the seizure of property (or money from the cash register). In those circumstances, any attempt to take Brownfield into custody would have been unlawful.[10]

Second, the white version of how Brownfield got hold of Scurry's gun is illogical. Experienced barbers with razors in their hands are not clumsy people. If Brownfield's razor hit the floor, it was not by accident. If it did hit the ground, it could have done so because the police officer's demeanor was very startling or because Brownfield was ordered to drop it and complied. One thing about the razor is certain, however: not even the whites accused Brownfield of trying to use the razor as a weapon.

Third, police officers seeking to arrest someone typically do not extend the courtesy of picking up things suspects drop, at least not until after the suspect is handcuffed. It is a simple matter of personal safety—secure the suspect first and then search for and secure any potential weapons. If Scurry acted to the contrary, he acted foolishly.

Fourth, in the ordinary course of the performance of their duties, law enforcement officers may have to run, jump, climb, crawl, stoop or bend over any number of times during the course of a day for one reason or another. Because they do, they generally secure their weapons so they do not come out of the holster accidentally. Loose weapons can be dangerous for a variety of reasons: they can discharge accidentally, they can fall into the hands of criminals or they can fall into the hands of curious children. The notion that Scurry's weapon was out of its holster accidentally, therefore, strains credulity. Either that or Scurry was careless with his weapon.

CHAPTER XIII

INSURRECTION AND INQUISITION

To this day, South Carolina's procedure for picking juries for a coroner's inquest is fraught with potential for abuse.[1] Rather than providing for a selection process aimed at impaneling an impartial jury, the law allows coroners to hand pick those who will serve. In 1900, the coroner selected fourteen names. Twelve had to be sworn as jurors. The only limitation was (and is) that the jurors must otherwise be qualified for jury duty. At the time of the inquiry into the death of J.C. Scurry, the list from which the coroner chose names was limited to registered voters.

The job of coroner is an elected office in South Carolina. It does not require special education or experience, or a legal or medical background. For many years in Georgetown (and to this day elsewhere) undertakers held the office, which, while always on-call, was considered part time. Being coroner was good for business. The job only became a full-time position in Georgetown in the late 1990s. A former sheriff's deputy is the incumbent.

Once a coroner's jury is sworn, the coroner, as presiding officer, decides who can testify and the extent of their testimony. He[2] is not bound by the rules of evidence and can allow or bar presentation of any evidence he likes. He can even bar lawyers from participating. While he can request the assistance of the solicitor's (district attorney's) office, he is not required to do so. His decisions on matters of physical evidence or testimony are not subject to appeal. Additionally, he can hold those who disagree vocally with his rulings in contempt of court and have them jailed and/or fined.

At the conclusion of the hearing, the coroner charges the jury by telling them the nature of the decision they have to reach, "whether the deceased came to his death by mischance and accident or by felony; and if by felony by the act of God or of man; and if he died of another's felony, who were the principals and who accessories, and who threatened him of life or murder, and with what instrument he was struck or wounded; and if by mischance or accident, by the act of God or man."

If, based on the evidence the coroner allows to be presented, the jury decides the death was the result of a felony by another person or persons, the matter is bound to the Court of General Sessions. Once there, it is the responsibility of the prosecutor's officer to decide whether the case will be presented to the grand jury. Meanwhile, the only responsibility of the coroner at the conclusion of the hearing is to turn the records of his inquiry over to the clerk of court.

The archives of the Georgetown County clerk of court's office still contain the records of the coroner's inquest into Scurry's death. Among those records is a document indicating that an all-white coroner's jury was selected, summonsed and viewed Scurry's body. The jury then recessed and, a few days later, convened at the Georgetown County Court House. There, they heard the testimony of Dr. T.P. Bailey. He told the assembled jurors:

> *Someone came in hurriedly and called me to a lot near the Windsor hotel and, going to the place designated, I found Mr. J.C. Scurry in the rear of Washington's barber shop on the ground wounded and bleeding. I made an examination and found two wounds about the abdomen and one flesh wound. One was located on the left about the neighborhood of the short rib, the other on the right, lower down toward the hip. There was an abrasion somewhere between the two wounds. I also observed his hand was bleeding but made no special examination as it was a matter of minor importance. I think it was his left hand. This occurrence was Saturday evening late. Five or six o'clock. In the meantime, Dr. Black came in and I stated hurriedly that I had given him a hypodermic injection. Mr. C.W. Scurry, brother to the wounded man, came up about this time and asked that Dr. Black and myself accompany his brother to his house.*
>
> *When we got him around to the house, we could not at that time tell positively the ultimate effect of the ball in the abdomen but if it penetrated the cavity death would inevitably result as a consequence of internal bleeding. I probed for the ball and could not find it. I think that the abdominal wound on the right side unquestionably caused his death.*

The next day, Sunday, almost everyone in Georgetown went to church, blacks to theirs and whites to their own. The events of the day before undoubtedly were the subject of many a conversation as folks congregated outside and, later, around Sunday dinner tables.

The peace of the Lord's day was disrupted Sunday evening. Some "hot-headed"[3] armed whites gathered in front of Scurry's brother's house and decided to lynch John Brownfield. In furtherance of their plan, one or more of these vigilantes went to one of the volunteer fire stations on Front Street three or four blocks away,[4] rang its bell and called out "fire" and "help." This tactic was intended to create a diversion that would result in black volunteer firemen responding to the call while the white mob went to the jail, got their hands on Brownfield, brought him outside and hung him.

A mulatto merchant W.R. Woodbury heard of the plot around ten o'clock in the evening and reported it to the sheriff. The sheriff assured Woodbury that the prisoner would be protected. Woodbury told others, too. In a letter to the *Georgetown Times* on October 6, 1900, he acknowledged that he told George Herriot, the black superintendent of education, about the situation. He denied using his place of business, "Ford and Woodbury," as a place for blacks to congregate and plan a riot. By whatever means, rumors about the threat to lynch Brownfield circulated around the black community.

On Sunday evening, September 30, 1900, a crowd of "a thousand or more Negroes, men and boys, got up a regular whoop" and, chanting "Free John," marched through the streets and assembled at the county jail. Some were armed with pitchforks and rakes. A few carried firearms. The demonstrators threatened to "burn down the town and used other alarming language"[5] if anything happened to Brownfield. As a little more than four thousand citizens of all races, sexes and ages were living in the city at the time, this group represented a majority of the town's black adults. All of who presumably had sufficient regard for Brownfield to leave their homes on an otherwise restful Sunday evening to protect him from being lynched.

Meanwhile, among the armed whites at the scene were a number of members of the Georgetown Rifle Guards, of which Scurry was a member. How these individuals knew what was going on, who had summoned them to the scene, the motive for their presence or the level of "hot headedness" of each are not recorded anywhere. One thing is certain; they had not been called out by the governor, the mayor or the sheriff. Any conclusions regarding those facts can only be surmised from the surrounding events. But the presence of armed angry whites and armed angry blacks created a tense and extremely volatile set of circumstances.

Georgetown County Jail, circa 1900. *Courtesy of the Georgetown County Library Morgan Collection.*

The rear door of Mayor Morgan's house, circa 1900. *Courtesy of the Georgetown County Library Morgan Collection.*

Into this scene walked Mayor W.D. Morgan, the elected official with ultimate responsibility for protecting lives and property as well as maintaining the peace. He lived a square city block away from the county jail and one block in the other direction from Washington's barber shop. He became aware of each event as it was unfolding. He undoubtedly was distressed to see the assembling of an armed, angry mob that included members of the militia he had helped organize a quarter century earlier.

If behavior under pressure is any measure of a man, Morgan's character was clearly revealed in the next few hours. An even-tempered, almost serene person, he walked to the jail. The demonstrators parted as he waded calmly into the middle of the crowd and directly up to the most vocal of the black demonstrators.

What happened next is described in court records of the trial of the case of *State of South Carolina v. Cupid Haynes* in the archives of the clerk of court for Georgetown County. Haynes was tried on the charge of incitement to riot.[6] At Haynes's trial, L.S. Ehrich, a member of the Georgetown Rifle Guards, was called to testify. He said: "On the night of September 30, I was standing on the street near the jail and saw Mr. Morgan go into the crowd there assembled. I got near enough to see that he was having an altercation with someone and I went up through the crowd. I found that the man he was talking to had a musket and I wanted to see who it was. It was Cupid Haynes, the defendant. He was talking to the crowd and said he 'be dam'd' if he was going to leave nor should anyone get his gun. He appeared to be belligerent and appeared to hold the crowd there for as soon as he left it, the crowd dispersed. I could see that his conduct to the Mayor was defiant and insulting."

Morgan was called as a witness too. After identifying himself and the office he held, he told the jury: "On Sunday night, the 30th of September, I was called to go to the jail where a multitude of people had gathered. I gathered from the people that they were there to prevent what they said was the probability of lynching of John Brownfield. Things looked serious and I proceeded to say something to quiet the people. Among the number of people there, this defendant was present with a gun and in a terrible rage and his attitude was very menacing and terrorizing to the crowd. I ordered him to desist and go home but he was defiant and stood his ground saying he'd be damned if he would leave: He had as much right to be there as I and would not leave. He was the most bold and defiant of the crowd and his conduct very menacing. He used the most threatening speeches and was very insulting in his words and demeanor."

William Alex Small confirmed the mayor's testimony. "I was at the pump at the jail near where the crowd was. I saw Morgan go into the crowd and I then went up to where the crowd was. I then saw Mr. Morgan [who only had one arm] try to get the gun from Cupid who said it was his gun and he would not give the gun up. 'Dam'd if I'll give it up as I am Mayor tonight.' He said he was going to stay there til the crowd...would listen to him....The Mayor told him to go away, but he wouldn't go."

Even Cupid Haynes, testifying on his own behalf, admitted he was there "all right, with his gun."

As these events were unfolding, a shot rang out. It had been fired by a member of the Georgetown Rifle Guards. Someone screamed in pain. It was Josiah Doar, the editor of the *Georgetown Times*. He had been struck in the knee by the bullet. The resulting wound crippled him for life, not only physically but spiritually. For while he was able to promptly forgive the white Rifle Guard who shot him, he blamed blacks for his fate for the rest of his life. This measure of this man can be found in the pages of the *Georgetown Times* while under his stewardship. It became a forum for white supremacist sentiments. Meanwhile, armed with only the force of his character, Morgan continued to maintain control over the situation despite the confusion created by the trigger-happy white. The crowd peacefully dispersed after Cupid Haynes and about twenty others were arrested.

Immediately after calming everyone down, Morgan conferred with prominent blacks—Alderman Baxter, School Commissioner Herriot and attorney J.L. Mitchell—about what to do next. Morgan then consulted with white merchants and politicos, including Dr. J.R. Sparkman; Major B.A. Munnerlyn and Captain S.M. Ward of the Rifle Guards; Senator LeGrand Walker; and Alderman T.G. Tarbox.[7] Most of the whites were members of the Rifle Guards. Others had family members who were. Their advice was predestined. They wanted the mayor to use force. Morgan knew that, but he also understood that force would result in a horrible bloodbath with many victims on both sides. That put him in the position where he had to carefully maintain a balance between the black majority and the white minority if his beloved community was to be saved from self-destruction. So he persuaded everyone that it would be best if he were to contact the governor and ask for outside help. At 12:50 a.m. Monday, Morgan wired the governor and asked that several disciplined infantry companies be dispatched to Georgetown.

Revealing its own sentiments, the *State* newspaper characterized the communication this way: "Order Col. Sparkman commanding troops and Capt. Ward, of Rifle Guards, to report to mayor and sheriff with companies to preserve order. Negroes are gathering in large numbers. The trouble is caused by a negro killing a white man last night. Later troubles feared tonight. Order quick and answer."[8]

What the mayor's telegraph actually said was: "Yesterday afternoon a white man was shot by a negro. The negro was arrested and placed in jail. The white man died today. Tonight, about half past eight o'clock, cries of fire were raised. The alarm came to our surprise. We learned about a mob of negroes at the jail. It appears that they had heard that an attempt would be made to lynch the negro murderer and they gathered for the purpose of preventing that. The police being small were almost powerless to disperse."[9]

The actual text of the telegram is noteworthy because it made no mention of the dead man being a constable. It did not characterize what was occurring as a riot in progress. It did not ask for the assistance of the local Rifle Guards. Instead, it specifically told the governor that a crowd was gathering to prevent a lynching and asked for outside help.

The real context of the communication between the mayor and the governor meant little to the press of the day. As reported by the press, the reason troops were called in was because "the representative people here wanted no half-way business and wanted the colored people to know that there were other white people besides those living in the city limits. It was the moral effect that was wanted, hence there was great satisfaction."[10]

In the interim, someone described by the press only as a "leading citizen" sent a telegram to the governor. It read: "My personal opinion that we may need some good friends. Tensions very high and negroes defiant. Slightest circumstance would precipitate trouble." A few minutes later, the mayor sent another telegram, stating: "Send here at once four companies of infantry and Gatling gun squad. Much excitement and threats of burning. Must be here by dark. Wire number of men coming and when they will be here."[11]

The governor promptly responded. Within a short time, an infantry company from Sumter, some sixty miles to the west, was on its way to Georgetown. Three more companies of riflemen made their way from Charleston, sixty miles to the south. The Charleston companies were placed under the direct command of Mayor Morgan. The state adjutant general sent a telegram to the governor confirming that he would "send tomorrow all carbines on hold and one thousand cartridges. Sent express this afternoon two thousand cartridges."[12] At the same time as all these troops were being mustered, members of the Georgetown Rifle Guards assembled at their armory. Morgan would not allow them to leave. Treading that fine line that separated the city from chaos, he let them stay in uniform but told them to stay out of sight so that the volatile mixture of suspicious and angry local blacks and vengeful local whites would not spiral out of control.

At 11 o'clock in the morning on Monday, October 1, 1900, Mayor Morgan telegraphed the governor, saying "Mob cleared off streets finally without assistance of military. Everything quiet now, but tension great. Have ordered dispensary and beer privilege closed and want them closed as long as necessary. Will keep you posted."[13] The governor authorized the closings.

Meanwhile, the mayor sent a telegraph to a his brother-in-law in Buffalo, New York, that read, in part, "I am keeping my head and doing the best I know how," and asked that his brother-in-law "Keep from Aggie and Katie, [Morgan's sisters] if possible."[14] He also issued a Proclamation reading:

> *To all whom it may concern:*
> *WHEREAS it has come to the knowledge of the municipal Executive of the city of Georgetown that divers civil-minded persons have associated themselves together within the city for purposes which have a tendency to riot and disorder and therefore in violation of the public peace. AND WHEREAS such persons have failed or refused to disperse when required to do so by the authorities of the city, NOW THEREFORE, I, W.D. Morgan, Mayor of the City of Georgetown do hereby call upon all persons so assembled or who shall assemble within the City of Georgetown for any unlawful purpose to immediately disperse and retire to their homes and cease their mutinous and riotous conduct and I hereby call upon all good and law-abiding people to assist the executive in his efforts to preserve good order and the public peace.*

The Sumter company arrived first. The presence of an outside military force apparently was reassuring to everyone. With its arrival, those milling around the jail went home, secure in the notion that there wouldn't be a lynching. The Georgetown Rifle Guards continued to follow Morgan's order to stay out of sight. The situation began to settle down.

On Tuesday morning, headlines in the *Georgetown Times* shouted:

> # All Laws Set At Defiance
> ## The City Threatened; Aid Asked For
> ## A mob of negroes takes possession of the city

"Chief of police McKeithen[15] did all he could," according to the article. "He had several arrested, but what could a force of five policemen do with such a throng? Mayor Morgan appealed to Alderman Baxter and several other prominent colored men to help persuade the negroes to go home, but in vain.

White militia preparing to parade through town, circa 1900. *Courtesy of the Georgetown County Library Morgan Collection.*

There were no overt acts on the part of the negroes. They screamed and threatened and no one, of course, felt comfortable."[16]

Curiously, the constable was not eulogized in any newspaper, either at the time of his death or thereafter. Nor did the city council adopt a resolution honoring his service.

On Tuesday, Major Henry Schachte, a battalion commander from Charleston, arrived with 185 men. They bore the colorful names and insignia of the "German Fusiliers," the "Lafayette Division" of the South Carolina Naval Reserves and the "Washington Light Infantry." They brought a Gatling gun and a Hotchkiss one-pounder rapid-fire gun, extremely modern and high-powered weapons at that time.

At the request of the white advisory board, a parade of 280 armed soldiers marched through the streets of Georgetown. Participating were Schachte's men, a company from the Sumter Light Infantry and assorted members of the local Hampton Imperial Guards on horseback. Forty members of the Georgetown Rifle Guards—namely, F Troop of the Third Regiment of the South Carolina Volunteer Infantry—were also allowed to show their colors. This was "the largest military demonstration seen in Georgetown since the war for Southern independence. The troops marched through the principal business and residence streets. The Gatling gun and Hotchkiss rapid fire guns were in the line of march, in the charge of details of the German Artillery and Naval Reserves."[17]

Then, the editor's attitudes hemorrhaging into the news pages (and ignoring the common interest of both the white and black communities in the maintenance of the rule of law), the newspaper opined, "The colored people know and have seen unmistakable evidence that the blood of the white man works wondrous fellow feeling, and there is but the need of a hint of danger to bring hundreds, yea, thousands, to the rallying point.[18]

According to Rogers' *History of Georgetown County*, "The main point made on that October 2 was that the white population of Georgetown could depend upon overt support from the white population of the rest of the state."[19]

There were no further demonstrations once the militia arrived. There were also no further efforts, or rumors of efforts, to lynch Brownfield, at least in the traditional manner.

Word of what had happened in Georgetown spread around the region. On October 3, 1900, the *Florida Daily Times* reported on these events. On October 5, 1900, Mayor Morgan wrote to the editor saying: "I thank you very much for your complimenting me in the issue of your paper of the 3rd. It was very gratifying to have the approval of my friends at home and abroad and especially of the recent troubles in our city. I am happy to say that peace and order have been restored without shedding blood."[20]

Within a week, "Mayor Morgan promptly took the bull by the horns." Eleven black men and ten black women—those arrested by the police chief and his men at the outset of events—were tried in municipal court by the mayor, found guilty of causing a disturbance and fined between $50 and $100, depending on the severity of their conduct. Three defendants were able to pay the fines. "The others are boarding at the Hotel de Skinner [the county jail] and will vary the monotony of said residence by work on the street chain gang," the *Times* reported.[21]

On October 10, 1900, the Georgetown Rifle Guards called a special meeting. The minutes of that gathering indicate that twenty-four new members were inducted. The minutes also report that the guards received a letter from the South Carolina attorney general "felicitating the various military companies for their exemplary conduct during the threatened riot. Secretary was instructed to have same published in the *Times*."[22] Then, at their next special meeting on October 24, 1900, the guard members learned that the group had received $225 in contributions during the preceding two weeks, an amount greater than their ordinary annual budget.[23]

CHAPTER XIV
FEARFUL TIMES

GEORGETOWN TIMES EDITOR JOSIAH DOAR was seriously wounded in the knee outside of the county jail on October 1, 1900. He remained under the care and treatment of Dr. C.W. Bailey for the next ninety-nine days.[1] His unidentified temporary replacement wrote a column titled "A Question of Simple Justice" in the October 13, 1900 issue. There was an election coming up. Filing dates had passed. The white Democrats had submitted their candidates and the black Republicans had submitted theirs under the fusion agreement between the two groups. There was no time to change. "The bargain is already made. The county convention and executive committee have already pledged us to this course....The general election is near at hand." There was insufficient time to organize a write-in campaign and, if the attempt was made on one side, it would be made on the other. Blacks still represented a majority of registered voters in Georgetown; whites could lose all voice in local government if the fusion agreement fell apart.

Against that background, the stand-in editor of the *Georgetown Times* attempted to persuade everyone to maintain to the political status quo.

> *What do we see? We see the mob, for a brief space, triumphant, at last brought to its senses. We see our mayor winnowing out the innocent from the guilty, and imposing the utmost severity of punishment upon the offenders. We find the best element of colored people supporting him in upholding the majesty of the law. We see Alderman Baxter cooperating with Mayor Morgan in endeavoring to quiet*

> *the disturbance on Sunday night. We see Herriot, Bolts and others counseling their people to a quiet obedience of authority. We find that Mitchell, the colored lawyer, does not appear as the counsel, nor any other of the colored leaders as bondsmen for the misguided rioters. Surely such conservatism and good sense on their part deserve to be recognized. And shall we seek instead to visit upon these men the sins of their ignorant and fanatical colored brethren....*
>
> *Every good citizen, be he white or colored, feels the importance just now of being specially careful to cultivate the spirit of harmony between the races. These leaders of the colored people we have mentioned, and doubtless others who we have not mentioned, have made their contributions toward this object. Now let us hold out an olive branch. Certainly nothing should be done to widen the breach between us. We say once more, let us stand by our party pledge. With us it is at once a question of honor, and of simple justice.*[2]

One week later, the *Times* reported, under its "News Items" that "Editor Doar is still confined to his bed, and is flat on his back." Also, under the headline of "Another Matter of Simple Justice," the *Georgetown Times* prejudged which version—black or white—of what had happened to be true. Siding, as always, with whites, it editorialized: "If ever there was a time when a court of justice should assert itself, we hope it will be done at the November session of this county. The juries should make short and swift work of the Negro murderer, John Brownfield. The respectful members of his own race have assured us in unqualified terms of his bad qualities, and he should be made an example of.

"When Brownfield had disarmed Mr. Scurry, and had secured the only pistol between them, he should have stopped in his murderous work and simply held Scurry at bay. Instead of which he deliberately shot every barrel into his victim.

"Unless this murderer is convicted, the courts of justice of this country should be abolished altogether."

Nothing in the newspaper indicates that its reporter spoke with eyewitnesses to the shooting. The newspaper did not reveal who "the respectful members of his [Brownfield's] own race" might have been nor the "bad qualities" that this full-time barber and part-time volunteer fireman might have had, other than his having been registered to vote but having not paid his dollar poll tax. Whatever those "bad qualities" may have been, they had not prevented a thousand of his neighbors from turning out at the county jail to prevent him from being lynched. Those qualities also had not prevented members of Bethel AME Church from taking up a collection and hiring two attorneys, J.L. Mitchell of Georgetown and W.J. Whipper of Charleston, both of whom were black, to represent Brownfield.

Within a week of the prejudicial pretrial editorial in the *Georgetown Times*, Brownfield was indicted by an all-white grand jury for capital murder. The case was scheduled for trial during the term of court immediately following later in the same month.

At the time Brownfield was charged with a crime leading to the gallows, more than 80 percent of Georgetonians were, in whole or in part, of African descent. So too were 52 percent of all registered voters in the city of Georgetown. The percentage was much higher in the county.

Grand juries are supposed to be made up of people qualified to serve on jury duty. In 1900, that meant only registered voters. Selection of grand jurors was to be done in the same way as the jury venire for trials. Either a blind person or a child is supposed to pick the names at random, a process that statistically should have resulted in a panel generally reflective of the racial makeup of the registered voters in the county.

The absence of blacks on the grand jury did not go unnoticed. Instead, it sparked a motion to quash the indictment because the three white "jury commissioners appointed to select the grand jury which found and presented said indictment, selected no person or persons of color or of African descent, known as negroes, to serve on said grand jury; but, on the contrary, did exclude from the list of persons to serve as such grand jurors all colored persons or persons of African descent...because of their race and color; and that said grand jury was composed exclusive of persons of the white race, while all persons of the colored race or persons of African descent...consisting of and constituting about four-fifths of the population of the registered voters in said city and county of Georgetown, and although otherwise qualified to serve... were excluded therefrom on account of their race...; that such discrimination is a denial to [Brownfield] of the equal protection of the laws, and of his civil rights guaranteed by the constitution and laws of the United States, all of which the defendant is ready to verify."

At the beginning of each term of court, all the court personnel—bailiffs, the court crier, the clerk of court, the sheriff or some of his deputies as well as the solicitor or his[3] assistants—assemble before the judge arrives. Defendants are then transported to the courthouse from the county jail. In the days discussed here, the transport of pretrial detainees and other prisoners was accomplished in a barred, horse-drawn wagon. Defense attorneys are generally in the courtroom by the time their incarcerated clients arrive. Upon his arrival, Solicitor Wilson dismissed an indictment against A.P. Hazard, a white man, for adultery arising out of his "habitually cohabiting and having unlawful intercourse with" Marie

Georgetown County Court House on the left. Georgetown Rifle Guard Armory on the right. Circa 1900. *Courtesy of the Georgetown County Library Morgan Collection.*

Hutchinson, a "colored" woman. The charge was dismissed on Hazard's written promise to have nothing further to do with Miss Hutchinson and never to commit adultery "in Georgetown County" again.[4]

Brownfield was transported the one block from the county jail to the county courthouse at the beginning of the November 1900 term of court. When he entered the court room, he saw something that distressed both him and his attorneys. Every member of the jury venire was white. Because Georgetown was an overwhelmingly black community and the victim in the case was white, Brownfield's attorneys moved to quash the jury venire and select another. The grounds for the second motion were the same as that relating to grand jury selection.

Before any business of the court proceeds, the jury venire is "qualified." The process involves making sure that everyone present is a resident of the county; is a registered voter[5]; does not have a prior criminal record; can read, write and speak the English language; and is not a law enforcement officer or employed within the four walls of the courthouse.

The trial judge in Brownfield's case was Earnest Gary. He was white and had presided in Georgetown many times before. He was familiar with the makeup of the community. Everyone stood when he entered the room as the court was called to order. "Oh yea, oh yea, the honorable Court of General Sessions for the County of Georgetown. All those having business before this honorable court draw near and rise for the Honorable Earnest Gary, Presiding. God save the State of South Carolina and this honorable court."

Judge Gary said, "Call your next case, Mr. Solicitor." John S. Wilson would have responded, "*The State of South Carolina v. John Brownfield.* Indictment for murder."

Judge Gary would have then asked if there were any pretrial motions. There were. Both had been filed by the defendant. Brownfield's attorneys would have then stated the nature and grounds for their motions—to quash the indictment and, if that were unsuccessful, to quash the jury venire and pull another. As part of their argument on these motions, Brownfield's attorneys offered to present evidence of the intentional exclusion of blacks from both panels. Judge Gary told them that such proof was "not necessary." This seemingly polite rebuff would later serve a fateful and venal purpose. Judge Gary then heard from Wilson (who was white) who spoke in opposition to the motions. Judge Gary then denied both defense motions.

Arraignment followed, a process during which the indictment is read aloud for everyone to hear. "That John Brownfield,...on the twenty-ninth day of September, in the year of our Lord one thousand and nine hundred, with force and arms, at Georgetown, in the County of Georgetown, and State of South Carolina,...in the peace of God and of the State, then and there being, feloniously, wilfully, and of his malice aforethought, did make an assault...with a certain pistol, loaded with gunpowder and leaden balls, and...John Brownfield,...had and held...James C. Scurry, [and did] then and there feloniously, wilfully, and of his malice aforethought, with the said pistol loaded as aforesaid, did shoot, hit, penetrate and wound; give to the said James C. Scurry thereby, in and upon the body of him...two mortal wounds, of which said mortal wounds, the said James C. Scurry thence continually languished until the thirtieth day of September, in the year of our Lord, one thousand and nine hundred he there died...[all of which was] against the peace and dignity of the State."

Arraignment includes a request that the defendant enter his plea. "How say you, John Brownfield, to the felony wherein you stand indicted, guilty or not guilty?" Brownfield responded, "Not guilty." He was then asked, "And how shall you be tried?" "By my God, my country and a jury of my peers," he responded. "May God grant you a true and just deliverance" was the reply.

Any general inquires to the entire jury venire from either the prosecution or defense would have been posed at this point. Standard questions involve whether any member of the jury venire is related by blood or marriage; has social or professional ties to the victim, any of the witnesses, any of the attorneys or the defendant; has heard about or formed an opinion about the merits of the case; and knows of any reason why he could not render fair and impartial jury service. For reasons that should become clear as this story proceeds, at least some potential jurors passively lied by not standing up in response to one or more of these inquiries. The truth was that a significant number of the members of the venire were members of the Georgetown Rifle Guards and should have been disqualified because of their association with the victim.

"Harken now as a list of jurors be drawn to be the trial jurors in your case. If you have challenge to them or any of them, you must do so as each is presented to the Book to be sworn. Mr. Clerk, let us have a jury," the judge would have instructed. At that point, names would have been pulled, one at a time, from a box and handed to the clerk. The clerk would have read the name aloud. The courtroom ceiling is nearly thirty feet above what was then an uncarpeted wood floor. The sound of each word spoken—as well as the chains binding the defendant as he walked down the aisle—would have loudly echoed from the plastered walls of the courtroom. (Even with carpeting added, the acoustics of the courtroom suffer from an echo to this day.)

As his name was called, each prospective juror would rise from his seat, come forward, enter through the swinging gate of "the bar" and stand facing the prosecution and the defense tables. Any inquiries of particular jurors—*voir dire*—would then occur.

Even though this was a capital murder case, there is no indication that extensive *voir dire* of prospective jurors was conducted. Instead, it appears that each side simply used peremptory challenges to excuse jurors. Peremptory challenges are those for which no reason has to be given. The prosecution struck four prospective jurors. Only one of the surnames is common in Georgetown today. The defense struck ten, almost all people with surnames of families prominent in Georgetown to this day. Of the fourteen men stricken from service on the jury, not one was a member of the Georgetown Rifle Guards. Because of that fact, it seems highly unlikely the question of whether any prospective juror "was associated with the victim in any way" was ever asked or, if asked, answered truthfully.

Even by the legal standards of 1900, blacks could not be systematically excluded from a jury. In 1896, during the same term as it approved the "separate but equal" doctrine in *Plessy v. Ferguson*, the U.S. Supreme Court held that a state could not, consistent with the Constitution of the United States, prevent otherwise qualified white and black citizens from sitting in the same jury box.

Today, lawyers are not permitted to use race, or racial stereotypes, to exclude individual jurors, even though peremptory challenges are intended to allow exclusion of individual jurors for no reason at all. The process, called a "Batson challenge," allows opposing counsel to question the exclusion of potential jurors by the other side. It places the burden on the acting lawyer to provide a race-neutral explanation for the strike.[6] The principle has gained such wide acceptance that the South Carolina Supreme Court has concluded that the term "redneck" is a racially derogatory term when applied exclusively to whites and, therefore, striking a potential juror because he looks like a "redneck" is unlawful. Similarly, striking a juror because he "shucked and jived" while approaching the bar has also been found to have violated the Equal Protection Clause of the U.S. Constitution.[7]

Once questioning (if any) of each juror was complete, the clerk of court asked, "What says the State?" The prosecution answered either, "Present the juror" or "We'll excuse this juror from the trial of this particular case." The clerk then asked, "And what says the defendant?" to which the response was either, "We'll excuse this juror" or "Swear him."

All the legal niceties aside, since jury selection was made from an all-white venire to which Judge Gary had already given a stamp of approval, it followed that an all-white jury was impaneled to try Brownfield. As it turned out, the trial jury included T.G. Tarbox, an alderman for the city of Georgetown who had urged the mayor to use force against rallying blacks a few weeks earlier. Tarbox was also a member of the Georgetown Rifle Guards. Five other members of the Georgetown Rifle Guards also served on the jury. They were Ormsby P. Bourke, J. Carraway, A.K. Dill, E.W. Kaminski and S.F. Croft. Shortly before the Brownfield trial began, Bourke, Carraway and Dill had served on the jury that had convicted Cupid Haynes for his colorful and boisterous participation in the demonstration outside the county jail the night Scurry died.

With an all-white, male jury in place, Brownfield went on trial for his life. Tarbox was appointed as foreman of the jury, and the trial recessed until the following morning, which was Wednesday.

The Georgetown County Court House was built by slaves in 1824. The plans for the building were drawn by Robert Mills, the architect who designed the Washington Monument. Georgetown County appropriated $12,000 for construction of this impressive, tall Greek-revival structure with six massive columns supporting the roof over the second floor balcony, from which the courtroom is entered by the general public. Granite stairs wind their way up to the courtroom's entrance from the first floor on each side of the face of the building.

Large and attractive arched windows line each side of the second floor. They allow plenty of sunlight to illuminate the courtroom. Before air conditioning, the windows could be opened to allow whatever cooling breezes might pass to enter the room during the stifling days of late summer and early autumn. While the courtroom has been renovated and expanded twice since, in 1900 it occupied the front two-thirds of the second floor. The jury room was on the right-hand side in the back, the judge's office was in the middle and a grand jury chamber was to the left in the back of the second floor. The rows of seating for the public in front of "the bar"-the railing that separated public seating from the working part of the courtroom-were elevated on wide stepped platforms from the main aisle to create an amphitheater effect. While this dramatic arrangement has since been removed, one like it can still be seen at the Robert Mills-designed courthouse in Williamsburg County, some forty-five miles inland. It is still in use.

In 1900, all of the county's elected officers—the clerk of court, the treasurer, the auditor, the sheriff and the coroner—had offices in the cavernous first floor of the building. The walls of the building being nearly four feet thick, the well-insulated first floor remained naturally comfortable, particularly when aided by the cross ventilation created by opening its opposing windows and doors.

When Brownfield entered the court, he would have been directed to the "dock"—a raised, enclosed space where, during criminal court, prisoners stood when brought to trial. The dock in Georgetown was an elevated platform surrounded by a decorative railing. It was constructed on wheels so that it could be easily moved out of the way when other court business was being conducted. Brownfield would have stood in the dock during all proceedings before opening statements.

There is no transcript of the trial of Brownfield. The reason for that will become clear a little later. There is, however, sufficient historical evidence from which to draw a rough sketch of what happened. That is done in narrative form.

On Wednesday morning, the bailiff once again called the room to order and said, "All rise for the Honorable Judge Earnest Gary, Presiding." Everyone stood when the judge entered the courtroom and took his seat at the large, elevated, enclosed podium that is "the bench." He told everyone to be seated, and asked the solicitor and the defense if they were ready to proceed.

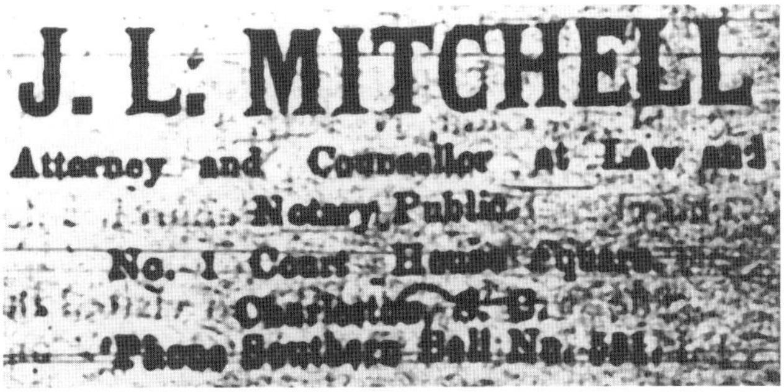

Advertisement for J. L. Mitchell in the *Georgetown Advocate,* August 2, 1902.

"The state is ready, your honor."

"The defense is ready."

In addition to the numerous spectators, the judge and the bailiff, others present included Brownfield, his attorneys Mitchell and Wipple, Sheriff McKeithen, the court crier, the court reporter, Wilson acting on behalf of the prosecution and an attorney assisting him, J.A. Kelly of Kingstree.

Opening statements followed. Wilson spoke first. In the style of the times, he thanked the jury for the willingness to serve, characterizing their service as an important duty. He told the jury of the charge against Brownfield. He mentioned that, according to law, the burden of proof was on the state to prove the charge against the defendant "beyond a *reasonable* doubt." (Prosecutors frequently put emphasis upon the word "reasonable.") With a minor amount of flourish, he told the jury that he gladly accepted that burden and that he would prove "beyond *any reasonable doubt*" that Brownfield had murdered J.C. Scurry "coldly, callously, cruelly and with malice aforethought." Wilson, who had a reputation as a colorful speaker and courtroom performer, probably pointed at Brownfield while addressing the jury and identified the victim as "white Georgetown constable James C. Scurry." Given the attitudes of the day (and a tradition of courtesy among lawyers to avoid objections during opening and closing statements if possible), it is unlikely that there was an objection to racial references. Even if there had been, Brownfield's black defense attorneys would have been sharply rebuked by the judge as he overruled the objection.

The solicitor told the jury the state would prove that on the afternoon of September 29, 1900, Scurry had gone to Washington's barber shop to collect a poll tax and fine from Brownfield. "The defendant wanted to vote like you and me, but he hadn't even bothered to pay his $1.00 poll tax like he was supposed to do."

"When Constable Scurry went into the barbershop, he told the defendant there [pointing at Brownfield] that if he wanted to vote he had to pay his taxes. Scurry told the defendant that he had a warrant that had been issued by Magistrate Hucks. The defendant, who was shaving some customer, turned toward Scurry and said something very angry and disrespectful which undoubtedly shocked Constable Scurry. He dropped his razor when he turned. Scurry reached over to pick up the razor for the defendant, Scurry's service pistol fell from its holster. Before he could pick it up, in less than the blink of an eye, the defendant seized hold of that pistol and started shooting at Mr. Scurry, emptying the gun of all its balls into his victim. Then, in an effort to escape your justice for what he did, the defendant tried to run away. But he got caught. Ya'll know what happened next. He's here now to face your justice."

Having not-so-subtly reminded the jury of the disorders in town without referring to them directly, putting a human face on the victim by using his name and title, and always referring to Brownfield as "the defendant" to dehumanize him, the solicitor once again thanked the members of the jury for their service and apologized for any inconvenience to them for having been called. He told them that they held justice in their hands and that he knew they would do the right thing. In this case, the "right thing to do," he would have told them, would be to "find the defendant guilty of capital murder so he can be hanged."

After saying "May it please the court" or "With the court's permission," defense counsel rose and, with a touch of hand on his client's shoulder, said he represented "Mr. John Brownfield, a citizen of Georgetown from a fine local family who works as a barber and who gives his time to the community as a volunteer fireman." Counsel continued with something like: "Today is the most fateful day in John Brownfield's life. He stands before you accused of murder. You have the power to decide if he lives or he dies." Counsel said that the death of Scurry was "a tragedy for everyone—for his family, his friends, the entire community, including John Brownfield *and especially John Brownfield*." But after listing carefully to all the evidence and considering it closely in light of the judge's instructions on the law, he was certain the jury would conclude:

> *[W]hile a tragedy, Mr. Scurry's death was not a murder. For the evidence will convince you that John Brownfield only acted to protect his own life. He did what any normal man would do under the circumstances that suddenly came upon him. A gun was pointed at his head by a very angry man. In the heat of the passions of the moment, he pushed that gun away from his head. When his aggressor*

continued to come after him, a very frightened John Brownfield yanked the gun from Scurry's hand and fired it in self-defense. God, oh my God, does he wish that never happened. He understands the grief of Mr. Scurry's family. He understands it because he feels the grief and remorse and sorrow so deeply himself.

Now the burden of proof is on the State in this case to prove that John Brownfield is guilty of capital murder. That means that it has to prove "beyond a doubt" that John Brownfield acted with "malice aforethought." Now the judge will instruct you closely about what that means. But I believe he's going to tell you that it means that the State has to prove without a doubt that John Brownfield thought about what he was doing, knew it was wrong, didn't care and did it anyway. But the evidence in this case will come nowhere near proving that. It's going to show you that John Brownfield acted in self-defense.

Now the law does not require Mr. Brownfield to testify in this case. He has nothing he has to prove. The burden of proof of everything is on the State in this case. And the judge will tell you at the end of the trial that you could not hold it against John Brownfield if he didn't testify. But even knowing all that, I'll tell you right now that he will take the witness stand, be sworn to God and before you, and tell you exactly what happened; how belligerent his assailant was; how frightened he was; how everything happened so quickly that he didn't have time to think but acted solely on reflex and in self-defense, motivated only by the instinct everyone has for self-preservation.

John Brownfield will take the stand in the case, gentlemen of the jury, because he has nothing to hide. He knows that the truth will set him free. Thank you.

Once the defense attorney sat down, the judge said, "Call your first witness, Mr. Solicitor."

R.C. Davis was a young white man and a member of the Georgetown Rifle Guards. He had given a statement to the police about ten minutes after the shooting. After being sworn in, and giving his name and address, he was asked:

"Let me draw your attention to this past September 29, do you recall what day of the week that was?"

"Yes, it was a Saturday."

"Were you in Georgetown that day?"

"Yes, I was."

"Did anything unusual happen that day?"

"Yes."

"Tell the jury about that, please"

"Well, I was walking down Front Street late Saturday afternoon. When I got to

The office of Dr. Thomas P. Bailey, circa 1900. *Courtesy of the Georgetown County Library Morgan Collection.*

the vicinity of Front Street and Broad Street, I heard load noises. They sounded like somebody was shooting a gun. The noises sounded like they came from the barber shop just next to the Windsor Hotel, so I walked in that direction. When I looked in the window, I saw blood on the floor and Officer James C. Scurry headed out the back door. He was bent over, holding his stomach like he was hurt. I went in and followed him. There was a man—a negro man—sitting in the barber chair.

"Do you see that man in the courtroom today?"

"No."

"Go on please."

"Well, I stepped around the blood on the floor. It was near the chair where the negro was sitting and headed out the back door. I was concerned that Jimmy was hurt. When I got out into the back, I saw the defendant there pulling on the gate next to the hotel on Front Street. It seemed stuck, so he started climbing over the fence. I called out to him, but he didn't stop. He was in a hurry—a big hurry like someone running away from something."

"Objection. He is speculating about Mr. Brownfield's motives."

"Overruled. Continue Mr. Davis."

"Well, I walked over to Jimmy and said, 'You OK?' He said, 'Call a doctor, I'm bad hurt.' So I ran to Dr. Bailey's office on the corner just the other side of Broad Street and got the doctor."

Dr. Thomas P. Bailey died in 1904. He practiced medicine from a small, one-story frame house with a small front porch and an A-style roof for years. He had been active in post-Reconstruction politics in Georgetown.

"We hurried back to where Jimmy was lying together. Dr. Bailey said, 'What's wrong, Jimmy?' to Officer Scurry and asked if he could get up. Might have told him to get up. Jimmy said he couldn't get up. 'You don't know how badly shot I am. I am shot all to pieces and am going to die,' is exactly what he told the doctor. The doctor opened his bag and got out some bandages. He told me to go over to his office, get a litter and bring it back. I did that. When I got back, Dr. Black was there too. Mr. Rouse must come up after me, because I hadn't seen him there when I left to get Dr. Bailey. Anyway, Mr. Rouse had gone to get Dr. Black. Mr. Rouse and I put him on the litter and carried him to his brother's house around the corner on Screven Street—just up the street from here near the town clock. When he got there, he put his hands where the wounds were, tossing in bed from side to side, groaning. Somebody said, 'Those wounds don't look so bad.' He said, 'I'm shot more than you think.' He said that over and over for the next two or three hours. He also cried out, 'Oh, Lord, I'm going to die' a lot of times, too."

"Anybody else there?"

"Yes, me, Dr. Bailey, Dr. Black, Mr. Rouse and, a few minutes later, Dr. Sparkman came in just shortly after we got to Mr. Charlie Scurry's house. He's the family physician for the Scurrys and told me to go outside, which I did."

"Anything else?"

"Yes, I waited around to see if I could be any more help. Jimmy and I were good friends and fellow Guardsmen. Around 11 p.m., one of the doctors—I don't remember which one—called me into the bedroom, whispering to me just outside the door that I needed to witness a dying statement."

"And what did he say?"

"Objection, hearsay."

"It's a dying declaration—part of the res gestae. I'm going to allow it. Go ahead."

"Well, Charlie Scurry was in the room. So was Jonah Bourne and Taylor Ham. Jimmy was resting. I think the doctor had given him something for his pain. The doctor told him of the need for it. Dr. Sparkman told him something like, 'Jim, old boy, I am afraid the chances are against you.' He then told Jimmy that a statement had to be taken, 'otherwise there would not be sufficient proof' of who shot him. He seemed affected a great deal and his emotions did not permit his speaking for several minutes.

When he revived sufficiently, I asked him for his statement. He told me that he'd gone to Washington's barber shop with a warrant for John Brownfield from Magistrate Hucks. He told Brownfield he was there to collect his poll tax. Brownfield told him to get out, he'd pay the tax when he wanted to do that and there was nothing Jimmy could do about it. Brownfield was slinging his arms around while he yelled and acted disrespectful. The razor in his hand fell to the floor. Jimmy bent over to pick it up and his gun fell out of its holster. Brownfield snatched it up quick as a wink and started shooting at Jimmy. After he emptied the gun, he ran out of the back door. Not knowing at that moment how badly he was hurt, Jimmy went out the door after him. But that's when his wounds caught him. The rest I've already told you. I then went outside and wrote everything down. I went back into the room to get Jimmy to sign. I wasn't able to get it. He wasn't up to signing, and I wasn't going to try to make him do it. So I read it to him. He said it was right. Jonah, Taylor and Charlie were all there."

"Jonah Bourne, Taylor Ham and C.W. Scurry?"

"Yes, that's right."

"Where were they?"

"Standing right there. Heard everything."

"Objection, he can't know what they heard or didn't hear."

"Sustained. They can testify for themselves about all they heard."

"Did you stay after that?"

"Yes, I stayed 'til he died. Before he did, he asked Dr. Sparkman for some more morphine. The doctor said he had enough and couldn't tolerate any more. Jimmy said, 'It don't make any difference. I'm going to die anyhow and want to die easy.'"

"Nothing further for this witness at this time," the prosecutor said.

"Cross-examination?" the judge asked.

"With the court's permission" said black attorney J.L. Mitchell.

"Mr. Davis, you weren't present in the barber shop at the time of the shooting, were you?"

"No."

"So you don't know what happened in there, do you?"

"No, I didn't see the shooting if that's what you're asking me."

"Right. So you have no way of telling whether John Brownfield here [hand on shoulder] acted in self-defense or not, do you?"

"He shot and killed my friend."

"That's not what I'm asking. You don't know why your friend ended up shot, do you?"

"He shot him."

"But you don't know why, do you—whether it was self-defense or not—you didn't see what happened with your own eyes, did you?"

"No, I didn't see it. I know what Jimmy told me while he was dying and I believed him."

"Nothing further."

The next logical chronological witness would havc been L.M. Rouse, who had come to the scene of the shooting and gone to get help. The Rouse family and the Scurry family were related by marriage. Scurry was a boarder in one of the extended Rouse family homes. His testimony corroborated that of the preceding witness. Cross-examination of him would have focused on the fact that he was not an eyewitness to the shooting, so he could not shed any light on what happened inside the barber shop.

The next witness would have been from law enforcement. A black police officer, S.B. Moultrie, had stopped Brownfield as he was climbing over a fence. Brownfield had told the officer what had happened, undoubtedly telling him that Scurry had been the aggressor and the shooting had been in self-defense. The officer placed Brownfield under arrest and took him to the chief of police and then to the jail. The choice for the prosecution was whether to ask questions or try to avoid having the witness testify in detail about what Brownfield had said. "He told me he shot Mr. Scurry" is about as much testimony as the prosecution wanted from the witness. This, of course, would be an open invitation to the defense to probe further on cross-examination in an effort to get out the full story, assuming that, given the short period of time between arrest and trial, Mitchell knew whether the officer had exculpatory information. Even if he did, the black officer was riding on the horns of a dilemma. He had to choose between helping Brownfield and upsetting the racist, potentially violent white establishment that employed him, or betraying his soul and failing to remember anything Brownfield told him that was helpful to the defense.

After these witnesses had been presented, Wilson turned to the doctors, Bailey, Black and Sparkman.

Dr. Bailey would have simply repeated the testimony he offered at the coroner's inquest. As with all the witnesses for the prosecution, cross-examination would be limited. There would have been nothing to gain by attacking the doctor in any way. Jurors would resent that. The best that could be hoped for would have been to get the doctor to acknowledge that he was not an eyewitness to the shooting so he really could not offer any insight into what actually led to Scurry being shot.

A similar situation occurred with Dr. Black. He had told the coroner's jury that he and Dr. Bailey had probed the wounds together "as well as the restlessness of the patient would permit, but [we] were unable to trace the course of [the] bullets." He described the wounds. One was on the left side at the edge of the short ribs. Three or four inches below that wound was an abrasion that "evidently had been made by a bullet. The other open wound was on the right side of the abdomen, about on a line with the upper edge of the hip. On the left forearm were three bullet holes, two being made by one bullet, the entrance and exit for same." In a criminal trial today, these arm wounds would be described as "defensive," suffered when the victim lifted his arm instinctively to protect himself as the pistol was being fired at him.

"We did not find any balls," Dr. Black testified. He also indicated that he and Dr. Sparkman had dressed the wounds at the Scurry house.

Dr. Sparkman was a good witness for "death watch" testimony—to describe how the victim had suffered, physically and emotionally, during the hours between being shot and his death. He had seen his patient rolling in pain and described how only repeated injections of morphine eased that suffering. He had heard his patient express the fear of death over and over. He watched family members and friends as they tried to comfort Scurry as he was dying. He choked with emotion when he told the jury that, as the Scurry family doctor, he had cared for the victim as a baby, then as he grew into a little boy, then an adolescent and then into manhood. Having been so close, it was particularly hard for the doctor to have to say "Jim, old boy, I am afraid the chances are against you" and then watch him die.

Dr. Sparkman was asked to describe the grief of the relatives and friends when Scurry died. Defense counsel had to make a snap judgment about whether to object. The testimony would be inflammatory and highly prejudicial. On the other hand, an objection would anger and alienate the jury. Even if the judge sustained the objection, a curative instruction from the judge would do no good.

The prosecution could have concluded its case-in-chief with the testimony of the slain officer's brother, Charles W. Scurry. He had watched his younger brother agonize and die. Any cross-examination of him would have been foolish. He was, however, not listed as a witness in the Sessions Docket maintained by the clerk of court.

Today, trials of death penalty cases are bifurcated into a guilt phase and a sentencing phase. Part two only takes place if the defendant is found guilty during part one. Victim-impact evidence, including testimony from family members about their grief, is permitted only during the sentencing phase of the trial. That is the rule because it is deemed too inflammatory to be given to a jury that has yet to decide whether the prosecution has proven the defendant's guilt beyond a reasonable doubt. Juries are supposed to make unemotional decisions about the facts of what happened before getting to questions of mercy or the lack of it. In 1900, the procedure allowed for more of a free-for-all.

The state had presented evidence of a shooting, a dying declaration of the victim about how it happened, the defendant's spontaneous admission that he had shot Scurry, medical testimony linking the shooting to the cause of death and the death. Because there wasn't any direct evidence of malice aforethought, a motion having the effect of striking the murder charge and allowing the case to proceed only on the lesser included offense of manslaughter should have received serious consideration. No motion was noted in the record.

CHAPTER XV
THE DEFENSE

AS ANNOUNCED IN THE CASE *State v. Martin,* the distinction between murder and manslaughter is

> *founded on a thorough knowledge of the human heart, and framed in compassion to the passions and frailties which belong to and are inseparable from our natures. We look in vain through all classes of society, for even one individual who has such command of himself as to remain passive and unmoved when suffering under personal injuries. Passion arising out of even imaginary wrongs, frequently gets the ascendency of distempered minds, and even those that are better regulated are sometimes carried away by the ordinary "ills which flesh is heir to." These may, however, be subdued and overcome by a proper course of reflection and discipline, and it is our duty to keep them within proper bounds; but he who has suffered great bodily [harm]...does not stop to reason about the extent to which he will carry his resentment, and in proportion to the degree of provocation will be the almost certain excess of resentment; and if, under the influence of such an excitement, one man takes the life of another in whose wrong it originated, it is manslaughter, not murder. There must, however, be a provocation—a reasonable provocation and what will or will not constitute a reasonable provocation, is perhaps the only difficulty in applying the otherwise well-defined distinction between the crimes of murder and manslaughter. The line which distinguishes between those provocations which will and will not extenuate the office, is not, nor can it be, certainly defined.*[1]
>
> *Twelve men of the average of the community, comprising men of education and men of little education, men of learning and men whose learning consists*

> *only in what they have themselves seen and heard, the merchant, the mechanic, the farmer, the laborer; these sit together, consult, apply their separate experience (and observation) of the affairs of life to the facts proven, and draw a unanimous conclusion....It is assumed that twelve men know more of the common affairs of life than does one man; and they can draw wiser and safer conclusions from admitted facts thus occurring than can a single judge.*

Murder being potentially a capital crime while manslaughter is not, the distinction between murder and manslaughter was certainly important to John Brownfield. If a jury concluded that events unfolded so quickly that the defendant acted impulsively, rather than with malice aforethought, Brownfield could not be hung, only imprisoned, albeit for a long time.

Since there was no question about whether Brownfield shot (and killed) James C. Scurry, the only way for Brownfield to escape punishment completely was if he had an "affirmative defense." Those involve a defendant presenting facts that, if proven to the jury by a preponderance of the evidence, would excuse the killing.[2] In this case, that would involve self-defense. For self-defense to exist, the defendant must be without fault in bringing on the original difficulty. He must also have an actual belief that he was in imminent danger of losing his life or being seriously injured. It is the perception of danger that is important, not the actuality of it. However, the perception of danger must be reasonable to a person of ordinary prudence, firmness and courage (the jury).[3] The defendant can have no other probable means of avoiding the danger. He must flee if he can, except from his home or place of business.[4]

Brownfield described what happened in this way: "I was in my barber shop when Mr. Scurry came in to collect delinquent taxes under an execution issued by Magistrate Hucks.[5] Scurry told me that if I did not pay taxes that he would arrest me and I told him that he could not arrest me without a warrant.

"He grabbed me in the collar and threw a pistol in my face and told me that he would show me.[6] I caught the pistol with both hands and turned it to one side to keep him from shooting me and then wrenched the pistol from his hands and shot him several times. I left the shop and ran up the street but was caught by a policeman and put in jail where I have been ever since."

This quotation is not from his trial testimony. It comes from a newspaper interview several years later.[7] At trial, Brownfield was questioned about Scurry's overall demeanor—the look in his eyes and the tone of his voice when he entered the shop. Brownfield was questioned about the pace of Scurry's speech—whether he spoke slowly, at a regular pace or with a rapid tone. The shop that sold old-style Coca-Cola—the kind that "relieves fatigue"—was just across the street. Because many people in those days used cocaine and other drugs, their effects would have been well known, if not well understood by the jury. Any contribution of the effects of cocaine in these events, therefore, should have at least been explored. All of these questions would have been relevant to the issue of how aggressive Scurry may have been from the outset.

Moreover, Brownfield was questioned about the amount of force Scurry used when grabbing Brownfield by the collar. A demonstration of that action would have been useful. There should have been a line of questions about whether the gun actually touched Brownfield's face when pulled and, if so, whether it hurt when contact was made. If the gun did not come in contact with Brownfield's face, it would have been important to know how close it did come and how it looked at that distance. These questions were relevant to the sense of danger and urgency Brownfield was experiencing and, therefore, the issues of "malice aforethought" and self-defense.

On the question of multiple shots, the law today is that when a person is justified in taking the first shot in self-defense, he can continue to shoot until the danger to his life has ceased.[8] To emphasize the point that Brownfield continued shooting because Scurry continued to come at him, the defense needed to do three things: first, cross-examine those who came to Scurry's aid about finding him outside; second, ask Brownfield about whether Scurry continued to come at him and chase him outside after being shot; and third, ask the eyewitnesses about whether Scurry's attack continued after being shot.

Several eyewitnesses testified on behalf of the defense. They included Magistrate J.J. Hucks, to testify that he had not issued an arrest warrant,[9] and Stephney Johnson, the black store clerk who had been so solicitous of the whites who gave him employment and named him as third vice president in the white-dominated Tilden-Hampton Reform Club back in 1876. Johnson had also been a marshal in the Hampton Day parade honoring the visiting general during that same year. His testimony pointed the finger at Scurry as the aggressor and benefited Brownfield with self-defense. Given Johnson's personal history of accommodation to whites, it would be reasonable to expect that his credibility would not be seriously questioned.

Another of the eyewitnesses was Dick Chapman. Nothing is known about him, other than he corroborated Brownfield and Johnson's version of events.

In a brief news account about the trial, on November 14, 1900 under the headline "Court Calender," the *Georgetown Times* condensed the entirety of defense testimony into three sentences. "The next case to be tried was that of John Brownfield for the murder of Mr. J.C. Scurry. There was testimony, pro and con, Stephney Johnson taking the lead in lying all the way through, followed by Dick Chapman.

"Stephney swore point black that he was a witness to the shooting as well as other coons but competent and reliable gentlemen proved undoubtedly by their testimony that they were not telling the truth."

The insulting, racist characterization of witnesses as "coons" aside, this brief description reveals that after the defense rested, the prosecution called rebuttal witnesses to discredit the defense. Because these rebuttal witnesses could not have been eyewitnesses to the events in question (if they had been, they would have been called by the prosecution in the case-in-chief), the only role they could play would be to discredit actual eyewitnesses by placing those eyewitnesses elsewhere—to show that the defense witnesses could not have possibly seen what they claimed.

The "competent and reliable gentlemen" in question are listed in the Sessions Docket as Senator LeGrand Walker, C.L. Ford, S.S. Fraser and Laurens Mouzon. All four were members of the Georgetown Rifle Guards, of which the victim, six jurors and one of the doctors were also members. Shortly after the trial, Senator Walker, along with Laurens Mouzon, would become founding members of Georgetown's White Supremacy Club.

Summations followed. Solicitor Wilson, in his usual vigorous style, wound up the state's case, assisted by J.A. Kelly, Esquire of Kingstree.[10] "Lawyer Kelly in his speech admonished the jury while impartially weighing the evidence to pay proper regard to the principle of capital punishment in which only was protection against lynch law guaranteed."[11]

J.L. Mitchell spoke for the defendant. He thanked the jury for its attentiveness. He told them his client was presumed to be innocent and the burden was on the state to prove its case beyond all reasonable doubt. He pointed out that Scurry did not have a valid warrant and, therefore, did not have the legal authority to arrest Brownfield for nonpayment of poll taxes. He told the jury that it was lawful to resist an unlawful arrest. He referred to the testimony of the actual eyewitnesses establishing that Scurry had been belligerent and pulled a gun on Brownfield. He argued that Brownfield had no time to think, but only to react and, therefore, there could be no "malice aforethought." He emphasized how scared Brownfield was—scared for his life—and only acted in self-defense. He urged the jury to find Brownfield not guilty or, at worst, guilty only of manslaughter.

The Pastor and trustees of the board of Bethel AME Church sitting in front of newly renovated building, circa 1908. *Courtesy of the Georgetown County Library Morgan Collection.*

Brownfield's murder trial lasted two days.

"After weighing the testimony on both sides the jury came into the court at eight o'clock." The jury returned a verdict of guilty without a recommendation of mercy. "The death sentence will be passed on Brownfield this morning," the Georgetown newspaper reported.

When Brownfield was brought back to court and placed in the dock the following morning, Judge Gary, resplendent in his black robes, declined to extend any mercy. Brownfield was sentenced "to be hanged by the neck until his body be dead." The hanging was to take place three days after Christmas 1900. To that purpose, a gallows would have to be built in the private courtyard behind the same jail that housed the defendant (and from which some "hot-headed" citizens wanted to take him and lynch him).

The Sunday immediately following, people went to church and worshiped God, blacks in their churches and whites in their separate churches. That evening, Mitchell spoke to the congregation at Bethel AME Church. Bethel is a brick structure just down the street from the Episcopal church in Georgetown.

It is two blocks from the jail housing Brownfield and three blocks from the courthouse where Brownfield had been tried. Each structure—the churches, the jail and the courthouse—are impressive brick buildings. The churches each had large and devoted congregations composed of the most prominent members of Georgetown society, blacks at Bethel and whites at the other two. That is true to this day. Bethel's congregation had financed Brownfield's defense.

Mitchell's speech to Bethel's faithful was lengthy and passionate. He told the congregation that Brownfield would not be executed. He reassured everyone that the sentence of death that had been handed down would be reversed and a new trial ordered. He said the all-white jury had not been fair. On retrial, a mixed jury of black and white men could be fair and impartial.[12]

Mitchell pointed out that the prosecution's version of what happened did not make very much sense. No one disputed that there had been a disagreement and a shooting. But the prosecution's version of how Brownfield came into possession of the gun—accidentally dropped by a courteous Scurry was far-fetched. If there was "malice aforethought," it was that of an aggressive Scurry, not the genial Brownfield.

Mitchell said credulity was also strained by the notion that an otherwise unprovoked barber would simply pick up a fallen pistol and start shooting for no reason. That was especially true, Mitchell said, in an otherwise isolated community from which undetected escape was next to impossible.

Be all of that as it may, these are the sorts of issues that should have been decided by a dozen impartial jurors, not a jury stacked with vengeful whites, Mitchell said.

Brownfield's wife and sister passed the hat to raise money to pay for the appeal.[13]

The *Georgetown Times* reported the speech: "This kind of harangue coming from Mitchell has surprised a number of people, both white and colored. The white people of this city have always considered Mitchell one of its best colored citizens, and one who has heretofore conducted himself in a gentlemanly and conservative manner."[14]

"As a matter of fact, Brownfield had one of the most impartial trials that ever went before a jury," the paper brazenly asserted. The paper remained silent about Scurry's membership in the Rifle Guards, the presence of six Rifle Guards on the jury (including the jury foreman), five Rifle Guard witnesses and a Rifle Guard prosecutor.

Stating what was likely true, the news account opined, "If the killing had happened in any other place but Georgetown it is more than likely that

Brownfield would never have had an opportunity to be tried by a jury." The account failed to mention that Georgetown's whites had in fact tried to avoid a jury trial; it was Georgetown's overwhelming majority black population that had prevented a lynching—one outside the courthouse, at least. While they might talk about it, Georgetown's "hot-headed" whites did not yet have the gumption to take on a community with whom they had been fused into sharing power and that could defend itself. The town's white population had yet to become that brazen.

"Brownfield killed Jas. C. Scurry in cold blood and he must pay the penalty," the paper continued. Discounting the equal desire of blacks to live peaceful and productive lives, the *Times* warned that "[t]he white citizens of Georgetown are entitled to law and order, and the mandates of law must and will be obeyed."[15]

In the same issue, a notice to the Georgetown Rifle Guards appeared. It was printed in the column adjoining the report and critique of Mitchell's speech. It read: "[Y]ou are ordered to attend drill tonight and tomorrow night, Friday night, November 23rd. You are to appear in the armory at 8:30 o'clock with uniforms, arms and accouterments prepared for rigid inspection by the adjutant and inspector general.

"Any member of the company disobeying this order, without good cause, will be promptly court marshaled and discharged from the service."

Chapter XVI

Appeal for Justice

John Brownfield's execution was stayed pending appeal. Even in those days, appeals took a considerable period of time. The time would have been endless to a young man confined in a dank, stifling brick-walled cell just large enough for a cot and a chamber pot. While he would have been let out of his cell and into the jail's courtyard and while he could have visitors, the timing and duration of those would be at the discretion of the white sheriff and his white jailers. The despair associated with such close confinement was overwhelming.

On May 22, 1901, Brownfield escaped from jail. Somehow he obtained a leg from an iron stove and used it to scrape away the mortar between the bricks of the courtyard wall. He then kicked a small hole through the wall, squeezed through it and ran, fleeing through the adjoining yards and graveyards. His avenues of escape were almost nonexistent. He was captured by the new city police chief, J.D. Johnson, in less than an hour and placed back in his cell; his already strictly limited freedom restricted even further.[1]

While Brownfield languished in jail, his lawyers were busy with the process of appeal. Instructions on how to file an appeal to the South Carolina Supreme Court were set out in the Revised Statutes of South Carolina. A notice of appeal had to be given to the trial judge within five days of the conclusion of trial and filed with the clerk of court within ten days.[2] Within 10 days after receiving service of that notice, the trial judge had to file "the record and statement of all the proceedings in the case, and the testimony in writing taken at the trial and signed by the witnesses."[3] If this court-supervised process went astray, the

The remains of the wall surrounding the old Georgetown County jail as they appear today.

rules provided that "the Supreme Court may, in their discretion, permit such act or acts to be done at any time to perfect the appeal on such terms as may be just, provided that the Court shall be satisfied that the appeal was taken bona fide, and provided that notice of the same was given."[4]

The purpose of these rules and procedures was to bring uniformity to the appellate process. Doing so was supposed to ensure that everyone was treated equally and fairly, and that every important issue would be considered and heard by the South Carolina Supreme Court in an unbiased way. In addition, because this was a death penalty case, the appellate court was, at that time, charged with reviewing the matter *in favorem vitae*—in favor of life. That meant that the members of the appellate court would not stand on the ordinary formalities of the process but, instead, would carefully scrutinize the trial record to make sure justice had been truly served. Any error was supposed to be reviewed, regardless of if the defendant's lawyers had raised the issue.[5]

Relying on a comprehensive and fundamentally fair set of appellate rules to guide the process to a fair conclusion, Brownfield's lawyers initiated the appellate process on his behalf. The appeal they filed on his behalf can fairly be divided into three parts. One involved pretrial procedures. The second dealt with factual defenses. The last related to whether the law was properly explained to jurors.

Pretrial Procedures—Seeing No Evil

The Brownfield murder trial was infamous before it began. A black man had killed a white man in a small Southern town in 1900. The white man was a constable. There had been a threat of lynching. In response, blacks had demonstrated and protected the killer. This all had sparked negative pretrial publicity. Despite that fact, no motion to change the place of trial had been made. The defense lawyers, therefore, were not in a position to complain that the trial was held in an extremely hostile arena. No motion for continuance having been made, they also could not complain that the trial was held while emotions about the case were still supercharged. Obvious problems arising from the place and timing of the trial notwithstanding, the Supreme Court did not raise these questions on its own *in favorem vitae*.

Instead of focusing on questions of the highly prejudicial pretrial atmosphere, Brownfield's lawyers chose to focus on the obvious racial bias in the selection of the grand jury that indicted their client and the jury that decided his fate. The lawyers made this decision because the U.S. Supreme Court had previously ruled that intentional exclusion of blacks from juries violated the Fourteenth Amendment of the U.S. Constitution. In the case of *Gibson v. Mississippi*,[6] Justice Harlan reminded everyone that federal law required "no citizen possessing all other qualifications which are or may be prescribed by law shall be disqualified from service, as grand or petit jurors, in any court of the United States, or of any state, on account of race, color, or previous condition of servitude." While pointing out that a racially mixed jury is not guaranteed in every case, any intentional "denial of citizens of the African race, because of their color, of the right or privilege, accorded to white citizens, of participating, as jurors, in the administration of justice, would be discrimination against the[m]" and, therefore, a violation of law.

Selection of jury panels is very serious business. It is absolutely no exaggeration to say that the right of anyone confronted by the awesome power of the state to be judged by a fair and impartial jury of his or her peers is the single most important right in our federal and state constitutions reserved for those standing trial. The right to a trial by an impartial jury is the ultimate "separation of powers"—that ingenious American invention that divided the absolute powers of the monarchy into as many different hands as possible. By doing so, the founding fathers attempted to construct a system to prevent would-be despots and tyrants from using the power of the state to impose their will.

The first level of protection built into the system was to require indictment by a grand jury before an accused person could be put to trial. Grand juries are supposed to prevent overzealous prosecutors from running amok. Their proceedings are held in secret to protect the reputation of persons under investigation. They have broad subpoena powers enabling them to seek out any additional information they require. And before an indictment can be handed down, at least twelve of the eighteen members of the grand jury have to be convinced there is probable cause to believe a crime has been committed and sufficient evidence to link the accused to that crime. If so, an indictment is issued. If not, the case is dismissed.

As a check on the power of the grand jury, the prosecutor—be he a solicitor as in South Carolina or a district attorney elsewhere—has absolute authority to decide whether to prosecute a person who has been indicted or dismiss the indictment.

Next, to counterbalance the power of the grand jury and the solicitor should they proceed with a prosecution, the trial judge has the authority to dismiss a case if the state fails to present evidence as to each "element" of the offense for which the defendant has been charged.[7] The judge can also reduce the charge to a "lesser included offense" if some important element of proof of the crime as charged had not been presented. An example would be to reduce the charge from murder to manslaughter if there wasn't any evidence of "malice aforethought" preceding a killing.

The next level of protection is the right to a fair, impartial jury trial. Like the grand jury process, it places important decisions affecting the liberty of the accused in the hands of fellow citizens. They are selected from the community in which the offense was allegedly committed. They are supposed to be selected at random.

The jury is the ultimate arbiter of the facts—the group that decides, based solely on the evidence, what happened "beyond a reasonable doubt." Having done that, the jury is supposed to apply the law as the judge instructs and render a verdict of "guilty" or "not guilty." A trial jury traditionally comprises twelve people. Any decision as to guilt must be unanimous for a defendant to be convicted.

Appellate courts have no authority to second-guess a decision of a jury verdict of not guilty. They have no authority to second-guess the jury's conclusion about matters of fact. Their role, if asked, is to review whether the judge committed any errors in his rulings on any motions or objections and whether the judge properly instructed the jury on the law.

This delicate set of checks and balances works only if each decision-maker is fair and impartial. In an effort to ensure that is the case, many judges and most prosecutors are elected officials, answerable directly to voters. In South Carolina, most trial judges are elected by the legislature, which, in turn, is elected by the voters. In the federal system, judges are appointed by an elected president with the advice and consent of an elected senate. Grand jurors and trial juries are chosen at random from various lists. In South Carolina, those lists contain the names of registered voters, everyone with a South Carolina driver's license and everyone with an identification card issued by the South Carolina Department of Motor Vehicles. The selected individuals are summonsed to court and the list of eligible jurors is culled from that group.

This system of checks and balances can work well. Sometimes, as in the case of Brownfield, it becomes tainted by bias. When it does, doubt lingers as to whether justice was done.

Because of changes brought by advances in technology as well as a deeper respect for the rule of law, the procedure for selecting jurors in South Carolina has been substantially changed over the last hundred years.[8] There are a few similarities that remain from the time of the Brownfield trial. The law still designates each county's clerk of court, the county treasurer and county auditor as "jury commissioners." At the turn of the nineteenth into the twentieth century, as now, the jury commissioners are charged each January with the responsibility of selecting the names of inhabitants of their county who may be called for jury service during the year. The important similarities end there.

In 1900, a total of not more than 1/10 and not less than 1/24 of names of otherwise eligible people were to be included in this pool. Nothing in the law at that time required the selection process to occur under public scrutiny. The selection process was not done at random. Commissioners were to select "persons of good moral character, of sound judgment, and free from all legal exceptions," but did not define those terms.[9] There is no way to determine what criteria were used because the jury commissioners in 1900 did not have an obligation to disclose the names of people who were rejected.[10]

In 1900, the names of the chosen individuals were written on slips of paper, folded up to resemble one another as much as possible so that the names were not visible and placed in a bin or box that was secured with three locks. Each jury commissioner kept a separate key, supposedly as a way of preventing tampering. But since all of the jury commissioners did not have to be present when the box was opened, the keys could freely circulate among them, making the multiple locks more of a show of security than a reality.[11] The clerk of court was charged with the responsibility of keeping the box secured when not open.

When the time came to draw a trial jury venire—anywhere between one and three weeks before a term of court—commissioners would get together with the sheriff, shake up the jury box, unlock it and draw thirty-six names.[12]

This was to be done at the clerk of court's office.[13] The drawing was done in private and out of public view at the Supreme Court's specific instruction.[14]

In 1900, in Georgetown County, all three jury commissioners and the sheriff were white. They chose the names of the eighteen persons who served on the grand jury that reviewed the charges against Brownfield and framed a single-count indictment of murder rather than manslaughter. The same jury commissioners also drew the thirty-six people from whom the trial jury of twelve was later selected. Apparently these white commissioners believed only white men were of sufficient "good moral character" and "sound judgment" to serve in judgment of Brownfield.

To ensure that proper procedures were followed, Section 2400 of the Revised Statutes of 1893 stated that "at any time it shall be brought to the attention of the resident Circuit Court Judge of any circuit that an irregularity has occurred in the drawing of jurors...or that any act has been done whereby the validity of any juries drawn or to be drawn may be questioned [the circuit court judge had the power to] take such measures as may be necessary to correct the error." In a case decided a few years after Brownfield's case, the South Carolina Supreme Court said, "[W]e fully appreciate the very great importance of preserving the sanctity of the jury box, and the danger involved in tolerating any departure from the precautions which the Legislature has proscribed to safeguard it from improper manipulation."[15]

There was, therefore, a mechanism readily available to Judge Gary to correct any problems caused by attempts on anyone's part to manipulate the composition of the jury. The remedy was very much in his hands—that is, if he chose to use it.

Objections had been made to the racial composition of the grand jury and the trial jury venire. All fifty-four of those individuals—eighteen grand jurors and thirty-six venire men—were white. The duty fell upon the judge, if he were impartial, to make a reasonable inquiry. There was nothing hard about it. In point of fact, the process is simple. All Judge Gary had to do was to look at the white faces of the jury venire before him. If he then simply looked at the county voter registration list, he would have found that it stated the race of each voter. All he then had to do was count how many were black and how many were white. If he had done that, he would have discovered that a little more than half of the registered voters were black. The logical question would have been, therefore, how do we get an exclusively white jury venire out of an overall population that was just about evenly divided between white men and black men?

Today, a statistical test called a "bi-nominal probability model" would be done to determine the odds that this could have happened by chance. Those odds were very long indeed. Judge Gary did not have to be that sophisticated. All he had to do was to put his hand in his pocket and take out one unbiased coin—one with heads on one side and tails on the other. If he wanted to see how long it would take to fairly—randomly—produce the same result as before him, he could flip a coin enough times to produce an identical result.

First, for grand jury selection, the process would involve his flipping a coin in separate groups of eighteen flips each time. The groups are necessary because that is how many grand jurors there were in the panel, and he would test to see how long it takes to produce a panel of eighteen jurors of the same race (each race represented in this test by opposites sides of the same coin). Once he started flipping, he would have to continue until one of those groups came up only "heads" (or only "tails") eighteen times in a row. That total number of groups (here called X) would represent the same odds—one in X—or chances that the grand jury in the Brownfield case had been selected without race being a central factor.

Next, for the trial jury venire, he would have to flip the same unbiased coin in groups of thirty-six, the total number of people summoned for the trial jury venire. He would have to continue doing that until the same side of the coin—heads or tails—appeared thirty-six times in a row, all while keeping track of the total number of groups of tosses that were necessary to produce that result. That total number of groups (here called Y) would represent the same odds—one in Y—or chances that the trial jury venire in the Brownfield case had been selected without race being a central factor.

Gary's inquiry would not end there. He was dealing with a combination of results, not a single result. The combination was that both the grand jury *and* the trial jury had come up all the same—all white. To find out the chances of that happening at random, he would have to keep flipping his coin, first in sets of eighteen until the same side of the coin appeared eighteen times in a row *back to back* with the identical side of the coin appearing thirty-six times in a row. Only that result would represent the odds that the all-white combination that occurred in the Brownfield case had happened solely by chance.

If Judge Gary had started this process, his thumb would have gotten sore before he was able to conclude his experiment. That fact, standing alone, should have put a reasonably unbiased judge on notice that further inquiry was necessary.

Judge Gary did not try flipping a coin or make further inquiry. He did not ask to look at the voter registration list, even though it, like every other official document during those times, was maintained in offices located immediately below him on the ground floor of the Georgetown County Court House. He

Georgetown Rifle Guards and a stray dog on Front Street, Georgetown, circa 1900. *Courtesy of the Georgetown County Library Morgan Collection.*

did not ask the clerk of court or the sheriff, both of who were present in the room, to take the stand and testify under oath about how the selection process was conducted. He did not ask the bailiff to fetch the auditor and treasurer from their offices just downstairs to come to the court and testify.

Judge Gary apparently did not believe that even the appearance of impartiality in the case of Brownfield was worth a flip of a coin. Instead, he coolly told defense counsel that proof of their allegations of intentional racial exclusion was "not necessary," ruled against their motions and proceeded with the trial.

Judge Gary explained his actions this way. In his statement of the case to the South Carolina Supreme Court,[16] he said he denied the motions because grounds for them "did not appear from the records or otherwise; that, not being personally acquainted with the jurors selected, I could not assume the facts to be as alleged."[17]

This is sophistry of the highest order. The written motion was right in front of him. It specifically alleged that blacks had been intentionally excluded from the jury. The trial jury venire was sitting right in front of him. Nothing in the record indicates that Judge Gary was blind. If he had reasonable vision, he could see that every member of the jury venire was white. If he was blind, he could have asked the clerk of court, the bailiff, the sheriff, the court crier or even the jurors to describe the racial composition of the panel. In short, he was on reasonable notice that an inquiry was necessary. Instead, in this one sentence from his statement of the case, he proved his mettle, such as it was. While he may not have to be "personally acquainted" with the all-white jury panel, it is very clear that he was in bed with the people who handpicked it.

The reason that court records are kept is so citizens can look at the documents and see for themselves whether everything has happened legitimately. The court record in this case contains a remarkable statistical coincidence relating to selection of the grand jury and trial jury venire. That official record contains two other remarkable coincidences: first, six jury members, five witnesses and one prosecutor were all members of the same all-white paramilitary organization as the victim; second, the jury foreman was a local militiaman and prominent local politician who had been deeply involved in the situation from its outset. From these facts, the public was to believe Brownfield received a fair and impartial trial. Or, perhaps more accurately, certain members of the community were meant to understand that he had not and there was nothing they could do about it.

The opinion of the South Carolina Supreme Court in *State v. John Brownfield* is interesting in several respects. In upholding the conviction and sentence of Brownfield, that panel acted as if he were complaining solely about the absence of blacks from the panel, not their intentional exclusion. The court was able to do so because Brownfield's lawyers had not used the word "excluded" in framing the issue on the appeal in their "exceptions" to what had happened at trial. They stated, instead, that there weren't any blacks on the jury. As Justice Harlan had written in *Gibson v. Mississippi,* the mere absence of blacks from a jury panel, standing alone, would not be grounds for reversal. There had to be evidence of intentional exclusion.

The imprecise use of language by Brownfield's attorney may have been sloppy lawyering, but it should not have been fatal. By its own standards of the day, the South Carolina Supreme Court was not bound by semantics. It was supposed to do an *in favorem vitae* review of every appeal in a capital case. That meant the court had the power (and assumed the duty) to look at the content of the entire record in the case, including the actual written motions to see what the problem might be. As explained by the South Carolina Supreme Court some years later, in a capital case, "the Court is conscious of its duty to search the record *in favorem vitae*, and to give the defendant the benefit of any errors in the conduct of the trial which affects the merits of the cause, even though they may not be sufficiently covered by the exceptions."[18] This was not a matter within the discretion of the court, allowing it to give strict scrutiny to the trial record in some capital cases but not in others. Instead, "the duty of an Appellate Court in a capital case [is] to search the record for prejudicial error."[19]

Brownfield's written motions to the trial judge had specifically complained of *intentional* exclusion of blacks from the grand jury and trial jury venire, but his lawyers did not use the word "intentional" in their appeal notice. This gave the Supreme Court the opportunity to feign ignorance of the true grounds for appeal. This little bit of semantics proved quite important, for if the allegation of intentional exclusion were true, the most basic constitutional guarantee would have been denied Brownfield—the right to a fair trial by an impartial jury. The denial of such a basic right was grounds for reversal of the first conviction and the granting of a new trial.

Rather than acknowledge the true grounds for the initial objection—intentional exclusion of blacks from both the grand jury and trial jury venire—and find that Judge Gary's refusal to take evidence on the question of racial bias was grounds for a new trial, the Supreme Court turned a blind eye to the underlying issue. By doing so it gave tacit approval to Judge Gary's manipulation of the record and gave the impression that Brownfield's lawyers were at fault for not properly preserving the issue for appeal. During an *in favorem vitae* review, whether his lawyers had done so or not was irrelevant. Judge Gary had an affirmative duty to ensure that there had not any been tampering with the process of selecting those who were to decide the defendant's fate. Instead of fulfilling that responsibility, he refused to accept evidence about what amounted to preselection jury tampering or to look for it himself. It was now the duty of the Supreme Court to look into the matter further. It failed to do so, too. Instead, it shifted attention away from its own duty and that of the trial judge and onto the defendant's attorneys. In doing so, the South Carolina Supreme Court became complicit in a legal lynching of Brownfield.

Factual Defenses—Hearing No Evil

Having turned a blind eye to Brownfield's complaints of obvious racial bias in selecting the jury that tried him, the Supreme Court then turned to the record of the case.

The grand jury's indictment read that Brownfield had "with force of arms, at Georgetown..., in the peace of God...then and there being, [did] feloniously, wilfully and of his malice aforethought, did make an assault...with a certain pistol, loaded with gunpowder and leaden balls [upon] James C. Scurry,...did shot, hit, penetrate and wound; give to the said James C. Scurry thereby...two mortal wounds; of which said mortals wounds...he there died.

"And so the jurors aforesaid, upon their oath aforesaid, do say that the said John Brownfield...then and there in the manner and by the means aforesaid, feloniously, wilfully and of his malice aforethought, did kill and murder [James C. Scurry] against the form of the statute in such case made and provided, and against the peace and dignity of the State."

The important words in this indictment are "murder" and "malice aforethought." Unlike today in which killing a law enforcement officer in the line of duty is, in and of itself, a capital offense in South Carolina, the law in 1900 made no such special provision. Instead, the crime of murder, as well as the crime of rape, was punishable by death. Not all taking of human life is murder. Some killings constitute manslaughter. The latter involve any slaying that occurs in the heat of the moment, without premeditation or malice aforethought. The punishment for manslaughter is a long prison sentence, not the death penalty.

In the Brownfield case, a proper *in favorem vitae* review would involve checking the record to make sure evidence had been presented to prove all elements of murder. That, in turn, required the record to be reviewed for the existence of evidence of "malice aforethought." Without evidence of that, it could not have been a murder. It could only have been manslaughter, at worst.

In the law, malice is a word of art. It is "the intentional killing of a person, intending to do it, knowing it to be wrong, without just legal excuse." It is "a wicked condition of the heart; it is a wicked purpose; it is prompted by wicked, evil, depraved heart, devoid of social duty, and fatally bent on mischief." There can be no "excuse or extenuation."[20] Instead, there must be a deliberate intention to unlawfully take the life of another human being. It cannot exist when a person acts (or reacts) in the "heat of passion."

Scurry was armed with a civil execution for nonpayment of poll taxes when he went into Washington's barber shop looking for Brownfield. He did not have an arrest warrant; that fact is certain because the document was not introduced as evidence at the trial.[21] The document Scurry possessed authorized only seizure of money or property, not the arrest of a person. Nonetheless, Scurry attempted to arrest Brownfield. We know this fact to be true because both the prosecution and defense said so.

Knowing for certain, as we do, that Scurry had no lawful basis to arrest Brownfield, and also knowing for certain that it was Scurry who went looking for Brownfield and not the other way around, it is certain there wasn't any premeditation on Brownfield's part to kill Scurry. There is, therefore, enough information contained in the record on appeal to spark inquiry during an *in favorem vitae* review of the question of "malice aforethought."

But there was a problem. Before the Supreme Court could try to delve into this issue, it had to read the transcript of the trial to see if there was any evidence of "malice aforethought." It could not do that, however, because the record was defective. While it contained a history of the case, reprinted Brownfield's motions and set forth his grounds for appeal, the testimony was not included. Instead, as the Supreme Court's opinion notes, "under the word 'testimony' are the words '(Insert testimony).' This, however, did not make the testimony part of the [record]."

Brownfield's life was at stake. The Supreme Court was charged with the responsibility of reviewing the trial of the case to make sure no errors were committed. It did not do so because the print shop failed to include the trial testimony at the point where the words "insert testimony" appeared. Those two words are common and quite obvious instructions to the printer. If the trial transcript was not sitting in the print shop already, the printer had to walk down the street to the courthouse and ask the clerk of court (who, incidentally, was later elected secretary for the White Supremacy Club)[22] for a copy.

In 1900 when the record on appeal in the Brownfield case was prepared, there were two print shops in town. One was operated by the *Georgetown Times* under Josiah Doar, who was disabled during the demonstration to protect Brownfield from lynching. The other was operated by C.W. Rouse, kin to a trial witness and a member of the Georgetown Rifle Guards. Rouse was also kin by marriage to the Scurry family. J.C. Scurry lived in a boarding house owed by the Rouse family.

Without regard to which printer sabotaged the record sent to the appellate court, the omission should not have been fatal to the appeal. Section 349 of the South Carolina Code of Civil Procedure of 1893 allows the correction of an error. "When any party shall omit, through mistake or inadvertence, to do any act or acts necessary to perfect an appeal or to stay proceedings, the Supreme Court may, in their discretion, permit such act or acts to be done at any time to perfect the appeal on such terms as may be just."[23]

It was plain what had happened. And while Brownfield's lawyers had certainly been sloppy in not proofreading the record before (or after) it was filed, this was a review *in favorem vitae.* To properly fulfill its responsibility, the court had to review the testimony. It did not bother. Instead, it turned a deaf ear to Brownfield's plea for justice by allowing the saboteurs to prevail.

Questions of Law—Speaking No Evil

Every trial judge has an affirmative duty to correctly instruct the jury about the law as it applies to the indictment and any defense in the case. The process generally

Offices of the local newspaper and the Rouse print shop were located on the left side of the block. Georgetown County Court House at the end of the block. *Courtesy of the Georgetown County Library Morgan Collection.*

works this way: Lawyers draft proposed jury instructions, citing supporting legal authority for each proposal, and submit them to the court and opposing counsel. Each side gets an opportunity to object to any request. The requesting attorney is heard. Then, the judge decides whether to accept or reject the specific request.

The process does not end there. If a specific request is otherwise proper but not properly phrased, the judge should edit or rewrite it to be correct. The objective is not to decide who has the more clever lawyer. It is to make sure the jury is properly instructed about the law as it applies to the case. The judge also independently prepares instructions on the law. The lawyers are told of the content of the judge's instructions. Any objections are put on the record. At the conclusion of this process and after summations or final arguments are made to the jury, the judge instructs the jury and sends the panel to deliberate.

The surviving record of the case does not contain a complete transcript of jury instructions. It does, however, contain a list of those requested by the defense. Nonetheless, it is possible to reconstruct most of what was said to the jury simply by looking at the charge on the indictment and the applicable case law of the time.

Unquestionably, the Brownfield jury would have been told about the law of murder. Section 108 of the Criminal Statutes of South Carolina of 1893 defined murder as "the killing of any person with malice aforethought, either express or implied." Murder was punishable by death. "Malice aforethought" would have been defined in detail. Under existing law, it could not be implied simply from the fact that there had been a killing.[24] The prosecution had to prove, beyond reasonable doubt, that some circumstance existed to demonstrate a depraved spirit on the part of the defendant.[25] The premeditated use of a deadly weapon certainly would be one example.[26]

This certainly was an issue for an unbiased jury to decide in Brownfield's case. If, upon examining all the evidence, the jury could not unanimously conclude that Brownfield acted maliciously, the jury would have been told it had other choices. When on trial for the greater offense, the defendant could be found guilty of the lesser. That means members of the jury should have been told that if, from the evidence, they concluded Brownfield had acted instinctively and not in a calculated and malicious way, they could still convict him of manslaughter. Section 210 of the Criminal Statutes of South Carolina of 1893 defined manslaughter as "the unlawful killing another without malice, express or implied." Manslaughter was punishable by a sentence of up to thirty years of hard labor.

From the scant record that has survived in this case, it appears that Judge Gary did instruct the jury about Brownfield's affirmative defenses. He told the panel that an arrest without a warrant is allowed only in cases involving commission of a crime in the actual presence of a private citizen or an officer. He told the jury that officers serving an arrest warrant must show it to the person being arrested, otherwise the defendant could lawfully resist the arrest. "[A]n unlawful arrest vests no authority in the one arresting, hence one so arrested has the right in such case to use as much force as may be necessary to regain his liberty, even to the actual taking of life," the judge said. "If the evidence shows that the accused actually believed that he was in such imminent danger of losing his life, or sustaining serious bodily harm, that it was necessary, for his own protection to take the life of his assailant; and that the circumstances in which he was placed were such as would in the opinion of the jury justify such a belief in the mind of a person possessed of ordinary firmness and reason, the defendant is entitled to be acquitted."

In addition, Judge Gary told the jury that a person who was attacked with a deadly weapon was not obligated to retreat but could pursue his adversary until the danger had passed. He told the jury that while the prosecution had to prove its case for murder beyond a reasonable doubt, the defendant only had to prove his plea of self-defense by the greater weight or preponderance of the evidence. "[I]f, upon the whole case," the judge said, "there be any reasonable, well-founded doubt in the minds of the jury, growing out of the evidence, as to the guilt or innocence of the accused, such doubt must be solved in his favor, and he [must] be acquitted."[27]

Speaking in an entirely different context about how courts work, a well-respected local judge said recently, "Sure, they go along with you on the technical matters to make it look good, then they screw you on the big stuff where it hurts." This approach helps maintain the illusion of fairness.

It appears that Judge Gary did just that. Having done all of his violence to the defendant's right to a fair trial by allowing a jury to be impaneled that was racially, socially and personally biased, he could afford to appear fair on the record. Indeed, he had to maintain the illusion of judicial fairness for the conviction to survive appeal. As an experienced jurist, he would have known that it does not matter what the judge tells the jury if the jury has already made up its mind. In this case, twelve white men were from a larger jury venire that had been handpicked by the jury commissioners as predisposed to convict Brownfield of murder. Put more simply, while the Rifle Guards could not lynch Brownfield at the jailhouse, they did so at the courthouse, and the judge, while maintaining an air of impartiality, had joined the lynch mob.

Without an error in jury instructions, there wasn't any further basis for review of the conviction of Brownfield. Between the trial judge's winking at the stacking of the jury, the sabotage of the trial record by the printer and the passive review of the case by the South Carolina Supreme Court, John Brownfield's fate seemed to be sealed.

Chapter XVII
Roads High and Low

John Brownfield's appeal to the South Carolina Supreme Court was denied in early June 1901. The *Georgetown Times* of June 15, 1901 reported the news, again changing the story. By this time, the excuse that J.C. Scurry was trying to serve an arrest warrant had been abandoned by the white community. "Brownfield is the negro barber who killed a white deputy sheriff who served a delinquent tax notice on Brownfield" is how the newspaper described what had happened. Ignoring the white lynch mob that had been forming, the paper said it had been the "exaggerated accounts of the affair which nearly precipitated a race riot," thereby placing all blame for social unrest on the black community.

On August 7, 1901, the paper ran an item on the front page about the Ku Klux Klan. It characterized that terrorist organization as a benign social club. According to the article, the KKK had been formed in a law office in Pulaski, Tennessee, by bored young men "looking for ways and means of having a livelier time" and nothing more.

About a month later, the September 11, 1901 *Times* reported that "[a]n enthusiastic meeting" for the purpose of organizing "the White Supremacy Club" had taken place in a packed courtroom at the Georgetown County Court House.

> *In pursuance of a call duly issued, a meeting of the white citizens of the city was held at the court house on the evening of the 9th. The court room was packed. It was strictly a business meeting conducted in a strictly business way. No harangues were indulged in and no bombates furioso were expected or attempted. Every man*

present gave evidence in his prompt attendance in his bearing and in his action and speech of an enthusiastic purpose and determined resolve, all the more intense because quiet and suppressed. The proceedings were short and to the point, and in perfect harmony and unanimity prevailed from beginning to end.

A temporary organization was gone into with Col. J.R. Sparkman in the chair and J. Walter Doar as secretary. A permanent organization was then effected, with the Hon. Walter Hazard as chairman and Mr. Doar as secretary. On taking the chair Mr. Hazard addressed the meeting in a few well-timed and earnest words, briefly outlining the object of the meeting and counseling harmony and mutual forbearance. Mr. L. Mouzon then offered a set of resolutions providing for the future work of the White Supremacy Club and for the selection of an executive committee. These with sundry amendments were adopted.

The following officers of the club were then elected: S.M. Ward [the Rifle Guards' commander], President, LeGrand G. Walker [the state senator who had been a rebuttal witnesses at Brownfield's trial], Vice President and H.L. Smith [the clerk of court], Secretary....

The club has been organized by law-abiding white citizens in a lawful way and embraces in its membership very nearly the entire white voting population of Georgetown. There is no excuse or explanation demanded or required why this organization has been perfected just now. The whites had good reason—to say nothing of a paramount right for doing it, and they have done so. This paper does not claim to be official exponent of the views of the club, and, in holding the above sentiments, will not pretend to make any explanation or give any reason to the colored voters of the city. But in view of what has come to the editorial ear at sundry times since this white supremacy movement was first agitated we deem it best to admonish the misleading and misled colored voter not to jump at wrong conclusions; not to imagine, because there has been, heretofore, a fusion [agreement] in the city and county politics, that such a fusion has become like the laws of the Medes and Persians, and may not be altered; not to assume that such alterations may not be done with friendliness and without friction, as of right, and thus not to invite and precipitate a status of unfriendliness and friction; to realize and understand as in other cities and counties of the state—yea, in <u>all</u> other cities, towns and counties of the state—white supremacy has been achieved and now reigns without amenity and discord; to take notice that, in this movement, no race hostility animates the whites, but that if race hostility is engendered or injected into either city or county politics, this movement must not be blamed, <u>for they will have done it themselves and must be held responsible;</u> to apprehend first and last for the law abiding colored citizen, every right thinking white man *in Georgetown whom he has been associated in business, trade or labor relations, has and can have only kind and friendly feelings, and that if those relations are ruptured and those feelings changed into bitterness, it must not be laid at the door of this movement.*

The foregoing constitute several words to the unwise. A word to the wise is deemed sufficient. [Emphasis in the original.]

One month later, on October 12, 1901, the headline in the center of the front page of the *Times* boasted "Looks Like A New Republican Party. The Negro is Certainly Going to the Rear. Decent and Respectable White Men Appointed To Office."

"With such gentlemen as John G. Capers at the head of the republican party in this state, it ought not to take long to build up a decent opposition in this section of the country. A great many white men are known locally as 'democrats' simply to prevent Negro rule and to be in opposition to these people, whose rule simply meant corruption, rascality and fraud. Now that these black politicians are being relegated to the rear, it will be feasible to differ amongst ourselves and put that difference into effect by vote, untrammeled by fear of the 'nigger in the woodpile.' Why, even Booker Washington advises that the negro be dropped from politics. The sooner the better, we say."

The editorial onslaught continued November 2, 1901 under the headline "White Supremacy Now And Forever; Old Things...Passing Away Daily; No More Compromises And No More Dividing The Offices."

George Herriott was a prominent black man who lived on Pawleys Island and had served as school commissioner of Georgetown County for nearly twenty-two years. Troubled by the increasingly threatening tone of the newspaper, he wrote a letter to *Times* Editor Josiah Doar. Doar refused to print the letter. Instead, he reported he had received Herriott's letter that "deals with the white supremacy movement and gives some facts and figures (from the author's standpoint) for the consideration of our citizens. In addition to its length, we don't know that we would be subserving the public interests (nor Herriott's either) by publishing this article anyhow. The movement for white supremacy, as we understand it, is not directed against such good and respectable citizens as Herriott; in other words, there is nothing personal in it.

"There is a general feeling in our community that, the time has come for a change in our political condition, and that the interests of all our people will be best looked after by installing white men of known respectability and intelligence in all public offices," Doar continued. "A 'compromise' was good in its day and time, when it was necessary to divide the offices, but we have outgrown this method—'expanded,' as it were, from infancy to full grown manhood—and this method of settling our political disputes will no longer obtain. No harm is meant to the colored man, and no harm shall come to him; but times change, and men charge with them, and Georgetown is no exception to this rule."

A week later, on November 9, 1901, a letter to the editor appeared on the front page of the *Georgetown Times* bearing the headline "A Noble Tribute to the White People." Written by the Reverend R.B. Slater, "one of our best colored citizens," the letter reads:

> *Men are being lynched in different parts of the United States for stealing and for murder and other crimes. Even in South Carolina men have been lynched in the majority of the counties for the nameless crime [of rape]; but the white people of Georgetown county can come before God with their hands pure from the blood of their fellow men. Let the negro feel proud of the white people of this county. It can be said of the colored people that the nameless crimes have never been committed by any colored person or persons of this county. The white people should feel proud of the way in which the colored people of this county have behaved themselves, show to the negro that if he respects himself he will be respected and you will make him the equal of any nation on earth. It is said when we make one step towards God he makes two towards us with a heart full of love. When our white neighbor makes one step toward his colored neighbor he feels that he has been highly honored and will make two steps toward his white brother with a heart flowing with love for him. The rice fields have been drained by the negro, the fine mansions, good streets, public roads are the works of his craft and many other things that time will not permit us to name. And yet he does not ask for social equality among whites, neither does he desire to dine with them as Booker T. Washington did with the president. The negro only asks to be treated as a man and he will make his own way through life.*

This effort at appeasement of growing white hostility had no apparent effect.

Brownfield met with his attorneys and agreed to appeal his death sentence to the United States Supreme Court. On November 30, 1901, that tribunal notified everyone that it would hear the matter. The stay of execution, in place since the filing of the first notice of appeal, remained in effect.

Brownfield was sitting in his small cell at the Georgetown County jail when, on December 7, 1901, the *Georgetown Times* published a front page article under the headline "Our White Nominees for City Counsel; A set of Candidates to be Proud Of. Let Every Citizen Do His Best To Make Our Ticket Win." It congratulated Mayor William Morgan on being nominated and opined: "[H]e will assuredly be reelected, even the negroes offering no objection to his reelection. Mr. Morgan's whole soul and body are wrapped up in Georgetown, and whatever appertains to the welfare and growth of our little city is sure of an earnest advocate in him. He is particularly fitted for this position and has manifested judicial and executive qualities of a high order. Calm and well poised on all occasions, he never loses his self control or acts from impulse."

The article reported that Alderman T.G. Tarbox, who had served as foreman of the Brownfield jury, was seeking reelection to a second two-year term. The paper endorsed his candidacy. In an adjoining article, the paper reported, "It would not surprise us if 'our friends the enemy' did not put up a ticket." That same column contained a mystic paragraph reading: "K.K.K. - Jeroboam - I.I.I.-which is it? We have forgotten the countersign already. Give it to us again!" This preceded a reassurance saying: "Let not the colored people imagine for one moment that any of their rights will be ignored by the success of our ticket. They may not hold office hereafter, but they will be safe in every legal and moral right."

The black community was not reassured. Passive resistance to white domination surfaced. In the year following the trial and conviction of Brownfield, his fellow volunteer fireman expressed their displeasure by refusing their services. In a community in which most homes were constructed of pine, were heated with open fireplaces and used wood-burning stoves for cooking, fire was an ever-present hazard.

On June 19, 1901, the Board of Firemasters for the City of Georgetown met. The meeting minutes reveal "[c]onsiderable dissatisfaction among the colored fire companies and especially the Hestons. The chief considered it proper to have a called mutiny and investigate matters after hearing considerable complaints from city officials and citizens. Motion: That the Heston Fire Co. is not-at-present in the opinion of the Board performing its duties as she should. Board [should] appoint [a] representative to take charge until next annual election of officers. Present President's health makes him unfit. Board to appoint 60 new members."[1]

The January 4, 1902 *Times* asked: "Have We Any Colored Firemen Left Us! There is evidentially something wrong. Let our fire department authorities investigate." The article that followed reported that the two colored fire departments were "completely disorganized and rebellious and that the vast majority of them refuse to assist at all." During one fire, the Star Fire

Fire engine and members of Star Fire Company, circa 1900. *Courtesy of the Georgetown County Library Morgan Collection.*

Company's engine remained in the engine house even though it was only one hundred feet from the conflagration. White firemen forced open the doors of the engine house and brought the pumper into service. They had to do the same with the Heston company's engine. (John Brownfield had been a volunteer with the Heston fire company.)[2] Warning that unspecified "heroic measures" might have to be adopted, the newspaper urged local authorities to "[a]ct and act at once. The longer we dally with insubordination and rebellion the harder it will be to apply the remedy."

With municipal elections only a few weeks away, the *Times* reminded voters that, in order to vote in the 1902 election, all poll taxes due in 1901 had to have been paid in 1901. It also reported that as of January 1, 1902, in the city there were 523 registered voters, "of which about 110 are colored."[3]

A week before the election, the headline "White Supremacy Here and Everywhere" appeared in the center of the front page of the newspaper. The article that followed demanded "[u]nconditional surrender...of these 'niggers' in the Philippines. Just as long as these semi-barbarians continue to fire upon our flag, at our soldiers, let the warfare go on. That's the kind of an American citizen we are, and the Times...is proud of it. Not only white supremacy and intelligence and brains in Georgetown, but the world over."[4]

The municipal election was a rout. "Every man nominated by the white supremacy club...was triumphantly elected...and white supremacy is an accomplished fact." Each white candidate received 350 or more votes. The two black candidates received forty-six and forty-seven votes, respectively.

The only remaining black on the city council, "Alderman Baxter, on retiring,...made some remarks, saying that while he could not say that he left the council with regret, he did so with a conscientious belief that he had done his duty as he saw it; and regretted the new departure which practically debarred his color from participating in the deliberations of this body; but that he would ever be found doing his duty to his people and the city, and that the city would always find him a willing helper in time of need and a true conservator of the peace. He expressed the hope that the new council, in exercising its right to elect officers as guardians of the city's peace, would not forget to give the colored element representation."[5]

Left without a voice on the city council or in the press, Georgetown's blacks created an alternative forum for their views. The *Georgetown Advocate* circulated its first edition in June 1901. Under the motto "God bless all our people, both black and white," the newspaper was organized by two local black ministers—R.B. Slater and W.P. Carolina—and the former black superintendent of education, G.E. Herriott. In its second edition, it advised that its mission was "to better the condition of the people of Georgetown along all lines. We will condemn all wrongs committed by all persons. At the same time we will endeavor to do it in a manner that will continue to cultivate a spirit of union among both white and colored."

The same edition contained an editorial advising:

> *There are three essential things necessary to the success of the negro, as they have been to all other races who have attained the highest state of civilization. 1st, The cultivation of the mind; 2nd, the heart; 3rd, the hand. If the negro expects to attain to eminence as a race, he must not shirk honest toil, he must train the hand intelligently to perform the very best work. The mind must be cultivated to the very highest state of perfection and the heart to that degree of appreciation of the divine love of God toward all his creatures. With these three necessary qualifications, all other things that go to make up a strong, powerful and successful people will be in sight forthwith. In the first place if a race is industrious and frugal it will acquire wealth and wealth and power are hand maids.*
>
> *A race of paupers are only found in Potter's Field; a race of wealth as rulers of the universe. Then let the negro labor and save a part of his earnings; acquire*

> *property and learn to patronize each other in business. Don't go around abusing the white man because he has sense enough to stick to his people. Let us learn the lesson well. Let us strive by all means, like wise, to obtain an education.*[6]

In its next edition, on June 21, 1901, the *Advocate* took its first tentative step toward a separate equality. "[A]s a self-respecting people, we need and should have a place owned and controlled by ourselves in which to bury our departed dead. We need a cemetery. Ofttimes in 'Potter's Field,' parts of bodies are dug up in preparing a place for another silent sleeper. It is a disgrace, a burning shame that for so many years we have contented ourselves in part, (some have protested) to bury in a 'Potter's Field,' a place to be used for paupers, strangers and murderers. Let us bestir ourselves and prepare for the emergency that must surely come, that is, the closing of 'Potter's Field' by the authorities.

"Young man, I ask you are you willing to have your mother, your best earthly friends, buried in a 'Potter's Field'? God forbid! Let the cry be made loud and long. A cemetery is needed, one should be gotten, one can be gotten, one shall be gotten."

The resulting effort was successful. Even today, the dead are buried equally, but separately. In the intervening years, Potter's Field was abandoned and, without respectfully moving human remains, dug up to build stores, a bank and what was originally a gymnasium for an all-white high school.

Separate customs also surrounded celebration of patriotic holidays. May 10 was (and is) the observance of Confederate Memorial Day. It was (and is) a day of holiday recognized by Georgetown's whites, although less so in modern times. As part of that commemoration in the early 1900s, the Georgetown Rifle Guards would assemble in a show of force around the Confederate war memorial, then in the middle of town. Around the turn of that century, Georgetown's black residents organized a separate celebration on July 4. In 1902, they asked the mayor to be chairman of the event. His participation did not sit well with his fellow whites. On July 1, 1902, the Georgetown Rifle Guards convened a special meeting. The minutes from that assembly indicate that Senator LeGrand G. Walker "made one of his usual spirited talks. Raised warm applause. [He said that] the negro had held sway at [the] July 4th celebration long enough and that it was time for the white man to resume his rights and negate the negro the rear. He thought that the Georgetown Rifle Guards should endeavor [to do so] by turning out in full force."

The corrosive effect of racism wearing on him, Mayor William Morgan appeared at the meeting and apologized for his participation in organizing the July 4 celebration, explaining that he had been appointed to that position against his will by prominent members of the black community.

In the face of this growing racial animus, the July 5, 1902 *Georgetown Advocate* reprinted an article from the *South Carolina Standard* under the headline "Christianity Versus Race Prejudice" expressing the following sentiments.

> *To justify the enslavement of the negro the old advocates of slavery laid down as a fundamental proposition that the negro was naturally and inherently inferior to the white man, made so by God, and would ever remain so. This proposition is by no means dead, but it will die. The Bible was twisted and distorted to prove it, and the color, servile, lowly, and universally ignorant condition of the negro was cited to justify it.*
>
> *This doctrine was a virtual denial of the unity of the human race in Adam and the brotherhood of man. The natural result of such views was to engender harshness in the breast of the master toward his slave and contempt and race prejudice against any man with negro blood in his veins.*
>
> *This view of the negro gave special seats in the churches to negroes, produced the color line, introduced separate churches and schools for the races, and imposes "Jim Crow" [laws] upon us. The white man's prejudice against the negro is the natural outcome of the false and unchristian views he was taught to adopt relative to the negroes in the interest of selfishness. The negro's prejudice is the natural outcome of his sufferings and the wrongs perpetrated against him.*
>
> *Even now, to justify the unchristian sentiments and feelings now existent, well meaning southern white men addressing colored people in religious assemblies charge the whole deviltry to Jehovah saying, "God made us so," and some thoughtless colored brother swallows it down and gloriously cries, "That's so."*
>
> *The fact is, race prejudice is the result of oppression, selfishness, and pride; it is nurtured by inequality of conditions between men and differences of education and custom. God is not its author; and it is sinful to shirk responsibility thus for [holding] it in our breast.*
>
> *Nothing is clearer in our minds than the fact that race prejudice is against the whole spirit and genius of the gospel and the beneficent aims of Christianity. This will be seen by careful examination (1) of the life and teachings of Jesus Christ and (2) the teachings and practices of the Apostles....*
>
> *He had no prejudice against men because of their misfortunes, their lowliness and sinfulness; He bore the reputation of being the "friend of publicans and sinners." The Jews had "no dealings with the Samaritans." It is said that no race prejudice could be more intense than that formerly existing between the Jew and*

> *Samaritan; the Jew cursed the latter "publicly in his synagogue—prayed he might have no portion in the resurrection of life, and refused to admit him as a proselyte, proclaiming that his testimony might not be received, that he who entertained a Samaritan was laying up judgment for his children, and that to eat a morsel of his food was eating of swine's flesh." The Samaritan was not a whit behind a Jew in cursing his opponent.*
>
> *But behold the magnanimity of Jesus in preaching the good news to a sinful woman of Samaria at the well.*
>
> *The beautiful parable of the "Good Samaritan" is a bold rebuke of racial antipathies and teaches distinctly that a man of an opposite and hostile race may prove himself our brother and neighbor, more so than a man of our own blood and religious faith....*
>
> *Race prejudice is selfish, cruel, ungodly, un-Christian. The man who panders to it, and appeals to it, to sway the ignorant and carry a point, is a dangerous man, be he white or black.*
>
> *The negro has been a great sufferer by the existence and perpetuation of race prejudice, and he has more than anyone else to lose by its encouragement and continuance. The un-Christian demagogues who appeal to it, whether from white or negro pulpit, impose obstacles to the progress of the human race, delay the triumph of genuine Christianity, dishonor the religion of Jesus, contract the sympathies of mankind, and fan into flame the vile passions and cruel enmities of men. Such leaders are ignorant of their Bible and are very dangerous guides.*

In the same issue, the *Advocate* addressed the "[d]angerous doctrine" being proposed by candidates for governor in the upcoming election. White candidates were urging that the taxes paid by white people be applied to white schools and that the taxes paid by blacks be spent in the segregated black schools. Acknowledging that this proposal might have a "cheap and temporary popularity," the *Advocate* pointed out:

> *Should such a policy prevail in South Carolina and some 200,000 negro children in the state be made dependent for their education upon the taxes contributed by their race, not exceeding $50,000 a year, we would have a generation of negroes growing up in this State worse than any that emancipation has given them. The negroes of slavery period were illiterate, but they had been carefully trained, had never known license and were thoroughly under the control of the white people. A generation equally ignorant now would be disastrous to our civilization because the negroes now are free, have enjoyed the vices and immunities of freedom and may not be controlled*

> *by force. They can only be reached through their minds, they can only be influenced by considerations appealing to reason. Could we imagine South Carolina as a state with a large majority of its inhabitants—such majority being colored—ignorant of letters, unable to learn the delicacies...how would the State stand in comparison with its neighbors? It would be the blackest spot in the South; it would be avoided by every white man seeking a home; the neighboring states might flourish and advance but South Carolina under such a policy would remain stagnant....*
>
> *The advancement and the welfare of South Carolina depend upon the average condition of its people, the average enlightenment and wealth producing capacity of its people. If the negro is to retrograde, to be made unfit for any but the lowest class of labor, the general average will suffer and the State with it.*

These sorts of concerns and forecasts notwithstanding, South Carolina continued on the path of separate-but-unequal education of its citizens. In 1901, white schools had an average of around twenty-five students in their classrooms. The average was fifty-five per class for black students. White schools were open twenty-one weeks per year. Black schools were open an average of fourteen weeks a year. That year, $726,825 was spent educating 94,548 white children, and $211,237 educating 113,566 black children. White teachers earned an average salary of $138.91 a year. Black teachers were paid an average of $80.30.[7]

One white critic of the policy was of the opinion that depriving blacks educational opportunity "is based upon the false theory that degrading the colored people will elevate the white. The truth is that degrading the negro robs labor of its dignity, lowers the standard of manhood, and debases all alike. The true theory is that education—the development of power—add to man's efficiency in all the walks of life; the money spent in educating the child is returned to the state many times by the increased productivity of the man....

"We need longer school terms, better school houses and apparatus, better teachers and a more equitable division of school funds," the critic continued, "not between whites and blacks, but between colleges and the common schools....To rob the negro of his school is a step toward despotism."

The response of the Georgetown Rifle Guards was to obtain a Gatling gun, a fact noted in the minutes of the September 30, 1902 meeting.

Election season 1902 arrived with the *Georgetown Times* reminding its white readers that "you are expected to take your registration certificate and tax receipts with you and go to your poll and vote. The republicans have a ticket in the field. Lay aside everything, just for one day, and make the time, and exercise that God-given right—the ballot—and help us to wipe forever from our grand old county the last vestige of republican rule....

"From now until the election is over, when you meet a democrat, let your greeting always be: 'Met me at the polls;' and we will roll up a grand and glorious majority for white supremacy. We must not fail. By order of the Democratic Executive Committee."[8]

By this time, the changes in the law, editorial bullying, poll tax and literacy tests for the poor combined had their intended effect. For the first time since Reconstruction, an actual count showed there were more whites registered to vote in Georgetown County than blacks. Whites took political control under the name of the Democratic Party for more than eighty years thereafter. That dominion began to erode in the 1980s. When, during the last decade of the twentieth century, blacks amassed enough political influence to become viable candidates for countywide offices, threatened white office holders shifted their allegiance to the Republican Party.

Chapter XVIII

"Equal Justice Under Law"

Inscription chiseled over the main entrance to the U.S. Supreme Court

On February 25, 1903, the lawyers in John Brownfield's case assembled in Washington, D.C., to argue before the nation's highest court. J.L. Mitchell, W.J. Whipper and E.M. Hewlett appeared for Brownfield. Solicitor John S. Wilson and W.H. Townsend appeared for the state.

The U.S. Supreme Court had previously ruled that blacks could not be intentionally excluded from jury service and that to do so would violate a defendant's right to a fair trial. That precedent led Justice Oliver Wendell Holmes, writing for a unanimous panel, to recognize that Brownfield's case involved "questions of the gravest character." Rather than attempt to address those questions, however, the court did not reach them. Instead, like the South Carolina Supreme Court, the nation's highest court acted as if its hands had been tied by the lack of evidence of deliberate racial bias. Rather than acknowledge that the problem had been created by the trial judge who had rejected the defense's request by saying it was "not necessary," Holmes and his brethren simply accepted Judge Earnest Gary's excuse that "the statement of facts set out in the grounds for quashing [the grand jury and trial jury panels] did not appear from the record or otherwise" and that "[i]n the absence of any showing to the contrary, I was bound to assume that the jury commissioners had done their duty."

Judge Gary was not stupid. He could see the race of all the people in the town and in the courtroom. He could see the difference between the racial mix of the community and the racial composition of the jury venire. He was, therefore, on notice that something was amiss.

Judges are not required to be ignorant people and disregard commonly known facts just because those facts have not been placed in evidence. In appropriate circumstances, judges can fill in the gap by taking "judicial notice" of the existence of facts. These facts have to be matters of general knowledge and which are readily capable of verification.[1] Government records, including census data and voter registration records, are among the sort of information about which the court can take judicial notice.[2]

It was always well within the discretion of Judge Gary, the South Carolina Supreme Court and the U.S. Supreme Court to take judicial notice of the census data when deciding if Brownfield's appeal deserved closer scrutiny *in favorem vitae*. But, as one former member of the South Carolina Supreme Court was fond of saying, "the law is for everyone; discretion is for my friends."

In the Brownfield case, Judge Gary had exercised his judicial discretion to exclude the very evidence that would show whether the defendant was being tried fairly or being lynched, albeit in the courtroom. That he did so appears in the truncated record submitted to the South Carolina Supreme Court and the U.S. Supreme Court. This was a very clear abuse of discretion. Nonetheless, rather than take judicial notice of official records and remand the case to the trial court to give both sides an opportunity to present evidence on an issue "of the gravest character," Justice Holmes (and the court for which he was writing) upheld Brownfield's conviction for murder. That decision cleared the way for the hanging.[3]

The decision was announced in a brief memorandum opinion dated March 9, 1903. It was received with "satisfaction" among the white community in Georgetown. "Sheriff [J.J.] McKeithen will soon deal justice to the negro who caused so much anxiety and uneasiness on the part of our citizens during the uprising four [sic] years ago." The Georgetown Rifle Guards "held a very enthusiastic meeting," and forty-four men reenlisted and another twenty-nine applied for enlistment.

"The fragrant yellow jessamine are in full bloom around us....Rain, and still it rains," the *Times* reported on March 11, 1903. In that same edition, it told readers that municipal court had been convened, where Mayor William Morgan had sentenced Willie Watson to ten days for being drunk and W.B. Willis to ten days for cursing on the street; fined John Johnson $50 for making disrespectful remarks about ladies on the street; "two notorious characters" named Emma Smith and Clara Green were each fined $10 for being disorderly; and Belle Burgess "received her just deserts" for being disorderly and cursing on the street. The paper also reported that "Sheriff McKeithen may now prepare his noose for John Brownfield, for the U.S. Supreme Court has decided adversely to his appeal. The son-of-a-gun should have been hung long ago."

When the next issue of the local paper appeared March 14, 1903, a little more of the truth about what had happened was reported. Instead of J.C. Scurry having innocently dropped his pistol as he attempted to pick up Brownfield's fallen razor, as was initially reported and testified at trial, the *Times* reported there had been an altercation over the payment of poll taxes. And "when resistance was made and *Scurry pulled his pistol,* a scuffle ensued; Brownfield secured the weapon and turned it on poor Scurry." (Emphasis added.)

This is the "coon"[4] version—that Scurry had been aggressive when he entered the shop, pulled a gun and put it to Brownfield's head, and that Brownfield reacted in the heat of the moment. This version supported Brownfield's claims of self-defense or, at worst, manslaughter rather than murder.

By this time, the truth no longer mattered. Brownfield's conviction and death sentence had been upheld and there was no further appeal. As a practical matter, now that the legal lynching was nearly accomplished, acknowledgment that a black man could not defend himself without being hung only added to the already pervasive atmosphere of intimidation. That advanced the cause of white supremacy.

Rather than discuss any of that, the *Times* complained that "[t]his negro and his friends—and this murder—were responsible for causing the first riot in this community between the races, when the women and children passed a night of terror—the rabble surrounding the jail and taking possession of the streets armed with clubs and muskets, threatening dire vengeance and death to the white people...and bloodshed was only averted that night and later on by the calm and considerate action of the white people."

The article made no mention of the threatened lynching of Brownfield by "hot-headed" whites. It did not discuss the fact that the demonstrators had prevented a lynching, doing so with angry words, not violence. The "white people" responsible for calming the situation consisted of Mayor Morgan. Unarmed, he had been calm, courageous and persuasive. The other whites who had shown up at the jail had come armed and looking for trouble.

"The editor of The Times received a wound on that occasion which he will carry to his grave and which has crippled him for life. True, it was caused by the accidental discharge of a rifle in the hands of a careless soldier, but Brownfield's crime against the law was the reason for this soldier being where he was at that time, and armed as he was," the article states.

This paragraph provides a good example of how hatred twists logic. The article goes on to gloat, "[a]nd now there is a deal of quiet satisfaction in our midst that the law will be at last vindicated, and that John will get his just deserts." The article then reports (and threatens) that "[t]he negroes say they intend getting up a petition for imprisonment for life." The reporter then menacingly wrote, "We would like to know who would sign it."[5]

Judge Gary opened court on Monday morning, March 31, 1903 "promptly" at ten o'clock.[6] The "big and portly" Sheriff McKeithen and his deputy Captain George Durant were on hand with the court reporter, Robert Lathan. Henry Harvin was tried for stealing a hog owned by a Mr. Harrelson. When Brownfield's case was called, Solicitor Wilson told the judge that the official court documents had not been received. He would make a motion for re-sentencing as soon as he heard from the court.

In April 1903, the Rifle Guards had another meeting and reelected officers. Demand for the *Georgetown Times* reached an all-time high, and as many as one hundred disappointed readers were turned away at its offices because all copies of the newspaper had been sold.[7] The mayor was drafted into deciding who had the prettiest baby, and people began to complain about "dens and palaces of vice" and "resorts of pleasure" that had made an appearance in town, warning that Babylon "was more progressive even than Georgetown; and yet vice destroyed it."

Chapter XIX
Appeal for Mercy

The U.S. Supreme Court decision became final a few days after the end of the April 1903 term of court in Georgetown. That gave John Brownfield a slightly longer lease on his life. He met with his attorneys, who told him they would seek clemency from the governor. There is no record of their having done this.

Shortly after the court's decision was handed down, Sheriff McKeithen agreed to allow a reporter to interview Brownfield. The article appeared April 22, 1903.

> *The clanging of the massive iron doors as the bolts were thrown back aroused the prisoner from his cot in his cell where he had been quietly conversing with fellow prisoners through the bars. He immediately put on his hat and stood in the open door, apparently ready to meet any fate that might befall him. The negro is about 25 years old, tall, erect and his long confinement of nearly 31 months has reduced his weight to about 125 pounds. In answer to the question if he still felt confident that he would yet escape the gallows, he replied:*
>
> *"My chances now look pretty slim and I am the victim of Caucasian prejudice. I ought not to be hanged, for at the time of the trouble I was in my barber shop when Mr. Scurry came in to collect delinquent taxes under an execution issued by Magistrate Hucks. Scurry told me that if I did not pay taxes that he would arrest me and I told him that he could not arrest me without a warrant.*
>
> *"He grabbed me in the collar and threw a pistol in my face and told me that he would show me. I caught the pistol with both hands and turned it to one side*

to keep him from shooting me and then wrenched the pistol from his hands and shot him several times. I left the shop and ran up the street but was caught by a policeman and put in jail where I have been ever since.

"I am not responsible for anything else that happened. My attorney, Mitchell... has written me saying that a petition to the governor is being circulated asking him to commute my sentence to life imprisonment."

This is about the substance of his story. Noticing that he kept his hat pulled down over his eyes, he was asked to take it off, but he drew himself up and said: "No sir, I won't do that."

The sheriff, who was standing near, was appealed to and ordered the negro to take off his hat. He made the same reply to him but instantly it was snatched from his head and in the top was pasted a small mirror, in which, perhaps, he often admired himself, for the bump of self-esteem is very prominent on his cranium....

[After recounting the events that followed Brownfield's arrest, the article went on to report that] [w]hile the case was pending in the Supreme Court, a little more than two years ago, Brownfield burrowed a hole through the brick wall of the jail with the foot of a stove and made his escape but was captured within an hour. As soon as he learned that the state Supreme Court had decided against him, he attempted to end his miserable existence by taking an overdose of laudanum, but prompt medical aid saved his life....

Monday a week ago, Brownfield swallowed a large quantity of Paris green in another attempt at suicide but became frightened and sent for the sheriff and physician, who again saved his life. When asked why he made the attempt, he replied: "Any kind of death is preferable to the disgrace of being hanged by the neck until dead."

It is stated that his negro friends have about given up all hope, realizing that they have exhausted every means to save him.

Large sums of money have been raised in the negro church on his account.

The next term of court began June 15, 1903. At the beginning of the term, Judge Gary "complimented the people of the county upon their law-abiding character....He said [the county's] reputation for peacefulness and quietness could compare favorably with any county in the state."[1]

All of the cases scheduled for this particular term of court were disposed of on Monday and early Tuesday morning. Oliver Goldman was tried for robbery and larceny, found guilty and sentenced to serve two years on the chain gang. Isaac Waring was sentenced to serve two months for burglary and larceny. William Docker received an eight-month sentence for assault and battery

Mayor Morgan (front left with hat and mustache) and friends at Pawleys Island, 1902. *Courtesy Georgetown County Library Morgan Collection.*

with intent to kill. None of these defendants was represented by legal counsel. Stewart Bowens was represented by lawyer W.W. Pyatt and was acquitted of charges of burglary and larceny. Pyatt also won an acquittal for Gardner Gordon on larceny charges. A hog-stealing case against Henry Harvin was continued until the next term of court.

Hughey Flynn, alias "Silver King," was convicted for liquor-law violations. In sentencing Flynn and two others named Cannon and Roon, the judge lectured that these sorts of offenses flourished in Georgetown, along with bawdy houses, and complained that city hall and the police simply turned a blind eye to this sort of vice.

With the preceding legal affairs resolved, at eleven o'clock on Tuesday morning, June 16, John Brownfield was brought in chains before Judge Ernest Gary by the Deputy Sheriff George Durant. Sheriff J.J. McKeithen was already in the courtroom, as were Solicitor John S. Wilson, H.L. Smith, the clerk of court and a court stenographer named Latham. Brownfield was dressed in a pair of light-colored pants and a black cutaway coat, a low-cut vest, a high-standing collar and a dark tie. He was placed in the dock reserved for criminal defendants and his handcuffs were taken off. He looked around the room. His attorneys were not there. Newspaper accounts do not say whether his wife or any of his family members could bear to attend.

The solicitor read the original indictment against Brownfield. Judge Gary asked if the defendant had anything to say before sentence was passed. According to the local newspaper, "Brownfield said he would like to ask for mercy, but didn't think the Judge would grant it, but he would like to have a few words with the following named gentlemen: W.D. Morgan, J.B. Steele, D.J. Crowley and E.W. Kaminski."

This was a remarkable request. Criminal defendants typically do not ask to speak privately with municipal fathers before being sentenced, particularly when being sentenced for murdering a public official. They also do not usually ask to speak to a member of the jury that convicted them. E.W. Kaminski was one of the members of the Georgetown Rifle Guard who had served on the trial jury.

Even more remarkably, "These gentlemen were sent for by the Judge," the *State* newspaper reported, "and Brownfield then requested the judge to grant him the privilege of a private conversation with them."[2] Judge Gary granted that request. Meanwhile, "The prisoner seemed to be himself and acted in a calm and quiet manner throughout the proceedings which were of such fearful import to him."[3] Brownfield, the mayor and the three white civic leaders went into the jury room to talk, escorted by Durant.

There is no record of their conversation. The relevant facts surrounding the meeting are clear, however.

Brownfield did not want to die. From his perspective, he was a victim. He was minding his own business when Scurry came into Washington's barber shop late one Saturday afternoon. Brownfield was with a customer. He had customers, including Stephney Johnson, who were waiting. Everyone in the room knew Stephney. He had tried to cooperate with whites as far back as the formation of the Tilden-Hampton Reform Club years earlier. He definitely was not a troublemaker.

Brownfield didn't have any prior criminal record. He was a young man in his twenties at the time of this meeting. He and his wife Sibby had been married for two years in 1900. Sibby was a year older than John. They lived together in a rental house at 231 Prince Street in a part of the community called "Slab Town" because the houses had been constructed of slabs of lumber obtained from Atlantic Coast Lumber Company.

John and Sibby didn't have any children. Both could read and write.[4] Aside from working as a barber, John Brownfield had volunteered his time as a firefighter.

Morgan was familiar with the Brownfield family. Brownfield's father was a carpenter, and his mother had been a homemaker. He had three sisters and a brother. All five children had been born within five years of one another.[5] His

Front Street, Georgetown circa 1900 looking down the block in the direction where Morgan, Brownfield and the others worked.

cousin Timothy was also a barber. His cousin Elizabeth lived a block away on Prince Street and was a teacher. His uncle James had been a community leader. J.B. Steele had served with James Brownfield on the Committee for Public Safety that had been appointed after the 1874 Bowley/Jones riot—the disorders that had scared whites into reestablishing the Georgetown Rifle Guards. The Brownfields were a respectable family, and everyone in the room knew it.

Morgan and John Brownfield knew each other personally. Washington's barber shop was just a few doors away from Morgan's bank. Their business hours were about the same, except the barber shop was open on Saturdays and the bank was not. Each would have regularly stepped outside for a breath of fresh air on pleasant spring and fall days and nodded to one another. So, too, with J.B. Steele and D.J. Crowley. Their places of business were just across the street from the bank and barber shop. Kaminski Hardware was located one block away. There isn't a record of any prior conflict between Brownfield and any of these individuals. The fact that Brownfield asked specifically to speak with them can only indicate that he knew them well enough (and they knew him well enough) to represent his last hope.

Every member of the meeting was also acquainted with the Scurry family. The dead constable had been a horse salesman before getting a job in county government. The City of Georgetown purchased horses and mules from the Scurrys.[6] Yet while they all knew Scurry, there is no evidence to be found that they or the municipality had taken any action to mourn Scurry's death. While the November 1, 1900 minutes of the city council include a report from the mayor of the events at the jail and praise then Police Chief McKeithen for his bravery, Scurry is conspicuously not mentioned.[7]

The trivial nature of Scurry's business on the day he died would not have been lost on anyone either. The entire incident had been sparked by nonpayment of a $1 poll tax. Collection of delinquent taxes did not justify the use of a gun, even in 1900. The fact that Scurry had taken out his gun (a fact ultimately acknowledged even by the local white press) is strong evidence that Scurry was a menacing, belligerent, demanding, hot-headed aggressor and that his behavior was a substantial contributing cause of his own death. His removal of the weapon from its holster also gives rise to a legitimate question of whether, at worst, Brownfield's crime was manslaughter or, at best, self-defense.

The city fathers at the meeting would also have known that the grand jury and the trial jury had been stacked, whether they were willing to candidly admit it. They would have also known of the role of the Georgetown Rifle Guards in securing the conviction on the murder charge. They would have known that the printer—Rouse or Doar—sabotaged the record on appeal. While not much is known about the others at the meeting beyond their business success, it is certain that Morgan was too intelligent not to fully comprehend exactly what had taken place—that, while not lynched on the streets, Brownfield was lynched in the court.

Everyone at the meeting would also have been acutely aware of the danger of disorder if Brownfield were executed in the courtyard behind the county jail. The population of the community was 80 percent resentful blacks and 20 percent nervous whites. There had already been a large demonstration in Brownfield's defense. The black fire companies had revolted and refused to put out fires after the trial. While heavily armed, the white community in Georgetown was still heavily outnumbered, so any disorder carried with it the potential of a great deal of bloodshed on both sides.

None of the whites wanted to see the community in which he lived, worked, prospered and loved go up in flames. It almost had done so once within their memory, during the Bowley/Jones riot. The strong turnout for Brownfield at the time of his arrest and the fiery speech at Bethel AME Church about overt discrimination and an unfair trial were not reassuring. The latter had been so unnerving, in fact, to have resulted in public announcements of mandatory drills for the Georgetown Rifle Guards. So whether motivated by a sense that an injustice was occurring, a desire to protect their investments in the community, their personal friendships, simple curiosity or some combination, all the men who were summoned attended the meeting. They came to try to cool down an inflammatory situation. It is unlikely that there has ever been another meeting of this kind anywhere in American legal history.

The "conversation lasted some time," according to the *State* newspaper of June 24, 1903.

After a thirty-minute conversation, C.W. Scurry, the brother of J.C. Scurry, was asked to come to the court. He did and entered the jury room. "Much has been said as to what transpired in this room, when Mr. Charlie Scurry was called in; there are assertions and denials. But this remains true, that Mr. Scurry used some forcible language when he found that the interview was based on the hope of getting the murderer of his brother from out of the hang-man's noose. The whole miserable business, we have reason to believe, was planned by the negroes in advance."[8] According to the *State*, the enraged Scurry remained only a few minutes.

With the negotiation for Brownfield's life at an end:

> *Brownfield was brought back and put in the dock. When again asked by the Judge if he had anything to say, he replied that he would like to have his sentence extended so he could get up a petition on his own behalf. He also said "I thank you for your tenderness and your hospitality".*
>
> *Judge Gary said in part: "I trust you have availed yourself of the admonition I gave you in the first instance. Your case is without parallel. I hope you have put your house in readiness and have prepared to meet your God. Your case has been taken into the atmosphere of different courts and no error has been found. I cannot hold out any vain hope for you and cannot extent the time. My duty is plain. Therefore, you shall be taken back from whence you came, and there kept in close confinement in private, until Friday, the 26th day of June and then in private be hanged by your neck until your body be dead, and may God have mercy on you".*
>
> *Brownfield did not then shown any signs of nervousness. He was handcuffed and taken back to jail by Capt. George Durant, where he will remain until next Friday, when he will expiate on the gallows for his crime. The last hanging to occur in this county was that of Jerry Cox on December 21, 1888—twenty years ago.*[9]

The following day, the *State* newspaper reported that land purchased by the federal government "in the Radical days of 'good stealing,' the intention being to colonize thereon a lot of negroes with '40 acres and a mule'" was being put up for sale.[10] The article did not point out that, when the "good stealing" was over, almost all of the wealth of the South was in white hands, not black.

The following day, on Thursday, Morgan met with the board of the U.S. Corps of Engineers about making improvements to Georgetown's harbor. They discussed widening and deepening the channels in Winyah Bay from Georgetown to the ocean entrance to create a safer passage. They also discussed dredging the Black River all the way to Kingstree and clearing the channel in the Waccamaw River all the way to North Carolina. At the meeting's end, the men boarded a steamer and traveled to North Island to inspect the newly completed jetties at the mouth of Winyah Bay.[11] At the same time, the sheriff made preparations for the execution. The gallows was constructed, "the rope…stretched and greased and all of the deputies…appointed."[12]

On June 23, 1903, the weather in South Carolina was clear and sunny. The temperature ranged between a low of sixty-seven and a high of eighty-eight degrees. There was a slight southwesterly wind blowing about three miles per hour.[13] On that same day, a mob in Wilmington, Delaware, burned a black man at a stake within a few miles of the Mason-Dixon Line. The victim, George White, was accused of having stabbed and killed the daughter of a local minister. After an unsuccessful attempt to get the prisoner from the jail the day before, a mob of about four thousand men and boys "became inflamed with the spirit pervading the throng" and—armed with pistols, shotguns and other weapons—stormed the jail. Railroad ties were used to batter down doors. The warden used a fire hose to try to hold off the crowd. Shots were fired, and a few members of the mob were injured, only to be "quickly carried to the rear and attended by those who were not brave enough to be at the front." The crowd soon found the victim. "The cell doors were quickly battered open and the cowering accused man begging for mercy was dragged from the cell and the prison." When members of the crowd outside learned he was in their clutches, "a great cheer was sent up." The man was then marched to his death pyre and burned alive.[14]

On this same day, John Brownfield died. "The Murderer Escapes; Committed Suicide. John Brownfield Swallows Poison and is Dead. The Law Cheated Out of Its Just Deserts and All the Negroes Well-Pleased With the Results," the *Georgetown Times* reported June 24, 1903. The paper complained that "the majesty of the law had not been vindicated."

The same day, the *State* newspaper reported that "[a] negro was committed to jail yesterday charged with burglary and suspicions are held that he was the means of the transmission of some deadly substance to the desperate prisoner." In that same edition, an editorial appeared. It read, in part: "John Brownfield, condemned to die on the gallows in Georgetown next Friday, took his own life yesterday. Brownfield was a barber and belonged to the 'upper class' of negroes and every effort was made by his friends and relatives to save him. We have always questioned whether this man should have been convicted of murder. His case seemed to come in the manslaughter class."

Also in the same edition of the *State,* an article reported that the Columbia City Council had passed an ordinance segregating the city's streetcars by race. "Brother in Black on the Back Seat. Pleasant Trip Around Belt Now 'On Sunday Afternoon.' 'Jim Crow' Ordinance Passed" were the headlines. The next day's edition carried an editorial praising the law, saying that the protests of blacks should be ignored because "[u]nmindful of their offensive personality negro laborers, women of the street and others equally unknown to that state which is akin to godliness, have occupied front seats on the cars. The contaminated air is carried from the front to the rear of the cars and because of the sensitiveness of the olfactory nerves of the Caucasian, these negroes become a veritable public nuisance."

A coroner's inquest into the cause of Brownfield's death was conducted June 24, 1903. Fourteen white jurors (including three Rifle Guards) were appointed. Details about the inquest were reported in the June 24, 1903 edition of the *State.*

Around midnight Monday evening, the other prisoners heard Brownfield walking around in his cell. The next time anyone heard anything was just before daybreak on Tuesday morning. At that point, Brownfield was heard groaning. The jailer, a Mr. Fletcher, was summoned. He found Brownfield lying unconscious and frothing at the mouth. He called the doctor. By the time Dr. Robert Bailey arrived, Brownfield had no pulse. Dr. Bailey gave Brownfield an injection of strychnine and atropine. This produced an apparent temporary improvement but ultimately proved unsuccessful.[15]

An Irish prisoner named Flynn testified, saying, "Brownfield slept very soundly last night until about 12 o'clock, when he arose and retired to the closet, returning to his cot and again slept soundly." Additional testimony was offered by one Charlie Hanna, who "admitted giving Brownfield a drink of ice water that night."[16]

The *Times* carried the following report: "Several witnesses were examined, among them being Brownfield's sister, Anna Washington, and a little negro girl by the name of Jackson, who had been in the habit of carrying notes to Brownfield from his sister. There was nothing given in the testimony of the

"Slab Town" section of Georgetown where John Brownfield, his wife Sibby and sister Anna lived, circa 1900. *Courtesy of the Georgetown County Library Morgan Collection.*

witnesses examined throwing any light on the subject whatever, and no clue so far has been gotten which points to anyone giving him the poison. The jury is now dismissed, however, and probably further investigation will be made, and probably a detective will be employed to work the case up. It is believed that the poison was given to Brownfield since his re-sentencing on the 23rd, for Sheriff McKeithen searched Brownfield and his cell thoroughly before putting him back, and nothing was found. An autopsy was held and Brownfield's stomach, intestines and kidneys were taken out and sent to Columbia to Dr. Burney, the State chemist, for analysis. For some reason Dr. Burney could not make the analysis and they were sent to Charleston. The autopsy was in charge of Dr. R.S. Bailey, assisted by Dr. D.S. Black and Dr. C.W. Bailey."[17]

According to correspondence to Mayor Morgan, "As soon as the chemist reports his investigation, the jury will meet and return their verdict,"[18]

Dr. Bailey believed that the symptoms displayed by Brownfield were not consistent with a morphine overdose. In his medical opinion, they pointed to phosphorus or arsenic poisoning. "The theory was advanced that Brownfield committed suicide by eating match heads and this is one of the possibilities as several empty match boxes were found in the jail room. The whitewashers recently employed about the jail and the servants on the premises were put on the stand and closely questioned by the jurors with no new light being thrown on the [subject]."

During her testimony, Anna "took advantage of the occasion to thank the Sheriff and the jailer's wife for their kind treatment of Brownfield during his long confinement."

Sheriff McKeithen "had Brownfield's body buried in Potters field Tuesday afternoon, and it was not turned over to his relatives,"[19] denying the family the opportunity to bury their own (and preventing them from seeing the body). Meanwhile, a number of newspapers around South Carolina published "innuendoes and insinuations"[20] directed at the sheriff regarding Brownfield's death. A truthful response to those is buried in an unmarked grave in Potter's Field.

Chapter XX

"Eloi, Eloi, lama sabachthani"

Psalm 22:1; Mathew 46

ABOUT THREE WEEKS PRIOR TO his death, John Brownfield sent a prayer to the local newspaper with a request that it be published. The letter was held on file until after his death. Then it was printed.

> *Hear my complaint, O, men, in my prayer; preserve my life from fear of the enemy, hide me from the secret council of the wicked; from the insurrection of the workers of iniquity, for though knoweth it is not my will to provoke you to anger, for I was around you from boyhood and was never known to trouble this honorable historic city nor mistreat the white race until I was pressed to break the silver cord which led to the uproar in this city, cause the coming of the men in blue, while it did look like men of war, to think over my great distress my heart did pain, my eyes would quickly gather tears of sorrow, my flesh would tremble with sorrow and sadness.*
>
> *Oh! Men can you not have mercy on me, will you forever stand against the plea of my cry for mercy? Oh! Men, harden not your hearts for thou knoweth not the will of the Lord, He is mercy and is just to all mankind, He will hear us all and likewise pardon us, then why not thou, O men, pardon me; for thou knoweth that I was always for the up-building of your city of Georgetown for in many cases of fire, I have stood with the heat of the strongest and most ablest firemen in times of trouble, for at the tap of the bell night or day, you will find me in full speed making my way to the Heston, and in good short time we would be in good trim for battle for our aim is always to save. Now remember that our motto was to save and in*

time of fire I was never so proud that I would not go through a mass of smoke for the sake of savings and ofttimes I suffered cold from the bursting water over me to the angry flames.

Now I beg the citizens of this town as I have been turned down in every court I now call back to this honorable citizens of Georgetown, for the sake of our Savior Jesus turn me back up that I may not die this way, if it be thy will commute with me and give me a little chance.

Signed J.F.L. Brownfield.

CHAPTER XXI

DIVISION AND CONQUEST

As John Brownfield's body decomposed, so did race relations in Georgetown. On June 25, 1903, Alderman Moses resigned from the city council and moved to New York. He was given a silver cup for his "valuable and intelligent services" over the years by Mayor William Morgan.[1]

On June 26, 1903, Laurens Mouzon, a Rifle Guard member and one of the state's rebuttal witnesses at Brownfield's trial, wrote to the *State* newspaper protesting the editor's conclusion that Brownfield had been guilty of manslaughter rather than murder. The editor of the *State*—the person who had just a few days before praised the segregation of streetcars in the state's capital—revealed a little more background about what had happened and what issues should have been tried.

> *In response to Mr. Mouzon's first paragraph it is only necessary to remind him that a man cannot be arrested in civil process without a warrant and in few criminal cases is such summary action permissible by a deputy. Neither can a man be arrested or imprisoned for debt. At the time of the killing there was no evidence published of there being a warrant for Brownfield's arrest and we have never heard of such a warrant. Without one the constable acted not as an officer but as an individual. On this point hinges the question. If the proceedings of the officer were entirely legal and regular, the negro was deprived of the plea of "sudden heat and anger," as the officer under those circumstances is the embodiment of the law; if his arrest was not legal then the killing in sudden anger would have been manslaughter....*

> *We are not surprised that the people of Georgetown sustained the verdict. They are surrounded by negroes and at the time of this killing were threatened by a mob with the torch and the sword. But that does not affect our judgement on the facts of the case as they have come before us.*[2]

In a brief comment in its July 4, 1903 edition, the *Georgetown Times* informed readers of the exchange of correspondence in its "Brief Paragraphs: Local and General" in the center of its front page.

Meanwhile, the white community had taken control of the Fourth of July celebration that previously had been organized by blacks. "The Fourth of July was never celebrated in Georgetown so gloriously as it was done this year. In fact, last year was the first time since the war that it was even thought of by our white citizens as a holiday, and no observation was given it except by our latter day American citizens, whose political existence did not in the remotest degree darken the mental vision of the Sage of Monticello as he penned the immortal instrument that created a nation of free Americans.

"The work of the Fourth of July club...brought about the change, and hereafter the day, it is to be hoped, will be observed fittingly here, as elsewhere," the paper continued. "The military companies, the Georgetown Rifle guards, the Marion's Men of Winyah and the Hampton Imperial guards, were out in force, the fire department in line and a long line of carriages with prominent guests and citizens made up the procession."

Guest speakers included Congressman Scarborough, Mayor Morgan and, for the first time, Dr. Olin W. Sawyer made a public appearance.[3]

That day, the *Times* ran an article titled "The Rational View Lynching and Crime—A Bold and Clear Thinker Begins to See Light, Even in Chicago Where the Negro Sentiment is Strongest." The article read:

> *"I am no advocate of lynching or mob law, but I would rather see a community wrought up to the highest pitch over crimes that would seem impossible this side of hell than to remain apathetic" was the declaration of Rev W.A. Bartlett, of the First Congregational Church..., in a prelude on "Lynching From Another Point of View." Dr. Bartlett said, among other things:*
>
> *"I have seen so many sermons, editorials and resolutions denouncing lynching and mob law, that one would get the impression that the citizens who hang or burn the destroyer of life, home and all that is held sacred by womanhood are the real offenders, rather than the monster whom they destroy.*

> *"We seem to be so absorbed with the majesty of this vague term law that the notion appears to prevail that the real criminals are those who do not wait for legal processes and the violator of womanhood is the abused party.*
>
> *"We shudder at the torture of the criminal who is burned, but apparently forget to shudder for the innocent girl whose mental and spiritual agony is tenfold greater than that of fire. This is not the race problem, except so far as one race are the offenders. The white man who commits the same crime is just as guilty.*
>
> *"The indignant uprising of a community and some of the best men in it to avenge a wrong of such awful magnitude may be technically lawless, but the spirit that causes the uprising is the reflection of the highest civilization. There are crimes so dreadful that the pure and chivalrous and the strong find it well nigh impossible to endure the thought that such a degenerate should pollute the earth by his presence.*
>
> *"It is easy to theorize about the anarchy of mob law, but the same hand which penned the calm editorial might be the first to grasp the torch if it was a mother, wife or daughter who was the victim.*
>
> *"I say that when you look at lynching from another view point it is simply the bursting forth of an indignation and loathing that will not be checked. In the Old Testament days they made short work of such an offender.*
>
> *"Lynching is certainly a bad method and forms the habit of disorder, and makes men blood thirsty. But if it is to be avoided there certainly is call for a more sure and speedy trial of these wretches who often brazenly deny crime amid red tape of legal processes but confess abjectly when confronted with determined men. It is useless to bring to trial good men who rise up to protect their fireside. The community will not bear it. If men object to being burned let them cease from crimes which make a nation sick."*

The editorial onslaught continued in the July 8, 1903 edition in the center of the front page under the heading "The Mulatto Problem." In it, the opinions of one of the "best authorities on negroes and the negro problem" from Greenville, Mississippi, are reprinted from *Harper's Weekly.* The article expressed regret that the last census made no distinction between mulattoes and others.

> *American social policy has ruled that a drop of negro blood in a man's veins makes a negro. Mulattoes, quadroons, octoroons—all are negroes, all their abilities, aspirations, virtues, sense and failings are credited to the negro race. An able and good mulatto we think of as a credit to his race. His abilities and achievements are proof of what negroes may accomplish.*
>
> *Folly says Mr. Stone. The mulatto isn't a negro. His talent is Caucasian; his aspirations are born of white man's blood and white man's abilities; his meanness,*

> *when he is mean, is white man's meanness. Almost all the "famous men of the negro race" whom we hear about, from Crispus Atticus down to Booker Washington, were mulattoes. The true negro says Mr. Stone, is of a contented and happy disposition. When free from white or mulatto influence he is docile, tractable and unambitious, with few wants, and those easily satisfied. He inclines to idleness, and though prone to commit petty crimes, is not malicious, and rarely cherishes hatred. He cares nothing for "the scared right of suffrage," and infinitely prefers the freedom and privileges of a [separate street] car of his own to the restraint of one that he has to share with white people. But the mulatto, naturally enough, is quite a different creature. He aspires; he chafes, and chafing he stirs up the negroes over whom, through papers, pulpits and political associations he exercises tremendous influence. All but an insignificant part of the agitation over "negro enfranchisement," "negro [street] cars," "the negro's rights," "the lack of opportunity," "the injustice of race distinctions" comes from the mulatto or the white politician. The best mulattoes, like Booker Washington and Dubois, are great powers for good; a lot of others are very active powers for mischief. So says Mr. Stone, and he is seemingly right about it.*

Then, in a special feature appearing in the *State* from Georgetown dated July 16, the reporter stirred the pot of racial division further by gleefully announcing: "There is turmoil and discord among the brethren in black and tan of the several negro churches here. The color line is being tightly drawn by the mulattoes to the exclusion and consequent chagrin of the blacks. The pride of blood and alleged superiority of the intellect are with the former; while pride of birth and righteous indignation animate the latter. The trouble started with the attempt by the mulattoes to exclude black preachers from the city pastorates, and the resultant friction has extended to colored society in general. Thus it has become, in many instances, a family affair, and there is confusion worse confounded among them. The tans have secured an important victory in deposing the black editor of *The Advocate*, a negro paper published here, and installing a mulatto in his stead. The denouement of the muddle is watched for with interest and some curiosity."[4]

As a follow-up, on July 18, 1903, the *Times* ran a page-one story under the headline "The Race Problem" complaining there were more than 9 million "black-skinned people" living in the United States and that approximately one-fifth of the heads of households owned property, "where forty years ago they did not own even their own persons."

"In forty years more," the paper continued, "if they go on increasing as they have done since 1863, there will be about 30,000,000 of colored people in the United States, not counting the islands [that were U.S. protectorates]. And they will have a large property stake in the country too.

"What is to be done to make it possible for the white race to live with them in safety and peace? Lynching cannot be the final solution. Every county in the south, we believe, has school houses now for its colored children. Probably in that direction lies the hope of the future."

In an adjoining column, the *Times* reported that a municipal ordinance to ban "houses of prostitution," "gambling dens" and "blind tigers" (saloons) was defeated when all members of the city council, except the mayor, voted against it.

The next day, the results of the examination of Brownfield's viscera were published. In a letter to Georgetown County Supervisor J. Harlston Read, Dr. France L. Parker, an analytical and consulting chemist at the College of Charleston, reported that Brownfield's stomach and intestines "contain[ed] no traces of the poisons most commonly used by criminals and suicides; vis, Arsenic, Phosphorous, preparations of Copper, Mineral Acids, Strychnine, Opiates, Mercurial preparations, Antimoniacal preparations, cyanides, preparations of Iron, Carbolic Acid, Chloroform; and there is nothing to indicate the presence of other poisons in the viscera sent to me.

"If you want the investigation continued, it will be necessary for you to furnish the Liver, Spleen, Brain and Spinal Marrow. This will incur considerable additional expense, and the chances of positive results are doubtful."

Some head injuries—including trauma caused by a blunt instrument—can result in unconsciousness and foaming from the mouth. In light of that commonly known medical fact, the absence of a request to examine the prisoner's skull is conspicuous. White fears of another "Save John" rally at the jail, this time on execution day, would supply a motive. Apparently recognizing this possibility of foul play, the coroner's jury ruled that Brownfield had died "from some natural cause or disease, the result most probably of long and close confinement and great mental shock and depression" and, even though beyond the scope of its duties and outside its jurisdiction, adopted a resolution in support of Sheriff J.J. McKeithen, exonerating him of any wrongdoing. "The jury wishing to vindicate Sheriff McKeithen from the insinuations and innuendoes recently published by several papers, reflecting upon his honor and efficiency....Be It Resolved that...we are fully convinced that the criticisms of Sheriff McKeithen were premature and uncalled for, and we have the utmost confidence in his integrity and loyalty to duty."[5]

On September 12, 1903, the *Times* ran another front-page story under the headline "Anglo Saxon Supreme" offering remarks of John Temple Graves of Atlanta, Georgia.

> *He received an ovation after his effort, in which he discussed every phase of the negro problem. He stated that white supremacy was an unalterable fact; that the ballot of the negro was worthless whenever it was in the majority and the only remedy lay in a separation of races.*
>
> *The speech was eloquent and dramatic, as well as pointed and logical....*
>
> *Two opposite, unequal and antagonistic races are set side by side for government and destiny. One of these, by the record, is the strongest race on earth; the other by the record, is the weakest race on earth.*
>
> *The problem is one of irreconcilable elements....*
>
> *No statute can eradicate, no public opinion can remove, no armed force can overthrow the inherent, invincible, indestructible, and, if you will, the unscrupulous capacity of the Anglo-Saxon race to rule.*

With that, political fusion between blacks and whites was buried. After Brownfield's conviction, the newspaper had boasted, "The negro is certainly going to the rear." It also acknowledged what had been, and would remain true about Democratic politics in the South for decades in the future: "A great many white men are known locally as 'democrats' simply to prevent negro rule and to be in opposition to these people."

In mid-October 1903, the White Supremacy Club met and had a "general discussion" about these sorts of political principles. Dr. Olin Sawyer and Laurens Mouzon were noted participants. They were appointed to a "constitution committee" along with several other members to come back with proposals advancing the organization's aims.[6]

The club followed that meeting with another about a week later. The committee appointed a week earlier came back before the larger body and suggested the creation of two polling places "to provide for all white voters who have lived in the state for one year and in the city for sixty days—the election to occur on the second Tuesday in December." Also appointed was an executive committee, which included Sawyer, Josiah Doar and McKeithen. A proposed resolution calling for an increase in the mayor's salary to $500 per year was offered by Judge Henderson. After Mouzon and others commented about it, the resolution was referred to a committee. In the same edition of the paper, Sawyer announced that he was offering himself as a candidate for the office of mayor.[7] Mouzon's name was also mentioned as a possible candidate. W.D. Morgan, having been vilified for meeting with and seeking leniency for Brownfield a few months earlier, told people he would not seek reelection.[8]

Another announcement appeared in the paper under the headline "Not In The Race. Mr. L. Mouzon, Who Did So Much for White Supremacy,

Withdraws." In the letter to the editor that followed, Mouzon said "the main object of that candidacy and my subsequent humble efforts has practically beeen attained. White supremacy in Georgetown has become and I think will remain an indisputable fact. If my efforts have helped to establish that fact in any fractional degree, I have the satisfaction and pride of every white man who lent his assistance to the same. The results altogether have been gratifying."[9]

With Sawyer as the only candidate in the race, a number of businessmen in the city mounted a campaign to bring Morgan back. Their nominating petition detailed Morgan's substantial accomplishments over the years and asked him to make the personal, professional and financial sacrifices associated with the job for one more term while the planned municipal water and sewer systems were installed.[10] On November 14, Morgan announced that he would run again.[11]

Sawyer was a relative newcomer to Georgetown. He had moved from Edgefield a few years earlier to work for Atlantic Coast Lumber Company, which, ironically, had been attracted to Georgetown by the port improvements and tax incentives Morgan had spearheaded. In Edgefield, there had been some racial unrest, which had been dealt with aggressively by whites. Sawyer bragged about that and was critical of Morgan's handling of the "Save John" demonstration.[12] Sawyer, who was not a Georgetown resident at the time, said he would have used force rather than persuasion to quell the situation.

In what became an increasingly heated campaign, Sawyer's operatives accused Morgan of being a "nigger lover," in favor of integration of the schools and equal treatment of the races. Sawyer repeatedly said he was campaigning to "redeem Georgetown from the yoke of fogyism."[13]

An apparently self-confident young man, Sawyer also stopped Herman Schenk on Fraser Street in front of the Atlantic Coast Lumber Company and bragged that "I am as good as elected any how, in spite of the fact that you took around a paper and had every damned Jew, Dago and alien sign it against me."[14] Schenk responded that only qualified voters had signed the nominating petition and the voters would decide who would win the election.

At this point, the *Times* ran a front-page story listing the accomplishments of Morgan in one column and those of Sawyer in the next. It listed Morgan as (1) having served as chief of the fire department, (2) having served as mayor, (3) having developed a cash management system for the city, (4) having operated the city on a balanced budget, (5) having improved and added streets, (6) having made the streets cleaner, (7) having installed electric lights, (8) having municipal water and sewer systems on the drawing boards, (9) having increased the efficiency of the fire department, (10) having lowered the city's bonded indebtedness, (11) having lowered the interest the city paid on its bonds, (12) having brought improvements to the harbor and the port, (13) having secured federal appropriations for government buildings, (14) having supervised all city workers and (15) having not raised taxes in the process.

In the adjoining column, the *Times* listed that Sawyer had voted for a pay raise for policemen with a good bit of blank space below.[15]

Also on the front page, a letter to the editors characterized Sawyer as "a martyr, offering himself upon the alter of patriotism in the redemption of Georgetown."[16]

With accusations of Morgan being soft on blacks gaining a wider audience, he wrote a letter to the *Georgetown Times.* It appeared in the November 10, 1903 edition. It read, in part: "As a consistent member of the White Supremacy Club, I stand pledged to abide by the result of the primary, which will be held under its auspices. As a white man by birth, as a white man's man by association and heredity, as a warm and unflinching advocate of the right of dominancy by the Anglo-Saxon, I again pledge myself to abide by the result of said primary....But no matter who wins or who loses, let the white men not only stand together, but keep together."

Around this time, old friends came to Morgan's defense, albeit lukewarmly. Captain S.M. Ward, commander of the Georgetown Rifle Guards, and Mouzon of the White Supremacy Club raised their voices. Ward wrote to the *Times* acknowledging "while I did not approve of the manner in which the riot was handled that night I realized that Mr. Morgan had all the responsibility of the situation on his shoulders and while differing with him I knew from his past record and from what I saw him do that night that it was not a question of bravery on his part, but simply an honest difference of opinion, and that he was acting as he thought best for the interest of the community."

Mouzon had also disagreed with how the mayor had avoided bloodshed in September 1900. Mouzon had been very critical of Morgan at the time. "I do not mean to say that my views have changed as to his policy at the time I am bound to confess, notwithstanding my regret in doing so, that my views have not changed in this respect. But that was and is and will be for sometime a matter of difference of opinion, and whereas I criticized the man, I criticize now only his method....Suffice it to say, however, that every man did his duty to the best of his ability, as he conceived it to be, and whether right or wrong, there was no man among us more distinguished in patriotic sense, as he went alone unprotected and heedless into the thicket of the infuriated mob endeavoring to quell its tumult."

In the *Times* article "Exposing the Falsehoods and Insinuations Thrown at Our Candidate for Mayor," Doar wrote:

> *Everybody knows that Mr. Morgan went into the midst of the mob on that memorable night, taking his life in his hands, in order to quell the disturbance and disperse the crowd. At any moment a stab in the back or a blow in the head might have laid him low. But, without a moment's hesitation, he faced the danger and used all his powers of persuasion to calm the excited negroes. The personal courage and unflinching coolness which he displayed on that occasion would put to the blush the holiday bravery of some of the carpet-knights who are now so loud in their condemnation of his course....*
>
> *Georgetown is not yet quite ready to have her municipal government converted into a political machine as a stepping stone for the personal aggrandizement of ambitious agitators.*
>
> *It may be as well to remind some of our people that it is not necessary for us to import political prophets from Edgefield to tell us what true democracy means. The men of Georgetown are as brave and as true as any who ever fought the radicals along the banks of the Savannah River. When the men of Edgefield were struggling against the negroes with odds of perhaps two or three to one against them, they had thousands of Georgians at their backs ready to cross the river at a moment's notice and come to their aid, and many of them responded to the call. The white men of Georgetown, few in numbers, but indomitable in spirit, fearlessly faced odds twice as heavy and confronted dangers far more serious, though they were cut off from the world and had only their own courage and constancy to rely on. Thank you, we are not finding fault with the Edgefield type of democracy, but we have yet to see any reason for supposing that it was better or finer than the Georgetown type.*[17]

Then, just a few days before the election, on December 5, 1903, Morgan again wrote to the *Times* saying: "When the present municipal campaign was started, it was my hope and desire that all bitterness and personalities would be avoided, and a fair, manly contest engaged in between white men..., conducted on a high plane, under the auspices of the White Supremacy League [would result]....

"Reports are, however, being industriously circulated, especially among strangers, for the purpose of prejudicing them against me in the contest for the mayor's office, to the effect that I am a negro lover, not a democrat, nor a believer in white supremacy; and further that I am in favor of mixed schools and churches, and the social equality of whites and negroes. These reports I desire to brand as absolutely false. To those who know me all my life, it is not necessary for me to take this statement, but to those of my fellow citizens who have moved here within the last few years, and do not know me personally, I especially desire to make the above statement, and to say further that I have been a strict party man, and have never voted for any candidate... except regular nominees of the democratic party. W.D. Morgan

After serving twelve years as Georgetown's chief executive and presiding over its transition from an isolated backwater to a growing and vibrant economic community, Morgan must have found this turn of events to have been a bitter pill. In later years, Dr. S.S. Bruington, a black physician, wrote Morgan saying: "I have yet to find a man fairer than you in business transactions....As long as you live I know the Negroes in Georgetown have a very, very good friend; they have a friend that they can approach at all times....They tell me lots of things about the North and fairness of the white people to the colored, but I have yet to see any condition or any man that equals you."[18] For Morgan, the racism of the campaign with Sawyer was a spiritually heavy price to pay. But apparently he felt the circumstances required that he degrade himself in letters to the editor if he was going to be able to finish the work he had started. He also found himself in the politically demeaning position of having to debate Sawyer in the week before the election to bolster his chances of reelection.[19]

Morgan was reelected by an insultingly narrow margin. He received 286 votes, 257 of those being cast at the courthouse in the older section of Georgetown.

Sawyer's core constituency was among the new arrivals who worked for Atlantic Coast Lumber Company, an industry Morgan had lured to Georgetown by his good work. Sawyer's constituents resided primarily in the West End—the new part of the community built during Morgan's tenure. They had come from other regions of the South to oversee the work of indigenous black laborers for the company. Sawyer, billing himself as the friend of the working man, got most of his 267 votes on the West End even though the owner of Atlantic Coast Lumber Company, F.S. Farr, had written a letter to the editor of the *Times* (published on the front page on December 7, 1903) praising and endorsing Morgan.

Once election was reassured, at the December 1903 meeting of the city council, Morgan went back to work, backing passage of an authorization to plant four hundred more oak trees along the streets of Georgetown.[20]

Sawyer was finally elected mayor of Georgetown in 1916. He served two terms. White supremacist LeGrand Walker continued to serve as state senator until his death in 1920. During the last five years of his service, he was the president *pro tempore* of the South Carolina Senate.

Chapter XXII
And the Beat Goes On

W.D. Morgan served another term and oversaw completion of the municipal water and sewer systems. With an emerging industrial population, the political influence of Georgetown's merchants began to wane. Blacks were excluded from local politics, the polls and the economic mainstream, a state of affairs that lasted until the passage of the Voting Rights Act in 1965. Because the large majority of Georgetown's population was black, things remained otherwise outwardly genteel. All of the white rationalization of lynching to protect the virtue of white women notwithstanding, there was not even a threat of lynching for many years.

Around the time that Morgan retired from public life, C.W. Scurry, brother of the deceased officer, was elected sheriff in 1904 to oversee everyone's behavior. The first major disturbance he faced occurred in mid-May of 1907. At that time, a black man named Tony Scott was killed by a white store owner named Lallis Rhem near the Georgetown/Williamsburg County line. Scott had gone to Rhem's country store in a mule-driven wagon with his young son to make a purchase. Scott left the boy outside to tend to the mule while he went into the store. The mule became unmanageable, so the boy tied it to a post supporting the store's porch roof. The mule pulled free, bringing the roof down in the process.

Rhem became upset, came outside and "reprimanded"[1] the boy. Scott intervened to protect his son. A fight followed. Scott received a wound to his right temple and died. A coroner's inquest was convened on Sunday afternoon and the

Celebrants at party honoring W.D. Morgan. *Courtesy of the Georgetown County Library Morgan Collection.*

body was examined. The handpicked coroner's jury found no wounds "sufficient to have caused death and it was pronounced by both physicians in attendance that death resulted from heart failure, due to excessive...excitement."

"The negro element, unable to reconcile themselves to this decision became indignant and boisterous and formed a mob around the store. It was deemed advisable, to prevent further trouble, that sufficient military support be sent to the scene in accordance with orders from Governor Ansel. An armed guard was sent from Georgetown" the local newspaper reported. The governor had called out the Georgetown Rifle Guards because Sheriff Scurry and Williamsburg County Sheriff George J. Graham had wired for help, saying, "Race riot expected at this place."

With the appearance of a heavily armed white militia, the demonstrators went home without violence on a promise that a second inquest would be convened. In anticipation of trouble, the Rifle Guards were instructed to report to the home of Magistrate G.B. Nesmith where the second inquest was to be held. A special train of the Georgetown and Western Railroad transported the troops. Deterred by this show of white military might, there was no disorder, even though the outcome of the second inquest was the same as the first.

Shortly afterward, John Sampson, the reputed "ringleader of the mob" was arrested and jailed in Kingstree. Sampson had disarmed Scott's son who was looking to shoot Rhem. Rhem was not indicted, even though his "reprimand" of Scott's son and combat with the boy's father had caused the "excitement" that, according to the coroner's jury, had resulted in Scott's death . A proper charge, under the circumstances, would have been involuntary manslaughter or, at the very least, assault and battery of a high and aggravated nature.[2]

On May 23, 1911, Sheriff Scurry's son LeRoy was arrested and charged with disorderly conduct. He was found guilty and fined $12. The arrest warrant said LeRoy "did resist a lawful arrest by striking and fighting an officer of the said city, duly authorized to make arrest, and refused to submit to the said arrest." According to the South Carolina Supreme Court, "The case turned mainly on the issue whether the defendant was guilty of such disorderly conduct on the street as to justify the chief of police arresting him without a warrant."

At trial, the police chief, L.L. Bolick, testified that "[o]n last Tuesday morning, in the forenoon, Mr. [LeRoy] Scurry, the sheriff and I were talking. We first started talking on the sidewalk, and afterwards I got in my buggy. Mr. LeRoy Scurry came up while we were talking, and said these words: 'I told you...that you were a liar, and I still say you are a liar.' Then I appealed to his father, and told him I would not stand for that; if he called me a liar again, I would arrest him. Afterwards LeRoy said: 'Chief, I told you that you and Spry both lied, and I mean it.' I then started towards him, and he began to strike me several times about the body and arm....I had him about the neck with my left arm." The ensuing scuffle was broken up by Tom Skinner who happened to be passing by.

While LeRoy did not testify at his trial, his father, the sheriff, did. His account was much the same as that of the police chief, except that he added a little more background. He said the conversation between him and the police chief had been about LeRoy. The sheriff had been out of town. On his return, the police chief told the sheriff that "LeRoy tried to take charge of the town since you were gone. His mother told me that Mrs. Doar had the cow locked up...[and that Leroy] went on ridiculous." The police chief also told the sheriff that LeRoy had lied in court about the incident and that he had made the boy admit he was lying on the witness stand. The sheriff responded by saying, "Well, LeRoy is a boy and is hot-headed."

At this point in Scurry's recounting of events, LeRoy came up, called the police chief a liar and the two argued. Then, the police chief got out of his buggy and went to arrest LeRoy. A scuffle ensued, resulting in LeRoy's arrest for disorderly conduct.

In its written opinion, the South Carolina Supreme Court noted, "The scene of the disorder was immediately in front of the courthouse, and John Harrison, a witness for the defendant, testified that he heard the abusive language of the defendant in the aisle of the courthouse, where he was engaged in conversation."

The Supreme Court reversed the conviction of LeRoy, even though he had assaulted the chief of police in the process of being arrested. In doing so, it reasoned that conviction could not stand because the underlying arrest was unlawful. "A police officer who goes out of the course of his duty, and speaks so abusively of a citizen, in his presence, as to elicit language in reply which is no more disorderly, either in substance or in manner, than the language of the officer provoking it, is not justified in arresting, without warrant, the citizen for disorderly conduct in using the abusive language."[3]

In the case of LeRoy Scurry, violence in resisting an unlawful arrest was grounds for reversal. In the case of John Brownfield, it was not.

Between 1910 and 1920, the population of blacks in Georgetown declined by 1,649, while the population of whites increased by 1,096.[4] Atlantic Coast Lumber Company closed during the early stages of the Great Depression. In 1936, construction began on the local paper mill. It began producing pulp and craft paper in 1937.

In 1951, a drunken white man named Henry Jackson shot and killed "a colored policeman by the name of Lucius Jenerette" in Timmonsville. Jackson had taken a taxi home from a place where he had consumed beer and whisky. He told the cab driver to wait while he went inside to get the money to pay the fare. He never came out with payment and did not answer the driver's knock on the door, so the taxi driver summoned the police.

Officer Jenerette responded, returned to Jackson's home, and knocked on both the doors and the windows with his nightstick, all while announcing he was a policeman and there to collect the cab fare. The knocking woke Jackson's mother and a roomer named Cleveland. Jackson, meanwhile, was passed out on his bed. Cleveland woke him up and said that someone was outside. In response to the persistent knocking, Jackson's mother was saying, "Don't knock my door down." Jackson took out a gun and looked out a window. When he did, a flashlight beam shined in his face from outside the window, "and I couldn't see nothing." When asked what happened, he responded, "I snatched back on the hammer and turned loose."

"After it happened, he fell, and before I could get close enough to put my head down to hear what he was saying he done quit saying anything. His flashlight was on the porch about three feet off. I walked up between his legs and reached over and picked up the flashlight....When I picked up the flashlight, it was something or nother wet. I don't know whether it was blood or what. I took the flashlight and shone on him, and I looks, and it was the police."

In reversing the conviction of the white cop killer and granting him a new trial, the South Carolina Supreme Court said, "The test [of self-defense] is not whether there was testimony of an *intended* attack but whether or not the appellant *believed* he was in imminent danger of death or serious bodily harm, and he is not required to show that such danger actually existed because he had a right to act upon such appearances as would cause a reasonable and prudent man of ordinary firmness and courage to entertain the same belief." (Emphasis in the original.)[5]

In the case of Jackson, a reasonable perception of danger created by the otherwise lawful actions of a police officer supported a claim of self-defense. In Brownfield's case, danger perceived because of an officer's unlawful behavior did not.

According to the brochure produced for his funeral, "early in the morning on June 12, 1988, the angel of death came suddenly and claimed Henry Plucky Shubrick, Jr."

> *He was born on January 30, 1930 in Georgetown, and was the first child of Mr. Henry Plucky Shubrick, Sr. and Mrs. Janie Sands Shubrick, both now deceased. In August of 1971, he was united in holy wedlock to Miss Julia Waiters who preceded him in death.*
>
> *At an early age he became a Christian and was baptized at First Calvary Missionary Baptist Church under the spiritual guidance of Rev. G.G. Daniels. He received his education at Howard High School.*
>
> *To know Henry was to love him. He was loved by his family and friends and will be greatly missed.*

The deacons of his church were his pallbearers.

The "angel of death" that claimed Mr. Shubrick's life was a deputy sheriff for Georgetown County. Incident report number 88-1052 of the Georgetown City Police Department details what happened. The portion of the report written by hand reads as follows:

> *On 06-12-88 at 0030 hrs R/O [responding officer] was working a traffic accident at the corner of Church and Wood St. While working this accident R/O heard what sounded like another accident and went to investigate.*

Upon arrival R/O observed a B/M [black male] victim lying face down in the roadway in the south bound lane of Church St. R/O requested dispatcher to notify the E.M.S. unit. R/O then asked for any witnesses as to what happened so as to try to obtain information. No witnesses came forward.

[In the "witnesses" section of the incident report form appear the words] *"Unknown (uncooperative)."*

R/O asked for witnesses again and still no response from anyone. At this time the subject approached R/O and identified himself as the driver of the vehicle who hit the victim. At 0041 the E.M.S. – arrived on the scene. R/O started to get information from driver of vehicle at this time. E.M.S. attendant approached R/O and stated that due to the hostility of the crowd that had gathered on the scene that it would be best to move the body to the hospital. R/O consulted with the Supervisor – and determined this to be in the best interest and safety of all parties involved.

R/O observed a large crowd gathering and become very hostile towards E.M.S. attendants, R/O and other officers on the scene also towards driver of vehicle. R/O again consulted supervisor in regards to the safety of all parties at scene. [Supervisor] and R/O agreed that the driver of vehicle should leave the scene and go to county jail where he is employed as a Deputy Sheriff and wait for us to get to that location to continue with the reports. The driver of the vehicle left the scene and [Supervisor] sent R/O to Georgetown Memorial Hospital to continue investigation.

Upon arrival at hospital R/O was approached by E.M.S. attendant who stated that there was a disturbance in progress in the back of the ambulance.

R/O went to ambulance and observed the victim's brother shove an unknown B/M out of ambulance. R/O removed victim's brother from ambulance and led him to another area. R/O calmed him down and suggested he wait in the waiting room. R/O then went to morgue and met with Coroner – who stated that he had pronounced victim dead and that he would investigate further as to alcohol content and other substances that might be in the victim's blood. Coroner stated he would advise R/O of results when his tests were complete. At this time Coroner requested that R/O accompany him to waiting area to meet with victim's brother – to obtain information concerning positive identification of victim.

Upon entering hallway R/O and Coroner met with victim's brother who returned to morgue and positive identification was made and all information on victim was obtained at this time. Upon re-entering hallway R/O met with Sheriff – who stated that subject driver was in the waiting room. R/O, Coroner and Sheriff went to waiting room and met with subject. R/O asked subject driver questions concerning accident. Subject driver stated he was returning home from North Carolina traveling South on U.S. 17 (Church Street). Subject stated as he approached the 1200 block of Church St. he did not see victim until victim stepped into path of his vehicle. Subject states he tried to avoid victim but was too close. Subject also stated after impact he stopped his vehicle and pulled off roadway. Subject further states at that time he observed R/O on the scene. R/O asked subject for further information concerning accident report whether or not he had been drinking or using any type of drugs. Subject stated that yes he did. [The words "couple of drinks" were added to the report on the line immediately above with an arrow.] Earlier this afternoon in North Carolina. This was stated in the presence of R/O, [the] Coroner and [the] Sheriff –.

At that time R/O advised subject that I was going outside to check for damages to veh[icle] and to see where victim was struck by vehicle. R/O observed a dent on passenger side of hood also scrape marks above headlight and windshield was damaged. At this time Sheriff – and Coroner came out to veh[icle]. At this time Coroner while also checking vehicle removed a small piece of cloth material which matched victim's pants from underneath passenger side bumper. Sheriff — stated to R/O that he was personally going to take vehicle to County Jail and secure vehicle for any further investigation and [added by arrow "he let"] subject take his vehicle home. R/O did not administer any type of test to subject because subject had already left with Sheriff's vehicle. R/O attempted to locate subject before he left area but was unsuccessful. At this time R/O returned to scene of accident to obtain measurements and other information concerning accident. R/O obtained measurements and had earlier obtained a 12 oz can of Schaefer Beer which was not open but had been damaged due to impact. Can was placed into evidence at Georgetown Police Department. See Sketch for specific details concerning accident scene. The following people were notified concerning accident. Chief of Police –, Captain –, Investigator – and Highway Patrol Trooper – . Lt. – was also notified and met with R/O who both returned to accident scene and obtained specific details noted on sketch. Lt. – advised R/O to contact any witnesses and subject so statements could be obtained. While R/O and Lt. – were at accident scene the victim's sister approached officers and stated that she had heard accident but did not see the accident. She also observed several people who could be possible witnesses in the area but did not know there [sic] names. She stated she would try to obtain names of these people and that she would contact police department as soon as she could find out any information. Also area surrounding point of impact was well lit.

Pedestrian was wearing dark clothes. Pedestrian was wearing dark red and dark blue plaid pants, dark blue sweater with red and white stripes.

Attached to this handwritten incident report was a neatly typed "Supplemental Report." It was dated nine days later. It was prepared by a lieutenant.

> *On 13 Jun 88 the undersigned met with Georgetown County Coroner – at the Georgetown Police Department and discussed the facts surrounding this traffic fatality. Coroner – stated that based on his on the scene investigation and his personal contact and observation of the driver of the vehicle that struck the victim he felt that there was no criminal negligence attributable to the driver. Coroner – also added the driver – had offered in his presence and in the presence of Sheriff – to take a Breathalyzer or blood test if necessary. It was unknown if the reporting officer – had knowledge of this offer.*
>
> *On 14 Jun 88 at 9:15 AM, the undersigned officer met with and interviewed the driver. [He] related the events as they occurred prior to and after the accident. The officer requested a statement (written) from [him] and he supplied same (See attached to this report.) [The statement was not attached to the incident report when a copy was retrieved from the file.]*
>
> *On this same date writer met with and interviewed the reporting officer—. [He] stated that based on his investigation and assessment of the accident scene (physical evidence) and his interview with the driver it was his finding that [the driver] was driving too fast for conditions and was exceeding the posted speed limit of 35 MPH. This finding was indicated on the accident report. [The responding officer] further states that based on his personal observations and conversations with [the driver] that he had no probable cause to believe that the driver had been drinking or was under the influence of alcohol or drugs.*
>
> *The undersigned also questioned Officer – concerning the references in his incident report as to him being unable to locate or contact [the driver] after seeking him at the hospital. [The officer] states that it was his intention to secure a written statement from [the driver] and also offer him an opportunity to take a breathalyzer to substantiate his [the officer's] opinion that the driver was not under the influence. [The officer] also stated that he was not present when [the driver] offered to take a breathalyzer or blood test.*
>
> *Case closed pending receipt of additional information.*

Criminal negligence is the unintentional killing of another, without malice, while engaged in lawful activity with reckless disregard for the safety of others. Under South Carolina law, violation of a statue is negligence in-and-of-itself and is evidence of recklessness. The maximum speed at which a motor vehicle can be operated in an urban area where there are dwellings within one hundred feet is thirty miles per hour. It is for an impartial jury to decide whether criminal negligence exists in any given case.

Even though the investigating officer concluded that the off-duty deputy, who admitted having had something to drink earlier, was driving too fast for conditions, there was no coroner's inquest in this case.

A few years after this incident, the South Carolina Legislature amended the law to state the obvious. "A law enforcement department or agency may not investigate collisions in which a motor vehicle or an employee of that department or agency is involved that results in injury or death."[6] Shortly thereafter, the South Carolina attorney general's office issued a formal opinion stating that the language quoted immediately above "prohibits a law enforcement agency from investigating collisions in which an employee of that agency was involved. Looking at the grammatical arrangement of the sentence, and giving it its plain meaning, I would advise you that where a law enforcement officer is involved in a collision driving his or her private vehicle, that person's agency should not conduct the investigation....It would seem that such a conclusion is the logical intent of the statute, which appears to be to remove the appearance of impropriety or the possibility of a conflict of interest in the investigation of motor vehicle collisions involving law enforcement officers."[7]

A civil claim was filed on behalf of the dead man's estate. The estate was represented by an attorney who was then a member of the Georgetown County Council. He has since been disbarred for other reasons and subsequently jailed for failure to pay approximately $300,000 in alimony and child support. The civil case arising out of the death of Plucky Shubrick was settled for $15,000. No additional information was filed with the court and the entire matter was closed.

And the beat goes on.[8]

Epilogue

The Church of the Holy Sepulcher is considered by many to be the most sacred location in all of Christendom. It sits in the heart of the Old Christian Quarter of the city of Jerusalem. Its dome covers the site where tradition holds that Jesus of Nazareth was crucified, buried and resurrected. The last five Stations of the Cross are located inside the building.

Built originally by Emperor Constantine in the fourth century, the site has been destroyed by war, fire or earthquake, and rebuilt numerous times during its 1,600-year history. Over the intervening centuries, representatives of the Greek Orthodox, Armenian Orthodox, Roman Catholic, Egyptian Coptic Orthodox, Ethiopian Orthodox and Assyrian Orthodox churches have laid claim to the site. Since 1852, the rights and privileges of each of these communities have been protected by the *Status Quo of the Holy Places*. The document cedes control of the tomb of Jesus to the Greek Orthodox, Armenian and Roman Churches. While the center of the Sepulcher is shared by all, only Armenian and Roman Catholic monks can say Mass inside, except on Holy Saturday, when the Coptics get to do so. The rough-hewn chapel in the rear is used for Assyrian liturgies on Sundays. In the front of the Sepulcher, there is a large area reserved for use by the Greek Orthodox Church. The Armenians control the chapel at the site where Jesus was said to have been crucified. The Roman Catholics have an altar at the side of this same location. There is a ladder under a second-story window that is used to carry food to Armenian monks. The Ethiopians occupy the portion of the roof over the tomb. The status quo notwithstanding, there is a continuing dispute between the Coptic and Ethiopian Orthodox churches over ownership rights to the chapel.

The noise created by the priests, monks and visitors amid the conglomeration of altars, chapels and recesses of the candle-lit, gloomy and windowless stone cathedral creates an environment bordering on chaotic. In that place, each sect jealously guards the territory assigned to it. As one observer put it, "beneath every step and behind every pillar lies a potential minefield of centuries-old jealous quarreling among the denominations that share control of the church." Physical fights between these holy men are not uncommon. Since none of these Christians trusts the others, the ten-inch key to the building is kept by neutral Muslim neighbors—the Nusaibi and Joudah families whose ancestors were entrusted with it in 1178 by Salah el-Din (Saladin).

On a tour of Jerusalem a number of years ago, a Jewish friend hired an Arab guide to show him around. When they arrived at an important intersection, the guide offered a choice. In one direction were the Wailing Wall and Temple Mount. In the other was the tomb of Jesus. The guide recommended going to the Temple Mount because, as he said, "there's nothing in the tomb."

The guide's advice was historically and spiritually correct. The tomb is a dead and empty place, devoid of the spirit of the Lord. The pointless squabbling of the priests is evidence of that. That is not to say, however, that the rabbi does not live. His spirit is alive in the lessons he taught. Most important among them: Treat others as we want to be treated in return; love our neighbors as we love ourselves. To do otherwise is to dabble in the alchemy that turns gold into lead.

Likewise with secular history. Its lessons are not found by memorizing dates, adoring objects or worshiping ancestors. History is the ultimate school of hard knocks. Its study discloses the most important lessons from human experience. Everyone, to some degree, is a product of that experience. Reading about those experiences deepens understanding of what, why and how we and our neighbors believe, feel and act as we do. Understanding precedes forgiveness and acceptance. Acceptance breeds compassion. Compassion maintains peace.

As he aged and became more reflective, William D. Morgan penned words that, when viewed in the light of his life's work, show what had truly been in his heart all along. By the time he died at age eighty-five in 1938, he had abandoned concerns about politics and popularity. Instead, he focused on leaving behind something more enduring than his temporal works. Having never married and not having any children, he decided to leave a valuable legacy to those who, throughout his life, had been his family. In his last testament, Morgan asked for God's blessing on "my dear City of Georgetown and all of its people, both white and colored."

Most of the two thousand trees Morgan planted during his tenure in office still cast their cooling shadows over this oak-shaded colonial town and its people, "both white and colored." Those colors today include the whole spectrum of humanity.

NOTES

1 David H. Corkran, *The Carolina Indian Frontier*, Tricentennial Booklet No. 6 (Columbia, SC: University of South Carolina Press, 1970).

2 Robert Mills, *Statistics of South Carolina* (Charleston, SC: Hurlbut & Lloyd, 1826).

3 "Georgetown County, Where History Was Born," *The News and Courier* (Charleston, SC), March 21, 1965, supplement, 5.

4 See 42 U.S.C. 9607, *et. seq.*.

5 South Carolina Department of Health and Environmental Control, "In re: Georgetown Steel Corporation, CONSENT AGREEMENT," November 30, 1981; "Well Worries: State Finds Water at Steel Site Unfit," *Georgetown Times* (Georgetown, SC), February 1981.

6 Roger Regelbrugee, president of Georgetown Steel Corporation, in a letter to David Treme, administrator of the City of Georgetown, July 5, 1984, public records, City of Georgetown. See also "Agreement" between Georgetown Steel Corporation and the County of Georgetown, December 31, 1987, South Carolina Department of Health and Environmental Control.

7 "Order Granting Motion of GSC Remainder Corp. f/k/a Georgetown Steel Corporation to (1) Abandon Personal Property; (2) Abandon Environmental Permit; and (3) Reject Executory Contract," U.S. Bankruptcy Court, Western District of North Carolina, Charlotte Division, Case No. 01-30319 (GRH), filed February 20, 2003.

8 South Carolina Department of Health and Environmental Control, Office of Environmental Quality Control, Bureau of Land and Waste Management, "Postclosure Care Hazardous Waste Permit No. SCD 982 120 107," May 26, 2000.

9 Sierra Club/CUSP Newsletter, vol. 4, no. 3, October, 1981. Generally speaking, a gallon of gasoline can render 1 million gallons of water undrinkable.

10 U.S. Army Corps of Engineers, "Record of Decision, Permit #79-5R-319." See also, U.S. Army Corps of Engineers, "Army Engineers Deny Permit," December 14, 1984.

11 "IP Says It'll Rebuild Mill," *Georgetown Times*, January 14, 1982.

12 "Union Pacts With IP Set," *Georgetown Times*, January 12, 1982.

13 U.S. Environmental Protection Agency, "Dioxin Reassessment," 1994.

14 "IP decreases dioxin output," *Sun News* (Myrtle Beach, SC), May 28, 2000.

15 *Sun News* (Myrtle Beach, SC), June 2, 2002, 1.

Chapter II

1. Now Guinea, Sierra Leone, the Ivory Coast and Ghana.
2. Walter Edgar, *South Carolina, A History* (Columbia, SC: University of South Carolina Press, 1998), 157.
3. Charles Joyner, *Down by the Riverside: A South Carolina Slave Community* (Chicago and Urbana, IL: University of Illinois Press, 1985), 38.
4. Joyner, 44.
5. Walven, *The Slave Trade.*
6. Belinda Hurmence, ed., *Before Freedom, When I Just Can Remember, Twenty-seven Oral Histories of Former South Carolina Slaves* (Winston-Salem, NC: John Blair, Publisher, 1989).
7. Walven, *The Slave Trade*.
8. Benjamin Franklin warned long ago that those who try to trade freedom for security end up losing both.
9. Statutes at Large of South Carolina, no. 754, sec. VII (1715).
10. Statutes at Large of South Carolina, no. 476, sec. I–II (1722).
11. Christopher Boyle and James A. Fitch, *Georgetown County Slave Narratives* (Seaport Press), 6.
12 Joyner, 91.
13. George C. Rogers Jr., *The History of Georgetown County, South Carolina* (Columbia, SC: University of South Carolina, 1970), 344–345.
14. Statutes at Large of South Carolina, no. 586, sec. XIX (1735).
15. Ibid., sec. III.
16. Boyle and Fitch, *Georgetown County Slave Narratives* (Seaport Press), 46.
17. Statutes at Large of South Carolina, no. 586, sec. XIX (1735)
18. Ibid., sec. XIX.
19. Ibid., sec. XIII.
20. The otherwise unrationalized murder of a slave did not become a crime until 1821 when slaves became "people" rather than "property," but this distinction was only in the eyes of the criminal law, not the civil law. Rogers, 346.
21. Statutes at Large of South Carolina, no. 586, sec. XXXI (1735)
22. Ibid. sec VIII.
23. Ibid. sec VIII.
24. Statutes at Large of South Carolina, no. 2319 (1823).
25. Statutes at Large of South Carolina, no. 2361 (1825).
26. Statutes at Large of South Carolina, no. 2639 (1834).
27. Statutes at Large of South Carolina, no. 2639 (1834).

Chapter III

1. Robert Mills, *Statistics of South Carolina* (Charleston, SC: Hurlbut & Lloyd, 1826) "Georgetown."
2. Richard N. Côté, *Mary's World, Love, War and Family Ties in 19th Century Charleston* (Mount Pleasant, SC: Corinthian Books, 2001), 58.
3. Walter Edgar, *South Carolina, A History* (Columbia, SC: University of South Carolina Press, 1998), 70.
4. George C. Rogers Jr., *The History of Georgetown County, South Carolina* (Columbia, SC: University of South Carolina, 1970), 236.
5. Petition of William Vaught, South Carolina Archives, Document 1829-189-01.
6. Petition of William Vaught, South Carolina Archives, Document 1829-189-01.
7. Rogers, 224.
8. A similar distinct exists today between prisoners of war who are accorded rights of humane treatment by the Geneva Convention and "enemy combatants" ("terrorists") who are not. Those classified as "enemy combatants" are outside the protection of international law. See, for example, "Some 'High Value' Iraqis Detained Outside Purview of U.S. Command in Iraq," *New York Times,* May 17, 2004.
9. Ibid., sec XIV.

10. As part of research for another book, the writer asked one of Georgetown's preeminent attorneys, Meyer Rosen, about confessions by blacks in the 1950s. Mr. Rosen said, sardonically, that voluntariness depended upon which end of the belt had been used. Scars from buckles left evidence of involuntariness.
11. It is interesting to note, at that point, while death sentences are carried out immediately after trial in Communist China, an appeal is thereafter permitted to provide the family an opportunity to clear the name of the deceased defendant.
12. Petition of Francis Kinloch, South Carolina Archives, Document 1829-106-01.
13. Petition of John Coachman, South Carolina Archives, ND 1794, 778-782.
14. *Kinloch v. Harvey,* Harp. 509 (1830).
15. *Kinloch v. Harvey,* Harp. 51 and 52.
16. *Kinloch v. Harvey,* Harp. 508 (1830).
17. The practice of admitting unsworn testimony from slaves or Indians was formalized when codified in 1740 by Statutes at Large of South Carolina, no. 670, sec. IX.
18. Ibid.
19. Christopher Boyle and James A. Fitch, *Georgetown County Slave Narratives* (Seaport Press), 45.
20. Rogers, 346.
21. Max Farrand, *The Records of the Federal Convention of 1878* (New Haven, CT: Yale University Press, 1911–1937).

Chapter IV
1. Richard N. Côté, *Mary's World, Love, War and Family Ties in 19th Century Charleston* (Mount Pleasant, SC: Corinthian Books, 2001), 138.
2. Ibid., 146.
3. William Kaufman Scarborough, *Masters in the Big House* (Baton Rogue, LA: University of Louisiana Press, 2003), 176.
4. William J. Grayson, *The Hireling* (Charleston, SC: John Russell, Printer, 1854), cited by Katrina Paris Lawrimore, "The Economic Viability of American Negro Slavery: An Endless Debate," History 374, April 26, 1975. (Copies of Lawrimore's paper are maintained at the Georgetown County Library in the local history room.)
5. In her excellent treatise, "The Economic Viability of American Negro Slavery: An Endless Debate," Katrina Paris Lawrimore thoroughly surveyed scholarly debate over whether, as an economic matter, slavery was a profitable and, therefore, a sustainable institution. In reflecting on the work of other scholars, she recognized that most of them had missed the main point. The most important question to be answered, she observed, did not revolve around the dollars earned from the practice and whether those profits could be maintained as most scholars believed. The vast majority of antebellum planters made a lot of money. Ms. Lawrimore's analysis went further and deeper. She recognized that simple computation of the money amassed did not show the "profitability" of the institution of slavery. Those numbers simply represented "gross profits." The ultimate profitability of any economic enterprise, however, is measured by net profits, not gross profit. To arrive at net profits, she concluded, one has to subtract the misery, lost dreams and unrealized human potential from gross profits. Only in that way can the ultimate viability be properly answered in economic terms and in terms of common humanity. Stated concisely, she posits that the economic issue can only be answered by first answering the question, "Profitable for whom?"
6. Scarborough, 187.
7. Colin Powell with Joseph E. Persico, *My American Journey* (New York: Ballantine Books, 1995), 123.
8. Charles Edward Cauthen, *South Carolina Goes to War* (Chapel Hill, NC: University of North Carolina Press, 1950) 146–147.
9. Scarborough, 162.
10. When war erupted, less than 9 percent of South Carolinians owned slaves. Yates Snowden, LLD, *History of South Carolina* (Chicago and New York: Lewis Publishing Co., 1920), 654–655.

Chapter V

1. Colin Powell with Joseph E. Persico, *My American Journey* (New York: Random House, Ballantine Books, 1995), 148.
2. Professor Larry McGehee, Woffold College, "Southern Seen, Slavery's hold over the South," *Georgetown Times,* May 5, 2004, citing Scarborough.
3. Rod Gragg, *The Forgotten Front: A Military History of Georgetown County in the Civil War, 1861-65,* on file at the Georgetown County Memorial Library, 42–43.
4. United Daughters of the Confederacy, *Recollections and Reminiscences, 1861-1865,* vol. 1, SC Division, 1990, 391.
5. Gragg, 33–34.
6. "Recollections of Miss Georgie," Ibid., 24.
7. Gragg, 47–50.
8. Ibid.
9. "*The big mill to Laurel been burn right den. That the biggest mill on Waccamaw River. Twzn't the Yankee burn dem mill. White men have a idea the Yankee mean to burn [the] mill so they set'em a fire before Yankee come. Nothing left to Laurel Hill today but the rice mill tower. That old brick tower going to be there. Fire can't harm 'em.*" Recollections of Ben Horry as told to Christopher Boyle and James A. Fitch, *Georgetown County Slave Narratives* (Seaport Press), 33.
10. Boyle and Fitch, "Recollections of Ellen Godfrey, age 99," 18.
11. United Daughters of the Confederacy, Written recollections of war survivors, vol. 4, 492.

Chapter VI

1. United Daughters of the Confederacy, *Recollections and Reminiscences,* Nannie Beaty, vol. IV, SC Division, 1993, 462–464.
2. Ibid., 464.
3. Potatoe with an "e" is the preferred local spelling. Potatoe Bed Ferry is the site where Francis Marion, the "Swamp Fox," crossed the Black River during the Revolutionary War on his way to attack British troops occupying Georgetown.
4. Allen D. Thigpen, ed., *The Illustrated Recollections of Potter's Raid* (Sumter, SC: Gamecock City Printing, Inc., 1999), 32, 41, 42, 60.
5. Ibid., 62.
6. George C. Rogers Jr., *The History of Georgetown County, South Carolina* (Columbia, SC: University of South Carolina, 1970), 419.
7. *Reminiscence of Margaret Blanche Rouquie,* UDC, vol. 4, 493.
8. "Georgetown, Where History Was Born" supplement, *News and Courier* (Charleston, SC), March 21, 1965, 14.
9. Rogers, 419.
10. Ibid.
11. During the 1990s the ill-fated Confederate submarine *Hunley* was located and raised from Charleston Harbor. It sank during an attack that destroyed a naval blockade ship. The *Hunley* has been carefully excavated and preserved, as it should be. Meanwhile, promoters of this artifact of war tout it as the first submarine ever to sink "an enemy vessel." The ship it destroyed was, in fact, a ship of the line of the U.S. Navy, not that of an aggressive foreign power. Under the circumstances, it would be more accurate (and less offensive) to characterize the *Hunley* as being the first submarine to sink another ship during combat.
12. Sung by Aunt Ellen Godfrey, as told to Boyle and Fitch, 16.

Chapter VII

1. Max Farrand, *The Records of the Federal Convention of 1787,* 4 vols., (New Haven, CT: Yale University Press).

2. National Geographic Society, *Our World Heritage,* 1987, 181.
3. See note 1.
4. Christopher Boyle and James A. Fitch, "Recollections of Ellen Godfrey, Age 99," *Georgetown County Slave Narratives* (Seaport Press), 20.
5. Boyle and Fitch, "Recollections of Mariah Heywood, age 82," 27.
6. Alan Conway, ed., *The Welsh in America: Letters from the Immigrants* (Minneapolis, 1961) 194-196, reprinted in *The Annals of America, Encyclopedia Britannica, Inc.,* vol. 10, 320–321.
7. T. Thomas Fortune, "The Common Cause of Negro and White Labor," *Black and White: Land, Labor and Politics in the South* (New York, 1884) 234–242, reprinted in *The Annals of America, Encyclopedia Britannica, Inc.,* vol. 11, 12–14.

Chapter VIII

1. Cyril Outerbridge Packwood, *Detour-Bermuda; Destination–U.S. House of Representatives: The Life of Joseph Hayne Rainey* (Hamilton, Bermuda: Baxter's Limited, 1977).
2. George C. Rogers Jr., *The History of Georgetown County, South Carolina* (Columbia, SC: University of South Carolina, 1970), 443.
3. Packwood, 9.
4. While in Bermuda, Rainey encountered Dr. Luke Blackburn. Blackburn was a Confederate sympathizer who treated yellow fever victims on the island. In an early attempt to use a weapon of mass destruction, Blackburn had the soiled clothing and blankets of his patients shipped to Philadelphia, Pennsylvania, and New York in hopes of spreading an epidemic in those cities. The effort was unsuccessful because Blackburn had chosen the wrong method. Yellow fever is spread by mosquitoes, not blankets or bed bugs. Rainey was called to testify at Blackburn's trial. Packwood, 13.
5. Rogers, 442.
6. Packwood, 17.
7. Congressional Record, 42nd Cong., 2d sess., 393-4.
8. Congressional Record, 42nd Cong., 2d sess., 1439.
9 Packwood, 18.
10. Congressional Record, 43nd Cong., 1t sess., 344.
11. Packwood, 29–30.
12. Congressional Record, 42nd Cong., 2d sess., 1439–1443, 3382–3383.
13. Packwood, 23.
14. Christopher Boyle and James A. Fitch, *Georgetown County Slave Narratives* (Seaport Press), 26–29.
15. As part of the effort to extend economic freedom to newly emancipated slaves, a Freedman's Bank was established. It contained the deposits of black people—day laborers, farmers, maids and the like. In a harbinger of things to come more than a century later, in 1870, greedy white bankers proposed amending the bank's charter to allow half of all deposits to be invested in what were the day's equivalent of "junk bonds." Rainey opposed this, but it happened anyway. Jay Cooke and Company was allowed to borrow a half-million dollars secured by junk bonds. When the bonds proved worthless and the bank failed, thousands of newly freed slaves lost all their savings.
16. James G. Blaine, *Twenty Years of Congress,* 2 vols. (Norwich, CT: Henry Bill Publishing Co., 1886), 515.

Chapter IX

1. "Disgraceful Scenes," *Georgetown Times,* 1872, Morgan Scrapbook, Georgetown Public Library, vol. 2, 1.
2. Ibid.
3. Ibid.
4. George C. Rogers Jr., *The History of Georgetown County, South Carolina* (Columbia, SC: University of South Carolina, 1970), 459–460.

5. Rogers, 459–460.
6. Ibid.
7. Ibid.
8. "The Riot Last Week," *Georgetown Times,*1872, Morgan Scrapbook, Georgetown Public Library, vol. 2, 1.
9. Ibid.
10. Ibid.
11. Ibid.
12. Ibid.
13. Ibid.
14. Ibid.
15. Morgan Scrapbook, vol. 2, 7.
16. Katrina Paris Lawrimore, "The Georgetown Rifle Guards: An Institutional History," Master's Thesis, Department of History, University of South Carolina, 1979.
17. Lawrimore, 32, citing a newspaper clipping dated August 15, 1875, Morgan Scrapbook.
18. Ibid.
19. Resolution, Morgan Collection, South Caroliniana Library, University of South Carolina.
20. United States Census, 1880, Georgetown County, SC.
21. Morgan Scrapbook, vol. 2, 16.
22. Lawrimore, 40.

Chapter X

1. Congressional Record, 44nd Cong., 1t sess., 4645.
2. James G. Blaine, *Political Discussions,* (Norwich, CT: Henry Bill Publishing Co., 1887), 202.
3. Congressional Record, Appendix, 45th Cong., 3d sess., 264.
4. Congressional Record, 45nd Cong., 3d sess., 267.
5. *The Annals of America, Encyclopedia Britannica, Inc.,* vol. 10, 325–326.
6. Congressional Record, 43rd Cong., 1t sess., 344.
7. Congressional Record, 44th Cong., 1t sess., 1439.

Chapter XI

1. In addition, the District of Columbia gets three delegates.
2. This constitutional system was preempted in the 2000 election when the U.S. Supreme Court stopped the recount of Florida's popular vote, a decision that swung Florida's electoral votes to the candidate that had received fewer popular votes nationally. See *Bush v. Gore,* U.S. (2001).
3. In one of the numerous ironies of American history, Rutherford B. Hayes made it possible for the self-styled Southern "elite" to reestablish dominance. In his personal diary, Hayes wrote, "We ought not to allow a permanent aristocracy of inherited wealth to grow up in our country." He proposed limiting the amount any person could inherit, either individually or through a corporation, to an amount that, at 4 percent interest, would generate an annual income equal to that of the chief justice of the U.S. Supreme Court. The danger he sought to avoid was "the vast wealth owned or controlled by a few persons. Money is power. In Congress, in state legislatures, in city councils, in the courts, in the political conventions, in the press, in the pulpit, in the circles of the educated and the talented, its influences is growing greater and greater. Excess wealth in the hands of the few means extreme poverty, ignorance, vice and wretchedness as the lot of the many." Charles R. Williams, ed., *Dairy and Letters of Rutherford B. Hayes,* December 4, 1887, vol. 6, (Columbus, OH: 1924).
4. U.S. Census, 1880, Georgetown County.
5. "Harmony and Good Feeling Among Whites and Blacks!" *Georgetown Times,* September 17, 1870, Morgan Scrapbook, Georgetown Public Library.
6. Ibid.

7. Morgan Scrapbook, vol. 3, 4.
8. Ibid.
9. The requirements of the law were not always interpreted properly. One tale told to this author by an elderly Georgetonian involved the 1952 presidential election. After marking an otherwise secret presidential ballot, he was told to deposit it in the box marked either "Eisenhower" or "Stevenson." If he tried to preserve the secrecy of his ballot by putting it in the wrong box, it would not be counted.
10. Lawrimore, "The Georgetown Rifle Guards: An Institutional History," 44.
11. *Georgetown Times,* October 4, 1890.
12. *Annual Report, 1900,* State Superintendent of Education, Georgetown County.
13. *Plessy v. Ferguson,* 163 U.S. 537 (1896).
14. Ibid.
15. Ibid.
16. Art. III, sec. 33 of the South Carolina Constitution read, "The marriage of a white person with a negro or mulatto, or person who shall have one-eighth or more negro blood shall be unlawful and void." Related statutes extended the ban to marriage between whites and "any mulatto, mestizo or half-breed," and threatened ministers who performed banned wedding ceremonies with fines and jail. Sec. 1438 and 8571, Code of Laws of South Carolina, 1932. Upholding these provisions, the South Carolina Supreme Court opined that a marriage between blacks or reds and whites "strikes at the sanctity of the home, the security of family relationships, the legitimate propagation of the race to which one belongs, and at moral standards that have been recognized and enforced, voluntarily and by compulsion of law, since the foundation of this republic." *Grant v. Butt,* 198 S.C. 298, 17 S.E.2d 689 (1941). During this same era, the late Senator Strom Thurmond was a circuit court judge in South Carolina. He had fathered a child with a young teenage black maid in his family's employ about a decade earlier. The age at which a female could consent to sexual relations was sixteen at the time. Prior to sixteen, a sexual act by an older man with a female constituted the crime of rape.
17. Mark Curriden and Leroy Phillips Jr., *Contempt of Court* (New York: Anchor Books, a division of Random House, Inc., 2001), Appendix I.
18. Ibid., 23.
19. Yates Snowden, LLD, *History of South Carolina,* vol. II (Chicago and New York: Lewis Publishing Co., 1920), 12.
20. Letter from W. D. Morgan, intendant, City of Georgetown, to H. V. and H. W. Poor dated March 12, 1892, reprinted by Katrina Paris Lawrimore, *The Letterbooks of William Doyle Morgan,* History 791, University of South Carolina, Dr. Clyde N. Nelson, December 8, 1978, 25.
21. See, generally, Dennis T. Lawson, *Georgetown: The Morgan Years,* The Rice Museum, Georgetown, 1973.

Chapter XII

1. Morgan Collection, South Caroliniana Library, University of South Carolina, correspondence.
2. Office of the clerk of court for Georgetown County, November 1900, term of General Sessions. See also, Sessions Docket, November 1900.
3. Bonds, Nesbit and Woodson, *Afro-American Georgetown, SC Heritage, 1670–1960,* Georgetown County Library, LNR 974.757 BON, South Carolina. This publication indicates that in 1896 Washington's Barber Shop was located on the "East Side of Front Street below Broad." That shop is depicted on a map of the day as adjoining a hotel, with an intervening vacant lot, in the 700 block of Front Street to the northeast of its intersection with Broad.
4. The law was silent on why owning more than $300 in realty can serve as a substitute for literacy.
5. Code of Laws of South Carolina, sec. 216, 1893.
6. See Deed Book U-44, Office of the Register of Deeds, Georgetown County, 743.
7. *Saucier v. Katz,* 533 U.S. 194 (1991); *Harlow v. Fitzgerald,* 457 U.S. 800, 818 (1982).

8. *In the Matter of Samuel B. Mendenhall,* 316 S.C. 196, 447 S.E.2d 858 (1994); *In the Matter of Ferwell,* 316 S.C. 302, 450 S.E.2d 46 (1994).
9. "Woodrow Carter, The Matt Dillon of Georgetown," *Myrtle Beach Sun News* (Myrtle Beach, SC), April 8, 1979; "Georgetown's Infamous Bordello," *Tidelands Magazine,* 2002.
10. While a much criticized legal doctrine, under South Carolina law any person is entitled to use whatever degree of force may be necessary, including deadly force, to resist an unlawful arrest. This legal principle has been consistently followed in South Carolina since 1877, even in situations in which the arrestee had no way of knowing at the time whether the arrest was lawful. See *State v. Jackson,* 227 S.C. 271, 84 S.E.2d 681 (1955); *State v. Bethune,* 112 S.C. 100, 99 S.E.2d 753 (1919); *State v. Winbush, 9 S.C. 309 (1877). The Model Penal Code,* sec. 3.04(2)O(a)(i), 1962 followed in most other states, takes exactly the opposite position. In the long run, it is a better policy to not permit violent resistance of an arrest. Unlawful arrests are more properly remedied by dismissed charges, release from jail and, in severe cases, civil lawsuits for violations of civil rights. At least that way, everyone lives.

Chapter XIII

1. See, generally, *Code of Laws of South Carolina,* sec. 17-7-10, *et. seq.*, and its predecessor statutes. The relevant section of law for the Scurry Inquest was title IV, chap. XXXV, sec. 580, *et. seq.,* of the Criminal Statutes of South Carolina, 1893.
2. Georgetown has never had a female coroner.
3. *News and Courier* (Charleston, SC), October 2, 1900.
4. There were four volunteer fire companies in Georgetown at the time, two black and two white. The blacks were named the Hestons and the Stars. Bonds, Nesbit and Woodson, *Afro-American Georgetown, SC Heritage, 1670-1960,* Georgetown County Library, LNR 974.757 BON, South Carolina. The white companies were named the Salamander Hook & Ladder Co. and the Winyah Steam Fire Co. Winyah was the oldest, having been founded in 1849. W. D. Morgan was a member of this company. *A View of Our Past, The Morgan Photographic Collection,* Georgetown County Library System, 1993, 100–103.
5. *News and Courier* (Charleston, SC), October 2, 1900.
6. The indictment read, "Whereas, Complaint upon oath has been made by W.D. Morgan that on the night of the 30th of September 1900 at Georgetown in the State aforesaid Cupid Haynes did in a riotous and disorderly manner assemble with sundry other persons then and there together for an unlawful purpose and that the said defendant was armed with a gun and conducted himself in a very menacing manner towards the citizens and authorities of the City to the great disturbance of the public peace." The grand jury ordered Haynes be tried for incitement to riot.
7. George C. Rogers Jr., *The History of Georgetown County, South Carolina* (Columbia, SC: University of South Carolina, 1970), 482.
8. "A CRY FOR HELP COMES FROM GEORGETOWN: Race riot was threatened," *State* (Columbia, SC), October 1, 1900. The article noted that "[t]he negroes in Georgetown outnumber the whites overwhelmingly."
9. *Morgan Collection*, South Caroliniana Library, University of South Carolina, Box DC, September 30, 1900.
10. "All Laws Set at Defiance," *Georgetown Times,* October 2, 1900.
11. *State* (Columbia, SC), October 2, 1900.
12. Ibid.
13. *State,* October 2, 1900.
14. Telegram, Morgan Collection, South Caroliniana Library.
15. Police Chief McKeithen became a member of the Georgetown Rifle Guards when it reestablished itself in 1889. *Minutes, Georgetown Rifle Guards,* MS vol. 1889-1904, South Caroliniana Library, University of South Carolina, 18.

16. *Georgetown Times,* October 3, 1900.
17. *News and Courier,* October [date illegible], 1900.
18. Ibid.
19. Rogers, 482–483.
20. Morgan Collection, South Caroliniana Library, University of South Carolina, Box EA, October 5, 1900.
21. *Georgetown Times,* October 10, 1900.
22. Minutes, Georgetown Rifle Guards, South Caroliniana Library, University of South Carolina, Minute Box, 184–185, October 10, 1900.
23. Ibid.

Chapter XIV

1. *Georgetown Times,* January 9, 1901.
2. *Georgetown Times,* October 13, 1900.
3. The judicial circuit in which Georgetown is located has never had a female sheriff or solicitor. Women first began to serve as deputies in these departments in the late 1980s.
4. Sessions Docket, May 1900 term and November 1900 term, clerk of court, Georgetown County.
5. Today, being registered to vote is not a prerequisite to jury service. The list of potential jurors now includes everyone with a driver's license and those with state-issued identification cards. This approach greatly expands the pool of potential jurors.
6. *Batson v. Kentucky,* 468 U.S. at 89 (1986).
7. *Peyton v. Kearse,* 319 S.C. 188, 460 S.E.2d 220 (Ct. App. 1995); *State v. Tomlin,* 299 S.C. 294, 384 S.E.2d 707 (1989).

Chapter XV

1. *State v. Martin,* 216 S.C. 129, 57 S.E.2d 55 (1949).
2. See, for example, *State v. Wood,* 1 S.C.L (1 Bay) (1794); *State v. Franklin,* 80 S.C. 332, 60 S.E. 953 (1908), *aff'd sub. nom., Franklin v. South Carolina,* 218 U.S. 161 (1910). The law on self-defense is different today. A defendant does not need to establish his defense by a preponderance of evidence (that it was more likely than not that he acted in self-defense). Today, a defendant need only raise the issue. Once raised, the question becomes one addressed in the context of "reasonable doubt." *State v. Hendrix,* 270 S.C. 653, 244 S.E.2d 503 (1978); *State v. Bellamy,* 293 S.C. 103, 359 S.E.2d 63, 64–65 (1986); *State v. Addison,* 338 S.C. 277, 525 S.E.2d 901 (Ct. App. 1999).
3. See, from among any number of examples, *State v. Jackson,* 227 S.C. 271, 87 S.E.2d 681 (1955).
4. *State v. Jackson,* 227 S.C. 271, 87 S.E.2d 681 (1951) (as to the home or its curtilage) and *State v. Kennedy*, 143 S.C. 318, 141 S.E. 559 (1928) (as to place of business, even if the aggressor had a right to be there in the first place).
5. The document was never introduced into evidence, a fact reported by the *State* newspaper in 1903.
6. Mere words, no matter how provocative, do not justify assault. See *State v. Woodham,* 162 S.C. 492, 160 S.E.2d 885 (1931) in which the victim called the assailant a "God damned Dago son of a bitch." The insult, standing alone, was insufficient to justify violent behavior.
7. "John Brownfield Will Soon Hang," *Charleston News & Courier* (Charleston, SC), April 22, 1903.
8. *State v. Hendrix,* 270 S.C._653, 244 S.E.2d 503 (1978).
9. Sessions Docket, September 1900 term, office of the clerk of court, Georgetown. Being white, it may have been a reluctant witness.
10. The newspaper indicates that Senator LeGrand Walker aided with the prosecution on behalf of the City of Georgetown, but the Sessions Docket maintained at the clerk's office lists him as aiding the prosecution as a rebuttal witness.
11. *State* (Columbia, SC), November 17, 1900.
12. *Georgetown Times,* November 21, 1900.

13. Ibid.
14. Ibid.
15. Ibid.

Chapter XVI

1. "Cheated the Gallows," *Sunday Outlook,* Georgetown, SC, June 27, 1903.
2. Criminal Statutes of South Carolina, 1893, sec. 67–68.
3. Criminal Statutes of South Carolina, 1893, sec. 68. Sec. 74 says "the practice and proceedings in cases of appeal from the Court of General Sessions shall conform to the practice and proceedings in cases of appeal from the Courts of Common Pleas." Sec. 345 of the Rules of Civil Procedure requires that the record "shall be prepared by and under the direction of the Court."
4. Code of Civil Procedure, sec. 349. See previous footnote for applicability of the Rules of Civil Procedure to criminal appeals.
5. Because of the common complaint about the length of the appellate process, this pro-life review was abandoned in South Carolina in 1991. *State v. Torrence,* 305 S.C. 45, 406 S.E.2d 315 (1991). Bad lawyering is now reviewed as part of a process called *post conviction relief* (PCR).
6. *Gibson v. Mississippi,* 162 U.S. 565 (1896).
7. By way of example, the crime of burglary involves (1) breaking and (2) entering a (3) dwelling (4) at night (5) for the purpose of committing a crime therein. Unlawful entry into someone's house at noon without committing another crime, for example, would not be a burglary. It would be the "lesser included offense" of trespass.
8. Compare, for example, Code of Laws of South Carolina, 1976, sec. 14-7-110, *et. seq.* with Revised Statutes of South Carolina, 1893, sec. 2378, *et. seq.*
9. Revised States of South Carolina, 1893, sec. 2375.
10. *State v. Merriman,* 34 S.C. 16 (1891).
11. *State v. Merriman.*
12. *State v. Merriman,* sec 2392.
13. *State v. Merriman,* sec. 2389.
14. Ibid.
15. *State v. Smith,* 77 S.C. 248, 57 S.E. 868 (1907) upholding a murder conviction against a challenge that the jury venire was selected by two, not three, jury commissioners. No other irregularity was shown, so the deviation from procedure was deemed to be harmless.
16. *State v. Brownfield,* 60 S.C. 509, 39 S.E. 2, 4 (1901).
17. Ibid.
18. *State v. Simmons,* 208 S.C. 538, 38 S.E.2d 705 (1946).
19. *State v. Osborne,* 200 S.C. 504, 21 S.E.2d 178 (1942).
20. *State v. Doig,* 31 S.C.L. 2 Rich. 179 (1845); *State v. Gallman,* 79 S.C. 229, 60 S.E.2d 682 (1908).
21. The document was not among any of the numerous others maintained in the historical record in the archives of office of the clerk of court for Georgetown County, although Magistrate Hucks is listed as a witness for the defense in the Sessions Docket maintained at the clerk of court's office. See also, *State,* June 27, 1903, reply to a letter to the editor from L. Mouzon of Georgetown dated June 26, 1903. It notes that the document was never introduced into evidence.
22. *Georgetown Times,* October 28, 1903.
23. Sec. 74 of the Criminal Statutes of South Carolina of 1893 mandates that the Rules of Civil Procedure be applied to criminal appeals.
24. *State v. Alexander,* 30 S.C. 74 (1889).
25. *State v. Smith,* 2 Strob. 77 (1907).
26. *State v. Sisson,* 3 Brev. 59 (1812); *State v. Ferguson,* 2 Hill 619; *State v. Smith* (1907), *supra; State v. Levelle,* 34 S.C. 120 (1891); *State v. Jackson,* 36 S.C. 487 (1890).
27. Record on appeal and brief of the appellant, *State v. John Brownfield.*

Chapter XVII

1. Minutes, City of Georgetown Board of Firemasters, June 29, 1901, 7.
2. See the prayer of John Brownfield reprinted in *Sunday Outlook*, Georgetown, SC, June 27, 1903.
3. "Legal Jottings, More or Less Interesting," *The Georgetown Times,* January [date illegible], 1902.
4. *The Georgetown Times,* January 18, 1902.
5. *The Georgetown Times,* January 22, 1902.
6. *The Georgetown Advocate,* June 14, 1902.
7. "*The Advocate,* An Issue Fraught With Evil," *Georgetown Times*, July 12, 1901.
8. *The Georgetown Times,* October 22, 1902.

Chapter XVIII

1. *Parker v. Carolina Savings Bank,* 53 S.C. 583, 31 S.E. 673 (1898); *Moss v. Aetna Life Ins. Co.,* 267 S.C. 370, 228 S.E.2d 108 (1976); *Matter of Harry C.*, 280 S.C. 308, 313 S.E.2d 287 (1984).
2. *Richards v. City of Columbia,* 277 S.C. 538, 88 S.E.2d 683 (1955); *Parker v. Carolina Savings Bank, supra.*
3. *Brownfield v. South Carolina,* 189 U.S. 426 (1903).
4. "Court Calendar," *Georgetown Times,* November 14, 1900.
5. "John Brownfield, Convicted Murderer," *The Georgetown Times,* March 14, 1903.
6. "The Court of General Sessions of the County," *The Georgetown Times,* April 1, 1903.
7. "Demand for the Times," *The Georgetown Times,* April 18, 1903.

Chapter XIX

1. "Good Work of the Sessions Court," *The Georgetown Times,* June 17, 1903.
2. Ibid.
3. Ibid.
4. U.S. Census, 1900.
5. U.S. Census, 1880.
6. See, generally, minutes, City Council, City of Georgetown, 1900–1905, South Carolina Archives.
7. Minutes, City Council, City of Georgetown, November 1, 1900, 330–332.
8. "Good Work of the Sessions Court," *Georgetown Times,* June 17, 1903.
9. "Death Sentence Passed," *Sunday Outlook*, Saturday night edition, Georgetown, SC, June 20, 1903.
10. "Land in Georgetown Attracts Colonies," *State* (Columbia, SC), June 17, 1903.
11. "South Carolina News and Gossip," *State,* June 21, 1903.
12. Ibid.
13. "The Weather Yesterday," *State,* June 24, 2003.
14. "Northern Mob Burns The Brutal Negro," *State,* June 23, 1903.
15. "Cheated the Gallows," *Sunday Outlook,* Saturday evening edition, Georgetown, SC, June 27, 1903.
16. *State,* June 25, 1903.
17. "Cheated the Gallows," *Sunday Outlook,* Saturday evening edition, Georgetown, SC, June 27, 1903.
18. Ibid.
19. Ibid.
20. "Died of Natural Causes," *Sunday Outlook*, Georgetown, SC, July 18, 1903.

Chapter XXI

1. Minutes, Georgetown City Council, June 4, 1903, South Carolina Archives.
2. *State* (Columbia, SC), June 27, 1903.
3. "Georgetown's Celebration," *State*, July 17, 1903.
4. "Cullud Pussons And Coons," *State*, July 17, 1903.
5. "Died of Natural Causes," *Sunday Outlook*, Georgetown, SC, July 18, 1903.

6. "Reorganization of Club; A Municipal Primary," *Georgetown Times,* October 24, 1903.
7. *Georgetown Times,* October 28, 1903.
8. *Georgetown Times,* November 4, 1903.
9. *Georgetown Times,* [date illegible] 1903.
10. *Georgetown Times,* November 4, 1903.
11. *Georgetown Times,* November 14, 1903.
12. *Georgetown Times,* December 5, 1903 and December 7, 1903.
13. *Georgetown Times,* November 28, 1903.
14. *Georgetown Times,* December 7, 1903.
15. *Georgetown Times,* November 28, 1903.
16. Ibid.
17. *Georgetown Times,* December 5, 1903.
18. Correspondence to W. D. Morgan from S. S. Bruington, Morgan Collection, South Caroliniana Library, University of South Carolina.
19. *Georgetown Times,* December 2, 1903.
20. Minutes, Georgetown City Council, December 1903, South Carolina Archives.

Chapter XXII

1. "Trouble at Rhems; The Death of a Negro Arouses the Blacks," *Georgetown Daily,* May 22, 1907.
2. Ibid. While the law of involuntary manslaughter has evolved over the years since this incident, *State v. Bartlett,* 218 S.C. 415, 63 S.E.2d 56 (1951) provides a good review of the law up to 1951. Today, the law is codified in Code of Laws of South Carolina, sec. 16-3-50 (Rev. 1985) as involving "criminal negligence."
3. *State v. Scurry,* 90 S.C. 346, 73 S.E. 353 (1912).
4. George C. Rogers Jr., *The History of Georgetown County, South Carolina* (Columbia, SC: University of South Carolina, 1970), 510.
5. *State v. Jackson,* 277 S.C. 271, 87 S.E.2d 681 (1955). The court has recognized that there is no duty to retreat in the face of a perceived danger while in one's home, at work or at one's clubhouse. *State v. Marlowe,* 120 S.C. 205 (1922); *State v. Davis,* 214 S.C. 34, 51 S.E.2d (1948).
6. Code of Laws of South Carolina, sec. 56-5-760.
7. 1994 S.C. Op. Atty Gen 139, October 26, 1994; See, also, Informal Opinion, 1996 WL 494732, July 10, 1996.
8 "Beat Goes On" Sonny and Cher

Suggested Readings

Bolick, Julian Stevenson. *Georgetown Houselore.* Clinton, SC: Jacobs Press, 1944.

Boyle, Christopher, and Fitch, James A., eds. *Slave Narratives, Georgetown County.* The Rice Museum, Seaport Press, Georgetown, SC., 1997.

Cate, Margaret Davis. *Early Days of Coastal Georgia.* Univ. of Georgia Press, distributor, 1955.

Côté, Richard N. *Mary's World, Love, War and Family Ties in 19th Century Charleston.* Mount Pleasant, SC: Corinthian Books, 2001.

Curriden, Mark, and Phillps, Leroy Jr. *Contempt of Court, The Turn-of-the-Century Lynching that Launched a Hundred Years of Federalism.* New York: Anchor Books, A Division of Random House, 2001.

Devereaux, Anthony Q. *The Life and Times of Robert F. W. Allston.* Georgetown, SC: Waccamaw Press, Inc., 1976.

Edgar, Walter. *South Carolina, A History.* Columbia, SC: Univ. of South Carolina Press, 1998.

Georgetown County Library System. *A View of Our Past, The Morgan Photograph Collection depicting Georgetown, South Carolina c. 1890-1915.*

Gragg, Rod. *The Forgotten Front: A Military History of Georgetown County in the Civil War, 1861-65*. Georgetown County Memorial Library, n.d.

Gregg, Rev. Alexander, DD. *History of The Old Cheraws*. Columbia, SC: Clearfield Co., 1925.

Hurmence, Belinda, ed. *Before Freedom, When I Just Can Remember, Twenty-seven Oral Histories of Former South Carolina Slaves*. Winston-Salem, NC: John F. Blair, Publisher, 1989.

Joyner, Charles. *Down by the Riverside: A South Carolina Slave Community*. Chicago and Urbana, IL: Univ. of Illinois Press, 1985.

Lawrimore, Katrina Paris. "The Georgetown Rifle Guards: An Institutional History; Submitted in Partial Fulfillment of the Requirements of the Degree of Master of Arts in the Department of History, University of South Carolina, 1979." Walter B. Edgar, director of thesis. George C. Rogers Jr., second reader.

National Geographic Society. *Our World's Heritage*. Washington, DC, 1987.

Packwood, Cyril Outerbridge. *Detour-Bermuda; Destination-U.S. House of Representatives: The Life of Joseph Hayne Rainey*. Hamilton, Bermuda: Baxter's Limited, 1977.

Powell, Colin L., with Persico, Joseph E. *My American Journey*. New York: Ballantine Books, 1995.

Rogers, George C. Jr. *The History of Georgetown County, South Carolina*. Columbia, SC: Univ. of South Carolina Press, 1970.

Index

C

D

E

F

G

About the Author

Tom Rubillo has practiced law in Georgetown, South Carolina for over a quarter of a century. As an honors graduate of Fordham University and with a law degree from Rutgers University School of Law, he began his legal career as a legal aid lawyer in 1978. He has served as chairman of the Georgetown County Democratic Party, as mayor of the City of Georgetown and as senior attorney in the Fifteenth Judicial Circuit's Solicitor's Office. He now represents individuals in civil rights cases and victims of violent crimes. He has also taught government, law and ethics at area colleges.